ROUTLEDGE LIBRARY EDITIONS: FOOD SUPPLY AND POLICY

Volume 4

URBAN FOOD MARKETING AND THIRD WORLD RURAL DEVELOPMENT

URBAN FOOD MARKETING AND THIRD WORLD RURAL DEVELOPMENT

The Structure of Producer-Seller Markets

T. SCARLETT EPSTEIN

Routledge
Taylor & Francis Group

LONDON AND NEW YORK

First published in 1982 by Croom Helm

This edition first published in 2020
by Routledge
4 Park Square, Milton Park, Abingdon, Oxon OX14 4RN
605 Third Avenue, New York, NY 10017

Routledge is an imprint of the Taylor & Francis Group, an informa business

British Library Cataloguing in Publication Data
A catalogue record for this book is available from the British Library

ISBN: 978-0-367-26640-0 (Set)
ISBN: 978-0-429-29433-4 (Set) (ebk)
ISBN: 978-0-367-27574-7 (Volume 4) (hbk)
ISBN: 978-0-429-29673-4 (Volume 4) (ebk)

Publisher's Note
The publisher has gone to great lengths to ensure the quality of this reprint but points out that some imperfections in the original copies may be apparent.

Disclaimer
The publisher has made every effort to trace copyright holders and would welcome correspondence from those they have been unable to trace.

URBAN FOOD MARKETING AND THIRD WORLD RURAL DEVELOPMENT

THE STRUCTURE OF PRODUCER-SELLER MARKETS

T. SCARLETT EPSTEIN

Published in Association with
The Research Center for South West Pacific Studies
La Trobe University
Australia

CROOM HELM
London & Canberra

© 1982 T. Scarlett Epstein
Croom Helm Ltd, 2-10 St John's Road, London SW11

British Library Cataloguing in Publication Data

Epstein, T. Scarlett
  Urban food marketing and Third World rural development:
  the structure of producer-seller markets.
  1. Underdeveloped areas—Agriculture
  2. Underdeveloped areas—Food produce—Marketing
  I. Title
  338.1'9'091724   HD1414

  ISBN 0-7099-0911-X

Printed and bound in Great Britain by
Biddles Ltd, Guildford and King's Lynn

CONTENTS

PART THREE: THEORETICAL AND PRACTICAL IMPLICATIONS

CHARTS AND MAPS

Charts

Maps

GRAPHS

TABLES

To Sir John Crawford

with admiration
and thanks

ACKNOWLEDGEMENTS

This book is based on market studies in Papua New Guinea conducted over two years between 1967 and 1969, while the country was still a dependent territory under Australian administration. So many individuals and institutions have helped in one way or another in the preparation of the manuscript that it is impossible to name them all.

My foremost thanks are due to the many informants who patiently answered our probing questions without objecting to the inconvenience this often caused them. The collection of the survey data was facilitated by a number of administrative and educational establishments which readily made available the many helpers needed in the conduct of our studies. The numerous assistants who so diligently helped us, deserve a special vote of thanks. A. McCullough, who organised the survey of Koki market in January 1969 and Professor Williams, who while teaching at the University of Papua New Guinea volunteered to supervise the studies which W. Straatmans conducted at Goroka, Lae and Mt. Hagen markets also contributed a great deal. The late W. Straatmans must be specially mentioned here: as research officer for the New Guinea Reseach Unit at the time he was seconded to our market studies. His devotion and skill as fieldworker helped him to establish excellent rapport with informants from different kinds of background, which enabled him to collect a lot of detailed individual profiles as well as other relevant qualitative material besides the survey data. It is a pity that he did not live long enough to see the results of the studies to which he had made an invaluable contribution.

The processing of the masses of quantitative data we collected proved a mammoth task in which many people helped. Only a few can be acknowledged here and I apologise to those whose names are left out of this short list: M.W. Ward, who assisted in the identification of our informants' home villages and also prepared most of the maps; A. Cornish, B. Gothe and M. Rose of the Australian National University who did the initial sorting and programming of the data; M. Cruize, of the Center for Advanced Study in the Behavioral Sciences, Stanford, who completed the computer work; and Agnes Page, my secretary at the Center as well as Irene Williams, my secretary at Sussex, who typed the manuscripts.

The preparation of the first and earlier version of this manuscript was facilitated by a Fellowship from the Center for Advanced Study in the Behavioral Sciences, in California during 1974/5. The ideal environment for academic work which the Center provides and its friendly atmosphere is responsible for bringing these market studies to fruition. I am deeply grateful for the facilites the Center offered so generously and am honoured for having been selected a Fellow.

I acknowledge with thanks the constructive comments by Ray Bromely, Aline Quester, Paul Streeten and Pan A Yatopoulus, who devoted a lot of their precious time to working meticulously through my manuscript. I have learnt a great deal from them, but the final version is of course my own responsibility.

The earlier manuscript remained untouched until last year when W.R. Stent urged me to revise it and the La Trobe University Research Center for South West Pacific Studies offered to help with publication arrangements. Without this encouragement it would have taken a lot longer before the analysis of this mass of fascinating data would have become generally available.

Finally, my daughters Mickey and Debbie deserve special mention. They were only five and three years old respectively at the time of my market studies and bore bravely all the inconveniences my demanding work commitments imposed on them.

University of Sussex   T. SCARLETT EPSTEIN

PART ONE

I N T R O D U C T I O N

Chapter 1

THE WEB OF PRODUCER-SELLER MARKETS

THE CRUX OF THE ARGUMENT

This book discusses urban food markets(1) in a
developing country. It documents and analyses the
persistence of producer-sellers at Papua New Guinea
markets. In doing so it differs from most other
market studies, which assume that economic development inevitably necessitates the evolution of a
hierarchical central place market structure (e.g.
Bromley, 1971 and Johnson, 1970).
    The analysis presented here shows that hier-
archical structured wholesale/retail food trade is
likely to evolve only in countries with a strong
centralised political administration. China constitutes a good example of such a country. It provides
the basis for Skinner's classic model of a central
place market structure (1964). In fact he dismisses
as unimportant in China what he calls a 'minor market'. The sporadic occurrence of such 'green vegetable markets' in rural China, its limited functions
and its peripheral position with regard to larger
marketing systems led him to consider it apart from
the regular hierarchy of central places -- as a
transition type which in most cases can be interpre-
ted as an incipient standard market (1964:6). By contrast markets of this 'minor type' were still the
norm in Papua New Guinea at the end of the 1960s;
there was then no sign of them giving way for central
place oriented wholesale/retail food trading. This
phenomenon has to be seen in its overall social setting. Only then can it begin to make sense.
    Papua New Guinea is an ethnically heterogenous
country composed of numerous tribal units, who until
not so long ago were often involved in inter-tribal
warfare. Its socio-political framework thus differs
considerably from countries such as China which have
a traditional centralised administrative structure.

This difference is reflected in the persistence of producer-seller markets in Papua New Guinea. Since ethnic diversity and producer-seller markets occur in many of the recently established independent States not only in the Pacific region but also in Africa the arguments based on studies of Papua New Guinea markets should be applicable over a wide area of the Third World.

The problems posed in Developing Countries by urbanization and the accompanying need for a rural food surplus appear to be tackled differently in centrally administered societies from the way more diffusely organized and ethnically diverse communities deal with them. The book suggests that for this latter type of country a webbed system of food marketing is more appropriate than central place market trade (see Chapter 6).

In line with the general interdisciplinary approach used in this book Chapter 5 provides an analysis of the price formation process at producer-seller markets. Economic variables here are regarded as deeply embedded in the socio-political matrix of society. This kind of analysis indicates that market prices are decided by the interaction between supply and demand price ranges. The level and range of supply prices between the desired and minimum acceptable price in turn is determined by the different types of vendors frequenting individual markets. Likewise, buyers come to the market with a preconceived notion of desired and maximum acceptable prices. Different types of buyers behave differently in this context. This is reflected in the level and range of demand prices.

The theoretical propositions and practical implications discussed in the last three chapters of this book are based on carefully collated masses of quantitative as well as qualitative data collected at seven Papua New Guinea markets. The background of the markets studied and the detailed accounts of supply and demand are presented in Chapters 2, 3 and 4. The research on which this book is based was conducted during 1967/9 in what was then the Territory of Papua and New Guinea and is now the independent country of Papua New Guinea.

WHY STUDY PRODUCER-SELLER MARKETS?

These market studies followed my earlier research on the Gazelle Peninsula of New Britain in 1959 to 1961 when I investigated the process of economic development and social change in Rapitok, a Tolai village (1968). Together with my female village friends I then frequently visited Rabaul market, when they were taking some of their produce for sale. I went to buy some vegetables which were not available in Rapitok. Previously I had done fieldwork in South India (1962). There too I accompanied my village friends to the local market. Unlike the Tolai they all had trooped there to buy rather than to sell. I was thus struck by the different trading patterns that prevailed in Rabaul in contrast with Asia.

Unlike the severe competition between the many different traders and the extensive bargaining between them and buyers that goes on at South Indian markets, in Melanesia overt competition between sellers is largely absent; there is only rarely any bargaining or haggling. This novel phenomenon of producer-seller trade without competition and bargaining aroused my interest in Pacific markets.

Accordingly, in May 1961 towards the end of my fieldwork in Rapitok I agreed with Richard F. Salisbury, who had then just arrived on the Gazelle Peninsula that we should jointly tackle a study of Rabaul market (Epstein, T.S., 1961 and Salisbury, 1970) (2). Our findings were important inasmuch as they produced many more questions than answers. This encouraged more research at Pacific market places (Brookfield, 1969); such studies as were done treated individual producer-seller markets as isolated trading events. There was no systematic attempt to piece together into one country's marketing structure the different producer-seller markets that co-exist within it.

Our first study of Rabaul market had whetted my appetite to find out more about the role of producer-seller markets in the overall economy of Papua New Guinea. My chance to pursue these interests came when I returned to the Australian National University in 1966 after a spell of five years teaching at Salford University in England. Sir John Crawford, the Australian National University Vice-Chancellor, kindly offered me a Visiting Fellowship, and Ron Crocombe, then the Director of the New Guinea Research Unit in Port Moresby arranged for me to conduct research at some of the major markets in the country. By the beginning of 1967 everything was set for my market studies.

After pilot enquiries we selected as research sites three markets on the New Guinea mainland, namely Goroka, Lae and Mt. Hagen; three on the Gazelle Peninsula of New Britain, i.e. Kokopo, Rabaul and Vunapope, as well as the major Papuan market at Koki in the capital city (see Map 2.1). These seven markets were the biggest ones in the country at the

5

time and represented a morphology of producer-seller market trade in Papua New Guinea. They included a number of different ethnic groups, as well as a variety of ecological zones.

The ultimate aims in organizing these market studies were to develop theoretical as well as practical propositions which might help to improve intra-country food distribution in areas with a tradition of producer-seller markets. The analysis of the market data, I hoped, would enable me to explain the price formation process that prevails at producer-seller markets not in any abstract way as most macro-economists are apt to do, but rather in terms of the culture and perceptions of market trade held by those who themselves are directly involved in it. To satisfy my ultimate aims obviously necessitated not only a lot of detailed quantitative survey data but also various kinds of qualitative enquiries. This determined the research strategy I had to employ. Yet it was no easy task to translate this strategy into concrete methods and procedures of study.

I searched the literature on market studies for guidance; alas none was to be found. I thus re-examined the methods we had used in our 1961 Rabaul market study and tried to improve on what we had done then. The study design I developed was far from perfect, yet it was the best I could come up with at the time. As yet no comprehensive set of guidelines have been published on market studies in general and producer-seller markets in particular. Accordingly, in the Appendices I outline the methods I used in 1961 as well as in my 1967/9 market studies and provide samples of the questionnaires. This should not only aid other researchers in organizing their market enquiries, but enable the reader to judge the reliability of my basic data and the validity of my argument.

At Pacific market places, large numbers of small vendors sit on the ground. Each displays numerous items of fruit and vegetables. Crowds of potential buyers throng the area. Such markets are thus not easy objects for study. Anyone who has ever seen markets of this kind will no doubt appreciate the difficulty such a study poses.

To conduct random sample surveys of buyers and sellers would have been hard enough but what made it even more difficult was my insistence on the need to adapt the anthropological method of participant observation to the study of producer-seller markets. "One must get out into the field in a study of this type and investigate the subject at first hand by observing the actions of those participating in this type of price making as well as interrogating them" (Cassidy, 1974:5).

Our data collection began in February 1967 and was completed two years later. Altogether almost 7,000 vendors and 12,000 buyers were interviewed. Also a lot of qualitative data was gathered on the individuals and groups involved in the market trade as well as on the markets and their Hinterland. It required considerable time and skills to process this wealth of novel primary data. At the urgent request of the Department of Labor, Port Moresby, that had let us have eight trainees as market investigators at Koki, I wrote shortly after completion of our data collection a provisional account of 'Buyers and Prices at Indigenous Produce Markets' (1969:18). Yet for the more comprehensive analysis I needed many complex tables and calculations. While this was being prepared for me at the Australian National University I was invited in 1970 back to South India for a re-examination of the villages I had first studied 15 years earlier. This was an opportunity I was not prepared to miss, however committed I was to the analysis of my market data.

I assume that many social scientists who work on more than one problem at a time must periodically face a dilemma: which of their equally important areas of concern should they give priority in treatment. I struggled with this problem when I returned to Canberra after six weeks back in South India during which time I collected a wealth of fascinating material. The question was what I should do first: work on my market material or on my re-examination of the two South Indian villages I had studied years earlier. The difficulties encountered in processing my market studies through the computer and the long time all this took tipped the balance in favor of giving my South Indian material priority of attention. I completed a monograph (1973) and soon afterwards moved from Canberra to the University of Sussex where I took up an appointment at the Institute of Development Studies. Though I carefully packed and brought with me all my market data, new responsibilities prevented me from continuing work on them.

A Fellowship at the Center for Advanced Study in the Behavioral Sciences in California in 1974/5 enabled me to get back to my market material and its processing. I then managed to produce the first complete version of a manuscript. The colleagues who kindly agreed to read through this first draft made a series of valuable critical comments which indicated that revision was necessary before I could

7

contemplate publication. Unfortunately until recently my other work commitments did not allow me the spell of time I needed to rewrite.

I have given here a brief autobiographical account, not to outline my career but rather to explain why it has taken so long before my market studies finally reached the publishers. During this period of over ten years, which was one of radical economic as well as socio-political changes in Papua New Guinea my market data have obviously lost topical significance. At this point the reader may well ask whether it is worthwhile to publish material which is now many years out of date. After all I am not just attempting a historical presentation. I myself have seriously wondered this. After careful consideration I decided that there are good reasons why my market studies should still be of interest. The detailed information I have collected on prices of individual commodities as well as my analysis of market supply and demand should be useful information for the Government and peoples of the now independent Papua New Guinea. The rapid urbanization which has taken place in the country inevitably necessitates increasing food supplies for the growing numbers in towns and cities. My detailed accounts of trading patterns as they existed at the major markets in the country more than ten years ago, might suggest to politicians and administrators what may now be the most effective incentives to encourage growers to increase market supplies of locally produced foods. Moreover, the information on prices that prevailed for the various staple items sold at the different markets we studied at the end of the 1960s also provides useful data for the calculation of inflationary trends in locally produced food crops. As far as I could establish these essential data are not available anywhere except in my market material.

Finally, and more important still are the general theoretical and practical propositions which result from my careful analysis of the interlinkages between specifically economic and general cultural variables as they affect the trading behavior at producer-seller markets. Some existing monographs do treat peasant market practices (e.g. Cassidy, 1974; Szanton, 1972) but hardly any concentrate exclusively on producer-sellers, nor do they try to explain market behavior in terms of the vendors and buyers' own culture and their perceptions of what trading means to them. This kind of analysis can be developed only on the basis of carefully collected and collated numerical as well as qualitative accounts of the observed minutia of market trading.

8

The most interesting aspect of these producer-seller markets is their persistence. These Pacific markets do not seem to be transitional types. They give all indications to be more lasting features of food marketing. The reasons for their continued central importance become obvious only by taking into account the socio-cultural setting of the different categories of buyers and vendors which predominate at these markets. To appreciate these different categories necessitates an understanding not only of the economic aspects of producer-seller marketing but even more important of the social matrix within which this type of trading is deeply embedded.

Pacific markets are predominantly sellers markets where the majority of vendors are 'trippers' (see p. 146) and where the profit motive is only of marginal importance. The very nature of such markets sets serious limits to the radius of supply and demand. This in turn becomes a problem with increasing urban growth particularly if it involves long distance migration. For instance, a Tolai from the Gazelle Peninsula of New Britain has to pay more than four times the price for areca nuts if he buys them at Koki market in Port Moresby than what he is accustomed to pay in his home area. Conditions of such considerable price differentials between markets, which far exceed transport costs, frequently provide fertile breeding grounds for middlemen. Yet no such brokerage has developed in Papua New Guinea. In this case the advantageous economic circumstances were counterbalanced by socio-political variables; the indigenous population was for several good reasons not attracted to develop an intra-country wholesale-retail food trade, nor were they prepared to allow expatriates to get involved in buying and selling crops produced by small local growers.

I expect that the various readers will each find different aspects of this book of interest. Some may find a bit tedious my detailed accounts of demand in Chapter 3 and supply in Chapter 4. I hope they will bear with me. In reading the final three chapters it should become obvious that the meticulously compiled materials represent an essential part of my analysis. They constitute the individual bricks which are necessary not only to build a price formation model (see Chapter 5) but also suggest a webbed country wide producer-seller marketing system (see Chapter 6). The argument in a sense evolves like a detective story. Little pieces of evidence from a great variety of different sources have to be joined together selectively to help understand why producer-seller markets operate the way they do and more important why they are likely to continue to do so. This accounts for the structure of the book.

Those readers more immediately concerned with the development of Papua New Guinea may want to concentrate on the detailed accounts of supply and demand as it existed at the seven producer-seller markets we studied at the end of the 1960s; while others not familiar with the Pacific- scene, who are more concerned with the theoretical discussions of market trade may wish to focus on the last three chapters. Whatever part of this book may attract the reader's attention I hope that I manage to convey at least a little of the fascination Papua New Guinea in general and producer-seller markets in particular hold for me.

NOTES

1. The term 'market' has many meanings but the three that particularly concern us here are "(1) the market in the price making sense, (2) the market in the geographical, or place, sense" (Cassidy, 1974:32) and (3) the market in its socio-cultural aspect.

2. Salisbury concentrated on studying buyers and I focussed on vendors. This division of labor was in line with our respective expertize. Salisbury was new on the Gazelle Peninsula then, but was fluent in Pidgin, the *lingua franca* among most buyers, whereas I was already familiar with the local language (the Tolai are the dominant tribe on the Gazelle Peninsula and represent the majority of vendors at Rabaul market).

Chapter 2
MARKET SETTINGS

HISTORICAL BACKGROUND

An efficient system of distribution is an important
feature of each and every economy at all stages of
its growth. It assumes critical significance for
underdeveloped countries involved in the process of
commercialization (Abbott, 1958:2) and urbanization.
The bulk of the influx into Papua New Guinea towns
is derived from indigenous people who move from the
rural Hinterland either as a result of economic
forces and/or are attracted by all the new amenities
urban centers offer. The remainder of the growing
urban population is composed of expatriates who move
there either in an administrative capacity or as
professionals, skilled craftsmen and businessmen.
    The population trends displayed in Port Moresby,
the country's capital, indicate this rapid urbanization; its numbers increased by as much as 60 percent between 1966 and 1971 (see Table 2.1).
    The expatriate community's food requirements
can be -- and in Port Moresby in fact are(1) --
almost wholly satisfied by imported products. The
high cost of some of the imported food stuffs accompanied often by a taste preference for customary
diets means that the indigenous urban immigrant has
to secure his nourishment from supplies derived from
the rural Hinterland. In turn this necessitates a
surplus production of food in what used to be
largely subsistence units and a preparedness to market the surplus. Provided their home village is
situated near enough to the town, indigenous urban
workers may either commute or still live sufficiently close so as to be in a position to get
regular supplies of food from their kin and friends
in exchange for either gifts of cash or store goods
desired by rural dwellers(2). If, however, urban
employment involves long distance migration, as is

frequently the case(3), urban immigrants are wholly
dependent on purchasing all their food. Some of
their requirements are satisfied by buying imported
articles such as rice, tinned fish and meat, etc.
The proportion the imported food component constitutes in indigenous urban consumption is a function
of change in tastes as well as of the relative price
of imported as compared with local food items. The
degree of substitution by import varies for different items of indigenous consumption: rice is widely
accepted as a full alternative for root crops such
as sweet potatoes, yams and sometimes even for taro;
by contrast there is no direct substitute for areca
nuts, peppers and limes, though cigarettes and
tobacco may be regarded as indirect substitutes.
The increasing demand for traditional foods in
growing towns stimulates local producers to supply
more and more and results in the spontaneous emer-
gence of new markets in strategic places, while
already established ones continue to expand. There
are certain important aspects which are characteristic not only of all Papua New Guinea markets but
also occur in other less developed regions under
similar conditions.

First and foremost, there is a striking absence
of any wholesale transactions; practically all vendors sell what they themselves produce to buyers who
are the ultimate consumers. Therefore goods offered
for sale are largely restricted to indigenously
grown cash crops. This can be a vestige of traditional exchanges between different groups of peoples
conditioned by ecological variations and/or an
aspect of "primitive affluence" (Fisk, 1966:23).

Second, no goods are sold by weight; instead
produce is arranged in bundles sold for 10 cents(4)
each or multiples thereof. Price variations are
therefore expressed in terms of different quantities
sold per unit of money, rather than by way of different amounts of money charged for the same quantity of goods. This appears to be a frequently
occurring sales practice. In Mexico too "instead of
offering a fixed 'package' at a variable price, the
'package' is variable at a fixed price" (Cassidy,
1974:49).

Third, earnings derived from market sales constitute only a part, frequently only a minor part,
of many vendors' total income.

Fourth, produce markets are not only places
where food can be bought and sold but are also
social centers which provide an important link in
the social network of the indigenous population.
Cassidy argues that "socializing is more apt to be

practised between buyers who come from diverse areas to purchase their requirements and who eagerly seize the opportunity of exchanging 'news' and ideas with others" (1974:60). The same phenomenon of course also occurs in the context of sellers.

Within this overall framework of producer-seller marketing practices there exist certain variations in transactions resulting largely from differences in environmental and historical background in Papua New Guinea between Highland and coastal areas and also Port Moresby, the capital city. Though most of the individual tribal societies were part of an extensive network of trade links, on the mainland only a few of them actually had the institution of a market. By contrast the Tolai of the Gazelle Peninsula of New Britain have had market trading long before European contact. This trade was brought about by the different yet complementary ecology of coastal and inland Tolai and was facilitated by the use of *tambu,* (shell money). Danks, the first European resident missionary in the Tolai area reported on the use of *tambu* at many markets in the area (1887:315).

Shell money is still used as a medium of exchange between the Tolai sellers and buyers, though barter transactions seem to have disappeared altogether, at least at the market place(5), instead now the majority of sales are for cash. Early European observers were struck by the number of markets held by the Tolai and the extent of their trade. In 1888 a German expedition crossed the Gazelle Peninsula from Walaur to Kabaira. After two hours' walk it came to a spring where a market was held. In the course of the morning the expedition passed half a dozen other market places before it reached the middle plateau (Nachrichten, 1888:155). There existed a series of markets which linked the interior of the Gazelle Peninsula with the coast. The constant hostility between the settlements made long travel unsafe. Though open fighting was excluded from actual market places by the institution of the 'peace of the market', those going to and from were not so protected. Market values of all commodities were expressed in terms of *tambu* (Schneider, 1905:30). Even human flesh was sold for shell money. Parkinson relates that on average one human body was worth about 50 to 80 fathoms (1887:121).

Prices for some things seem to have been fixed, but for many articles they differed according to the state of supply and demand. For instance, when taro was plentiful it sold at one fathom for sixty, whereas when it was scarce the price rose to one fathom for fifty (Danks, 1887:307). Not only goods but also specialist services were paid for in *tambu*. The Tolai had a price for almost everything.

The New Guinea Annual Report for 1924/5, relating to the Gazelle Peninsula, states that "in Rabaul and elsewhere native markets are frequently to be observed where considerable numbers of natives congregate with their produce. In some cases these market places are merely a spot by the wayside on a coconut plantation, and they exist as market places only on account of native use and custom. Even in the township of Rabaul no provision has been made to accommodate the market in a suitable place or building" (C.o.A., 1924/5:28).

A few years later "a substantial native market in Rabaul was nearing completion.... The object of this market is to assist local natives in the disposal of fruit, vegetables and native foods to Europeans and natives in Rabaul" (C.o.A., 1927/8:59).

In contrast with the more formal market mechanisms operating among the Tolai, the characteristic mode of exchange in the Highlands of Papua New Guinea was between individual participants on a one-to-one basis. The periodic prestations at clan ceremonial grounds cannot be regarded as proto-markets. The main characterisitcs of pre-contact Highland trade were:

1. Men dominated all aspects of trade, though women might have played minor roles in the production of traded goods.
2. Transport time and difficulty were disregarded as "costs".
3. A good that travelled twenty miles over difficult country was "worth" no more than a similar good which was traded over only a couple of miles; risk to life and limb was the only meaningful transport cost.
4. The great ceremonial exchange cycles tended to take place within regions of similar resources, whereas trade was most vigorous between regions of great contrast.
5. The overlap between types of goods used in prestation on the one hand and in trade on the other was very large. In fact, only one type of product ceremoniously exchanged failed to occur anywhere in trade, and that was staple root crops and common green vegetables (Jackson, 1974:2). In fact "vegetable foods were available to everyone to be fed to pigs and these raised for

eventual exchange with shells" (Strathern, 1971:108).

The Highlanders like the Tolai valued shells. The Tolai had their *tambu* which they stored in large coils, while the Highlanders valued goldlip shells. These shells originated from the Gulf district and reached the Highlands through indigenous trade channels. One goldlip shell bought two pigs in the 1930s (Leahy, 1937:152). As the first patrols began to pass through the Highlands they brought shells with them and used them as payment for goods and labor to the delight of the indigenes. One of these patrols almost failed for lack of goldlip shells. Subsequent patrols learned their lesson and came well equipped with an abundance of these shells. Prior to the last war at the time of these first patrols Highlanders also valued empty rolls of films, which they used as pendants on necklaces. One such aluminium roll bought one 150-180 lb. pig. Expatriates in their attempts to endear themselves to the Highlanders and/or to make handsome profits sought to buy goldlip shells wherever they could obtain them reasonably cheaply. At one time when the New York mother-of-pearl market collapsed low-priced shells where shipped all the way from America to Papua New Guinea. The influx of these additional shells resulted in a valuable inflation. During the immediate postwar period from 1947-1955, the ownership or control of increasingly large quantities of shells, bird of paradise feathers or steel tools became the prerequisite for a Highlander to occupy any position of power and influence within his society.

Shells were widely used then for payment in the Eastern Highlands and sent across to the Southern Highlands. Many of the shells were hoarded with a view to profitable investment in bridewealth; the more shells a man could accumulate the more wives he could marry and the more children he could beget with the likelihood of producing daughters who in turn would earn shells in bridewealth.

After 1955 the demand for shell money started to decline in the Mt. Hagen and Goroka region and cash began to take over the important function of acting as store of value and medium of exchange. Traditional valuables, however, retained their importance in bridewealth and as ornaments. Yet it has become possible for a man, even if he is from the coast, to marry a Highland girl by buying pigs and offering cash instead of shells as bridewealth. He thereby buys himself into the trading network with

which as an outsider he otherwise has no connections.
The fact that New Guinea Highlanders and coastal people alike attached such great importance to the accumulation of valuables as a means to gaining prestige and power when they first came into contact with the wider economy is a reflection of their "primitive affluence" (Fisk, 1966:23). Only the pattern of their transactions was different: the Tolai traded in market places while the Highlanders exchanged items on a personal basis. The modern markets which developed in the Highlands and expanded on the Gazelle Peninsula thus have their roots in the traditional system of transactions, and they therefore started with a narrower radius of supplies than markets which were established and grew solely as a result of urban development, as for instance happened in Lae and Port Moresby.

In order to attempt covering the great variety of market conditions prevailing in Papua New Guinea it was necessary to study several markets. As already mentioned I selected Vunapope, Kokopo, Rabaul, Goroka, Mt. Hagen, Lae and Port Moresby (see Map 2.1). These markets represent different levels in the morphological development of indigenous produce marketing and include coastal and Highland markets as well as Koki market in the country capital of Port Moresby. Vunapope, the informal spontaneous market is the only one among the seven studied, which was not operated by one or another of the Native Local Government Councils.

Except for Kokopo and Rabaul markets which are the offshoots of traditional market place trading, all the other urban markets were first started by the Administration in an attempt to control the quality of indigenous produce sales and only subsequently put under the jurisdiction of the appropriate Native Local Government Council.

MARKET PROFILES

The market studies presented here show a clear distinction between Hinterland-rooted markets on the one hand and Urban-based ones on the other. Hinterland-rooted markets, as for instance Rabaul and Goroka are the sequel to traditional exchange arrangements and have a limited supply area. By contrast Urban-based markets such as Koki and Lae, which developed solely in response to growing urban demand for food, have a much wider radius of supplies and altogether a different marketing pattern.

16

Hinterland-rooted Markets

Vunapope which is situated about two miles from
Kokopo on the Gazelle Peninsula of New Britain, is
the smallest market included in this study. It
represents a spontaneous response to demand perceived by some enterprising women sellers outside
the Vunapope Catholic Mission hospital to supply
the needs of patients as well as of people visiting
patients. Similar to flower and sweet sellers outside Western hospitals Tolai women try there to sell
their produce to visitors who want to take gifts to
patients. On Saturdays some 20 or 30 vendors from
surrounding villages settle down at the road junc-
tion nearest the hospital. They display their goods
on leaves laid out on the ground in front of them
and approximately 200 people stop to buy some fruit,
areca nuts and leaves or cooked food. According
to Salisbury, "many of the vendors were maternity
patients awaiting or recovering from delivery. Husbands would bring a load of food for their wives,
and the wives would use some for immediate consumption, and some for sale, saving the money received
for later purchases" (1970:100). On the day of our
Vunapope survey all the vendors had come from nearby
villages specifically to sell their produce; none of
them were themselves hospital patients. On
Saturdays this small market can be regarded as an
offshoot of the somewhat bigger market which is situated right in the center of Kokopo township.

Kokopo houses the headquarters of a subdistrict, in
which there is a considerable number of large plantations employing indigenous immigrant labor. It has
two medium-sized European stores and a number of
smaller ones. The market site occupies approximately 600 sq. yards; it is controlled by the
Gazelle Local Government Council which in 1966 built
two large sheds to provide shelter for vendors (see
Map 2.2) and in July 1967 began to charge a fee of
10 cents per seller which was increased to 20 cents
in February 1968. On weekdays the market is only
sparsely visited: a few local women offer bundles
of cooked food and chewing requisites to some of
the laborers on nearby plantations who come to the
market during their rest pauses. On Saturdays over
200 vendors assemble at the market displaying a
great variety of produce to 1,200 potential buyers.

Rabaul Market ranks next in terms of effective demand,
though if the criterion is the level of supplies
Rabaul market is bigger than Koki. Rabaul is the

center of a thriving regional economy; it handles
the largest volume of crop exports (copra and cocoa)
in the whole of the Territory. The area is blessed
with highly fertile, volcanic soils. In 1966 the
town had a population of almost 11,000 of whom 65
percent were indigenes (see Table 2.1). The market
caters not only for the urban population but also
for a considerable proportion of the 60,000 Tolai
rural dwellers as well as for a good number of non-
Tolai plantation laborers. It is open six days a
week. Saturday is by far the most important market
day in the week; about 2,400 vendors offer their
produce to approximately 10,000 potential buyers
with a weekly turnover of about $8,500. A long
stream of traffic begins to arrive on Friday bringing sellers and buyers to the market. On Saturdays
from the early hours in the morning until midday
there is a great hustle and bustle when trucks and
utilities queue up for space to unload produce and
keen expatriate buyers try to purchase cheap high
quality articles before vendors have had a chance to
take up their positions and display their goods.

Rabaul market occupies an area of about one-
third of an acre half of which is taken up by sheds
forming a quadrangle; the remainder is open ground
shaded by large trees (see Maps 2.3 and 2.4). Most
of the produce of interest to expatriates, such as
lettuces, tomatoes, etc., is displayed on the tables
under shelter, whereas many of the items in the
indigenous diet are laid out on leaves in the open.
On Saturdays it is often hard to find a passage
between the masses of food offered for sale. The
market site, like that of Kokopo, is held under a
lease by the Gazelle Local Government Council, which
built the sheds and even installed electricity in
order to encourage Friday late night shopping, so
far without much success. The Council introduced a
fee of 10 cents per seller in Spetember 1961 and
raised it to 20 cents in January 1965. Many vendors
escape having to pay the fee; during my survey only
about one-third of sellers purchased tickets.

There is no regulation stipulating who can sell
what where in the market, yet as a result of informal customary practice sellers from one village
always tend to congregate in the same spot at the
market. For instance, Rapitok vendors still display
their produce in the shade of the same tree which
they have occupied since 1961. This informal seat-
ing arrangement facilitates social intercourse at
the market, which is very important, particularly in
the turmoil of Saturday crowds. Anyone who wishes
to establish contact with a person from a particular

village can find out quite easily where vendors from that village are located at the market. A similar informal allocation of space is noticeable at Koki, though it is not as strictly adhered to there simply because of the greater tribal heterogeneity.

Goroka is situated in the heart of the Eastern Highlands, which in parts ranks among the most densely populated areas in the whole of the Territory (Brookfield, 1963). The systematic exploration of the New Guinea Highlands began only in the 1930s. Until then indigenes lived in small and scattered subsistence economies.

Administrative control was established in the region shortly prior to the last war: the first permanent Patrol Post in Goroka (Eastern Highlands) was set up only in 1944. There were a few expatriates living in the region already before 1939, but their economic impact was hardly felt. It was only since the last war that increasing numbers of expatriates began to settle in the Highlands with the result of new towns growing in the area. In 1966 Goroka had a total population of 4,826 of whom 20 percent were non-indigenous. By 1971 the total population had almost trebled (see Table 2.1). This growing urban population needed to be housed and fed. The immediate local reaction to this new demand for their produce was to hawk food round the town. As mentioned already, the Highlanders do not appear to have a tradition of regular markets. Their customary exchanges have been conducted on the basis of personal relations. It is likely that in line with this, individual producers tried to establish more lasting relationships with their urban buyers and therefore hawked their produce round homes. Administration Officers became concerned about the quality of produce hawked as well as about prices paid in these transactions; moreover, they realized that produce marketing may provide a lucrative source of income for local growers. Accordingly, they arranged for the free distribution of vegetable seeds among indigenous cultivators and encouraged the preparation of market sites. Consequently, it was administrative initiative, rather than local spontaneity, that was responsible for the setting up of regular markets in the Highlands. Yet these markets were embedded in the immediate Hinterland.

Goroka market was established by the Department of Native Affairs in the latter half of 1957 on a site across the road from its present position. By 1961 it had developed to considerable size: at least 800 sellers are reported to have come to the market

from villages adjacent to Goroka and from the Lower
Asaro region. Vendors used to arrive about 9 am --
approximately two hours later than they do now --
and displayed their produce on wooden tables. Late-
comers often found all the tables occupied and had
to make do with displaying their goods on the ground.
Unfortunately, no estimate of turnover during the
earlier years is possible. However, reports indicate
that trading was quite brisk. Indigenous buyers
mainly purchased sweet potatoes, tobacco, pig meat
and such like staple articles, but they were also
keen buyers of European-bred ducks, which were sold
at the market at the price of 30/- each. Of 15
ducks brought for sale on one day only two remained
unsold, most of them having been bought by indigenes.
Small pieces of pork were sold for 5/- each and whole
pigs' legs for 30/- each. Expatriate buyers used to
come to the market about mid-morning, carefully
choose their purchases and spend amounts ranging
from 2/- to 18/-, with an approximate average of 10/-.
Vendors took their unsold produce to the hospital
were they traded it for soap, matches or margarine(6).

By 1962 produce marketing in Goroka had taken on
such proportions that the site had become much too
small and it was therefore at the end of the year
shifted to its present place. The Local Government
Council, in whom the market site is vested, has displayed great interest in developing Goroka's market.
Significantly, in 1963 two indigenous councillors
traveled across to the Gazelle Peninsula to find out
how the Gazelle Local Government Council was organizing Rabaul market and to see for themselves how in
fact it was operating. Subsequently, the market site
was fenced in, and sellers made to enter through one
particular gate and pay five cents each. Market fees
are collected by the Council and used to pay for the
cleaning and maintenance of the sheds and the market
site in general.

The Council tries to control the display as well
as the price of produce. Boards picturing different
items of produce are used to indicate to sellers
where to display what produce. However, in practice
this is very difficult to arrange simply because one
vendor frequently brings more than one kind of produce for sale. At the entrance to the market the
Council put up a large board picturing bundles of the
major items sold, indicating how much of each produce
should be priced 10 cents e.g. four cobs of corn are
priced 10 cents. This too in practice is difficult
to administer: first of all, prices are usually
determined by the interaction of supply and demand,
for which the Council does not seem to be prepared

to make allowances. Moreover, prices are influenced by the quality as well as size of goods sold. Thus for instance three first rate large cobs of corn may be sold for 10 cents while five small poor quality cobs may be bought for the same price. In practice therefore Council interference in produce marketing is limited to the collection of fees from sellers. Receipts of market fees in 1966 indicate that on Wednesdays the average number of vendors was about 430 while on Saturdays it was approximately 750. As already mentioned in that year Goroka had a population of 4,826.

Weekend visitors to Goroka sometimes increase the total indigenous population to about 40,000. The number of expatriates in town on market days is probably also considerably larger than census figures lead us to believe. A count of potential and actual buyers at Goroka market during February 1967 showed that the average number of individuals entering the market site was about 2,800 on Wednesdays and 3,200 on Saturdays, of whom approximately 50 percent actually purchased something. During the same month an average of about 750 sellers attended Wednesday markets and approximately 1,000 turned up on Saturdays; about 75 percent of all sellers were women. The estimated weekly market turnover was then about $3,500.

Mt. Hagen is the major town in the Western Highlands, where the first permanent Patrol Post was established shortly before the last war. In 1966 the town had a total population of 3,315 of whom about 15 percent were expatriates; by 1971 total numbers had more than trebled (see Table 2.1).

The first informal food supplies for the urban population were brought in by hawkers. It was not before the end of 1959 that the first market was established in Mt. Hagen. This was done at the initiative of the Administration who wanted some control over the health aspect of food marketing and therefore suggested that market place trading should replace the hawking of food produce. The first market was at the site where the bakery is at present. There were some very simple tables made of bush materials supported by wooden legs stuck firmly into the ground. Right from the start it was considered desirable to display produce on tables rather than have it exposed to dust by putting it on the ground. These early display structures were made by prisoners.

The first market sites were not suitably situated and therefore changed several times. Here too, as in Goroka, the Department of Agriculture, who then controlled the market, was keen to improve the quality of produce and distributed free seeds of European type vegetables, such as celery, lettuces and tomatoes, to local growers. Officials also sought to fix prices by organizing sellers' entry to the market and weighing and grading all produce brought for sale. These attempts at price fixing raised sellers' opposition and encouraged a return to hawking, which led to the removal of price control altogether. In 1963 and 1964 there was a native agricultural assistant always in attendance at the market but prices were allowed to find their own level.

In 1965 the Native Local Government Council took over control of Mt. Hagen market and moved it to its present site in 1966. The market was fenced; entry controlled through gates and a fee of three cents charged to anyone entering, buyers and sellers alike. Since the Department of Agriculture ceased to control the market it also discontinued the distribution of free seeds, which, it is claimed in turn resulted in a deterioration of the quality of produce, particularly European-type vegetables. Approximately 5,000 individuals entered Mt. Hagen in March 1967 about 50 percent of whom tried to sell something. There were then two weekly market days, i.e. Wednesday and Saturday; the total estimated weekly turnover during that month was $3,200. About half of the sellers were female; everyone entering the market still had to pay a fee, but many potential buyers slipped through the fence unnoticed.

Five of the seven markets I studied are Hinterland-rooted. This reflects the predominance of this kind of market in Papua New Guinea. It is in line with the country's ecology and level of urbanization.

Urban-based Markets

Such markets are the response to growing urban demand for food. They lack the traditional background of customary exchanges between different ecological zones.

Lae is one of the towns which was first started in German days. Unlike Rabaul which nestles in a homogenous tribal area, Lae is surrounded by many different tribal groups. After the 1937 eruption of Matupit crater near Rabaul the Administration decided to move its New Guinea Headquarters from the Gazelle Peninsula to Lae. The war intervened and immediately after it private initiative began to build up Rabaul

once more, so much so that the Administration had no
choice but to go along with this development. In
spite of this Lae overtook Rabaul in terms of population, which in 1966 numbered 13,341 indigenes and
3,205 non-indigenes; by 1971 the numbers had
increased by over 100 percent (see Table 2.1).

The Germans had equipped the Gazelle Peninsula
with a reasonably efficient road network, which was
further improved under Japanese rule during the last
war. Lae was not as fortunate in this respect. For
at least ten years after the last war growers who were
interested in supplying food to Lae had to walk the
distances and bodily carry their produce. Most of
these sellers were women. They used to arrive in Lae
on Friday afternoons, hawked their stuff round
Chinatown on Saturday morning and arrived back in
their villages late the same day. There are reports
which claim that the supply areas then were very much
the same as they are now except for the Highland produce which can be transported by road since the
Inland Highway was opened at the beginning of the
1960s. Vegetables were much scarcer than they are
now and there was therefore less competition.
Sellers had no difficulty whatsoever in getting rid
of all the stuff they brought for sale.

In 1957 the Administration established a market
(7) and attempted to channel food sales into market
transactions so as to be able to supervise the quality of produce sold. The social aspect of attending
a market where many individuals from different parts
of the Lae Hinterland could meet in one place
attracted indigenous vendors to selling at the market
rather than hawking their produce. In 1962 the
management and supervision of the market site was
handed over to the Leiwomba Native Local Government
Council. Since then the market site has been shifted
several times because of the reorganization of the
town it served. Significantly, Lae market was
modeled after Koki, the Port Moresby market; the
Assistant District Officer from Lae went to Port
Moresby in 1964 to study Koki market, while, as mentioned already, Gorokan councilors traveled to
Rabaul in 1963 to look at the operation of the market
there. Accordingly, a Board of Trustees was established to supervise Lae market, which like its Koki
counterpart received grants for maintenance from the
Administration, to supplement the income derived from
fees taken from sellers. In 1966 the market moved to
its present site(8). The Leiwomba Local Government
Council decided in May 1967 on the layout of the
market site(9).

Lae market operates six days per week; during

one week in August 1967 about 1,400 vendors and
12,500 buyers were counted at the market; with a
weekly turnover of approximately $4,400. Friday is
the peak market day when most buyers and sellers turn
up, unlike at Gazelle Peninsula and Highland markets
where Saturday is the busiest market day. Supplies
reach the market by various means: by individual
porterage, others by road or sea transport, some produce arrives even by air. The tribal background of
suppliers displays considerable heterogeneity; frequently vendors are indigenes from other parts of the
country who have migrated to the Lae area, rented
land near the town, and grow vegetables there for
sale.

Koki is the major market in Port Moresby. This
capital city has been expanding rapidly since the
last war. In 1966 the population numbered 31,983
indigenes and 9,864 expatriates; there are estimates
that it increased by 57 percent between 1961 and 1966.
Census figures for 1971 give a total population for
Port Moresby of 66,244, which indicates an increase
of 63 percent in five years (see Table 2.1). The
sprawling suburbs accompanied by shanti settlements
provide ample evidence of the town's rapid expansion.
The growing number of urban immigrants, who originate
from many different areas and tribal units, which
together compose Papua New Guinea need not only shelter in town but even more so food; most of these
people emerged only recently from subsistence living
and their customary staple diets vary from taro and
sweet potatoes to sago, bananas and coconuts.
    Before the last war there were only a few hun-
dred Europeans living in Port Moresby and no indigenous urban settlers. Local people in the neighborhood
lived in their traditional villages where they
followed their customary practices of fishing and/or
cultivating their food gardens (Belshaw, 1957). Only
occasionally did they hawk their food surplus around
expatriate houses in Port Moresby.
    The large influx of troops into the area towards
the end of the war not only increased the demand from
expatriates for food produce but also created indigenous demand by attracting an indigenous work force
to the town. The Army even encouraged locals to
start vegetable gardens on a large scale to insure
food supplies for its troops. The shortage of urban
housing forced many immigrants to the town from other
parts of Papua New Guinea to live on canoes at Koki
point. Villagers from surrouding areas began to
bring food supplies for sale to these Koki dwellers.
This gradually evolved into market place trading at

Koki which at first was conducted completely uncontrolled until market supervision was made the responsibility of the District Officer in the mid-1950s. Eventually the amount of food handled at Koki grew to such proportions that problems related to the town's economy and public safety began to emerge. Therefore, at the end of the 1950s a Market Board of Trustees was established and by-laws for the control of the market were brought into force. The area designated for the market included its present site, Koki point, the area now reclaimed and the island. The Board of Trustees demanded a fee from each vendor (10 cents until the mid 1960s when the fee was doubled) and used this income to supplement Administrative Grants to meet the maintenance and improvement expenditures required.

In terms of facilities Koki is the worst provided market of the seven sites we surveyed; most of the produce is displayed on the ground and by the end of the day is covered in dust. Unlike at the other urban markets, where sellers arrange their produce so as to tempt buyers, at Koki there is an obvious sellers' market. Vendors, many of them who come from long distances stay in Port Moresby until they sell whatever they brought; each secure in the knowledge that what is not sold on the day will be sold on subsequent days. Koki is a gathering point for people originating from many different parts of the country not only for the purpose of food purchases, but also to meet friends and relatives as well as to enjoy the excitement of the crowd. The meeting of large numbers in a confined area embodies political dangers. Koki has in fact been the starting point of many of Port Moresby's more serious riots. Language difficulties often spark off rioting. To ease this strain the market has been divided into tribal areas (see Map 2.5). Koki market is open seven days per week; weekends being the busiest days there. During one week in 1968 we counted about 50,000 individuals visiting the market of whom approximately 25 percent actually purchased something from the 2,500 vendors who had turned up to sell their produce. The estimated weekly turnover in May 1968 was about $18,500.

The market is fenced in; trading begins about 7 am and the site has to be cleared of people and produce by 6 pm every day; unsold produce can be locked away overnight in a hut on the market site. Koki market is wedged in between on the one side the sea, and on the other the main coastal road connecting the different suburbs of the town. There are always anchored a large number of house boats at Koki point, from where freshly caught fish is supplied.

Adjacent to the market site is a parking lot behind which there are a few Chinese general stores.

Improvements of facilities at Koki have for years been the concern of administrative officers, the Board of Market Trustees and the Native Local Government Council, however, not much had actually been done by 1968.

In 1967/8 Rabaul, Goroka, Mt. Hagen, Lae and Koki markets constituted the five most important ones in Papua New Guinea. There were then possibly another dozen or so markets resembling Kokopo as well as many smaller ones like Vunapope. Therefore, the markets I studied feature the country's market place trade almost in its totality. I began this market investigation in February 1967. Field work was completed two years later. At each of the five major markets studied data was collected during two different periods in the year to allow for seasonal fluctuations (see Table 2.2). Altogether 6,902 vendors and 11,720 buyers were interviewed.

NOTES

1. The present tense used here refers to the years 1967-70 when the studies on which this book is based were conducted.
2. These conditions apply in the case of the Tolai who works in Rabaul   the Chimbu who works in Goroka and to a lesser extent to the Hannaubadan who is employed in Port Moresby.
3. e.g. the Tolai or Highlander working in Port Moresby, or the Sepik and Kerema employed in or near Rabaul.
4. Australia's currency, which was used in Papua New Guinea, was pounds until 1966 when it was changed to dollars at the rate of two dollars per Australian pound.
5. R.F. Salisbury claims that "direct barter does occur in all (Tolai) markets but only rarely" on the basis of his studies of Rabaul and Kokopo markets which he conducted in 1961 (1970:181). In my Rabaul market studies both in 1961 and 1968 I could not discover a single barter transaction.
6. The account of Goroka market in the late 1950s is based on District Records and Patrol Reports.
7. The site was on the Markham Road between the European Cemetery and the new Angau hospital.
8. It is situated between Air Corps Road and Malaita Street.
9. There were to be two rows of tables with paths on the outside and space in the center for

vendors to market and watch their produce; 24 high
tables were to be purchased at £5 each in addition to
those already available. It was suggested that
European toilet facilities should be erected, but it
was unanimously agreed that this could not be done
as the standard of hygiene was insufficient to
warrant this expense.

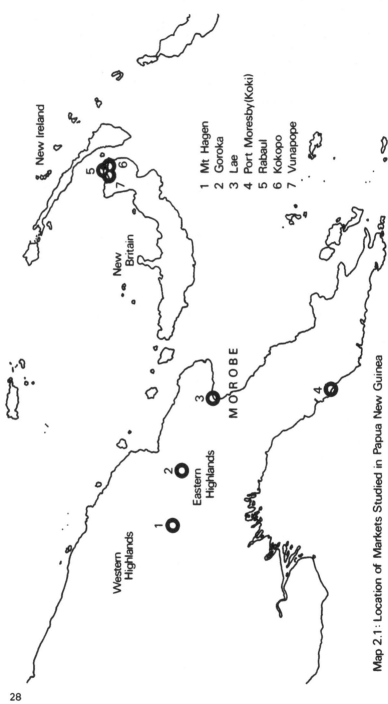

Map 2.1: Location of Markets Studied in Papua New Guinea

1 Mt Hagen
2 Goroka
3 Lae
4 Port Moresby(Koki)
5 Rabaul
6 Kokopo
7 Vunapope

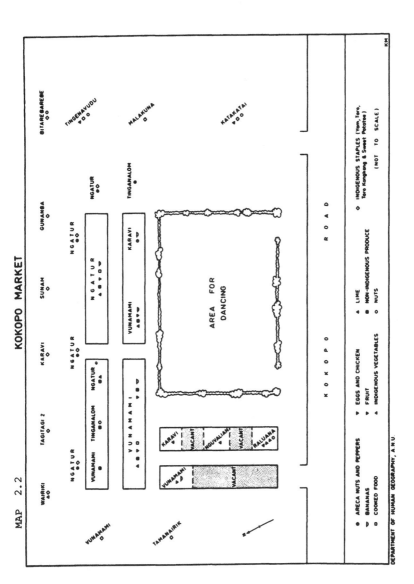

MAP 2.2

KOKOPO MARKET

AREA FOR DANCING

KOKOPO ROAD

- ♦ ARECA NUTS AND PEPPERS
- ♢ BANANAS
- ▫ COOKED FOOD
- ▼ EGGS AND CHICKEN
- ▽ FRUIT
- ▲ INDIGENOUS VEGETABLES
- ▴ LIME
- ■ NON-INDIGENOUS PRODUCE
- ○ NUTS
- ◇ INDIGENOUS STAPLES (Yam, Taro, Taro Kongkong & Sweet Potatoe)

(NOT TO SCALE)

KM

DEPARTMENT OF HUMAN GEOGRAPHY, A.N.U.

MAP 2.3

RABAUL MARKET

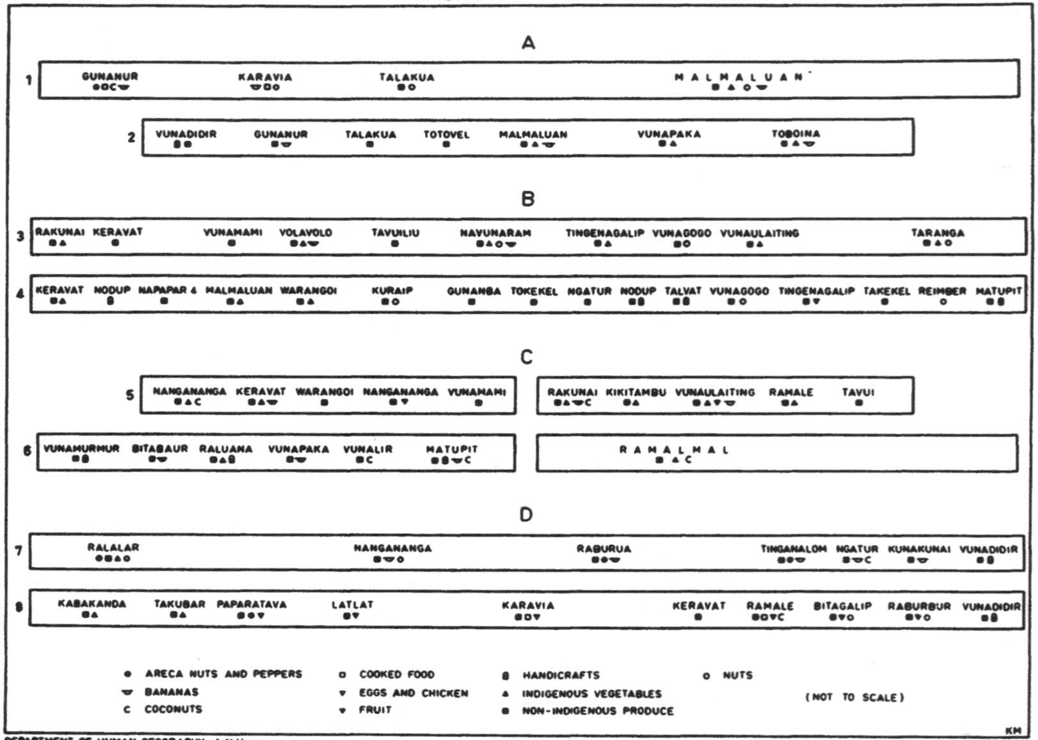

A

1 GUNANUR · ● C ▼

KARAVIA ▼ ● ○

TALAKUA ● ○

MALMALUAN ● ▲ ○ ▼

2 VUNADIDIR ● ●

GUNANUR ● ▼

TALAKUA ● ▼

TOTOVEL ● ●

VUNAPAKA ● ▲

TOBOINA ● ▼

B

3 RAKUNAI ● ▲   KERAVAT ● ▲

VUNAMAMI ● ●

VOLAVOLO ● ▲ ▼

TAVULIU ● ●

NAVUNARAM ● ▲ ○ ▼

TINGENAGALIP ● ▲

VUNAGOGO ● ○

VUNALILAITING ● ▲

TARANGA ● ▲ ○

4 KERAVAT ● ▲   NODUP ● ●   NAPAPAR ▲   MALMALUAN ▲   WARANGOI ● ▲

KURAIP ● ○

GUNAMBA ● ▲

TOKEKEL ● ▲

NGATUR ● ●

NODUP ● ●

TALVAT ● ▲

VUNAGOGO ● ▼

TINGENAGALIP ● ●

TAKEKEL ● ●

REMBER ● ○

MATUPIT ● ●

C

5 NANGANANGA ● ▲ C   KERAVAT ● ▲ ▼   WARANGOI ● ▲ ▼   NANGANANGA ● ▼   VUNAMAMI ●

RAKUNAI ● ▲ ▼ C   KIKITAMBU ●   VUNALILAITING ● ▲ ▼ ●   RAMALE ● ▲   TAVUI ●

RAMALMAL ● ▲ C

6 VUNAMURMUR ● ●   BITABAUR ● ▲ ●   RALUANA ● ▲ ●   VUNAPAKA ● ▼

VUNALIR ● C

MATUPIT ● ● ▼ C

D

7 RALALAR ● ● ▲ ○

NANGANANGA ● ▼ ○

RABURUA ● ▼

TINGANALOM ● ▼ C   NGATUR ● ▼   KUNAKUNAI ● ▼   VUNADIDIR ● ▼

8 KABAKANDA ● ▲   TAKUBAR ● ●   PAPARATAVA ● ●

LATLAT ● ▼

KARAVIA ● ▼

KERAVAT ● ▼ C   RAMALE ● ▼ C   BITAGALIP ● ▼ ○   RABURBUR ● ▼ ○   VUNADIDIR ● ●

(NOT TO SCALE)

● ARECA NUTS AND PEPPERS
▼ BANANAS
C COCONUTS

□ COOKED FOOD
▲ EGGS AND CHICKEN
▼ FRUIT

● HANDICRAFTS
▲ INDIGENOUS VEGETABLES
● NON-INDIGENOUS PRODUCE

○ NUTS

DEPARTMENT OF HUMAN GEOGRAPHY, A.N.U.

KM

MAP 2.4

RABAUL MARKET

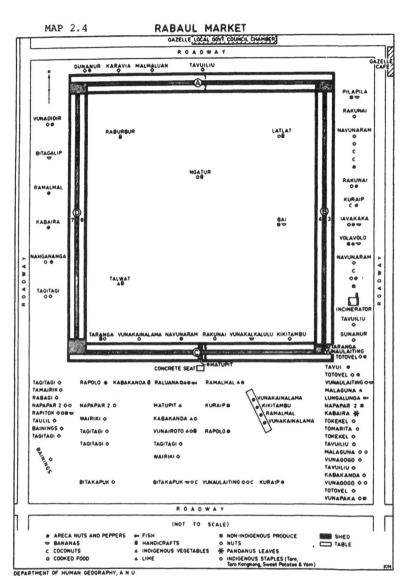

GAZELLE LOCAL GOVT. COUNCIL CHAMBER

ROADWAY

GAZELLE CAFE

GUNANUR KARAVIA MALMALUAN   TAVUILIU

PILAPILA ●▽

RAKUNAI ●▽

VUNADIDIR ◇●

NAVUNARAM
◇
C
C
C
◇

RABURBUR ▪

LATLAT ◇▪

BITAGALIP ◇●

NGATUR ◇▪

RAMALMAL ●

RAKUNAI ◇●

KURAIP C●

KABAIRA ●

BAI ▪▪

IAVAKAKA ◇●▪

VOLAVOLO ▪

NANGANANGA ◇●

NAVUNARAM
◇
C
◇● ·

TAGITAGI ◇◇

TALWAT ▲▪

INCINERATOR

TAVUILIU ◇

GUNANUR ◇

TARANGA VUNAKAINALAMA NAVUNARAM RAKUNAI VUNAKALKALULU KIKITAMBU

TARANGA ▽
VUNAULAITING
TOTOVEL ◇●

CONCRETE SEAT   ●MATUPIT

TAVUI ●
TOTOVEL ◇●

TAGITAGI ◇   RAPOLO ● KABAKANDA ▪ RALUANA ◇▲●◄   RAMALMAL ▲●
TAMAIRIK ◇
RABAGI ◇
NAPAPAR 2 ◇◇   NAPAPAR 2 ◇   MATUPIT ▲   KURAIP ●
RAPITOK ◇◇▪◄
TAULIL ◇   WAIRIKI ◇   KABAKANDA ▲◇
BAININGS ◇
TAGITAGI ◇   TAGITAGI ◇   VUNAIROTO ▲◇▪   RAPOLO ●
                 TAGITAGI ◇   TAGITAGI ◇
                                     WAIRIKI ◇

BAININGS

BITAKAPUK ◇   BITAKAPUK ▽◇C VUNAULAITING ◇◇C KURAIP ●

VUNAKAINALAMA
KIKITAMBU
RAMALMAL
VUNAKAINALAMA

VUNAULAITING ◇▽
MALAGUNA ▲
LUNGALUNGA ◄
NAPAPAR 2 ▪
KABAIRA ✳
TOKEKEL ◇
TOMARITA ◇
TOKEKEL ◇
TAVUILIU ◇
MALAGUNA ◇◇
VUNAGOGO ◇
TAVUILIU ◇
KABAKANDA ◇
VUNAGOGO ◇◇
TOTOVEL ◇
VUNAPAKA ◇▪

ROADWAY

(NOT TO SCALE)

● ARECA NUTS AND PEPPERS   ◄ FISH   ▪ NON-INDIGENOUS PRODUCE   ▬ SHED
▽ BANANAS   ▪ HANDICRAFTS   ◇ NUTS   ▭ TABLE
C COCONUTS   ▲ INDIGENOUS VEGETABLES   ✳ PANDANUS LEAVES
▫ COOKED FOOD   ▲ LIME   ◇ INDIGENOUS STAPLES (Taro,
                                                 Taro Kongkong, Sweet Potatoe & Yam)

DEPARTMENT OF HUMAN GEOGRAPHY, A N U

KM

31

MAP 2.5

KOKI MARKET

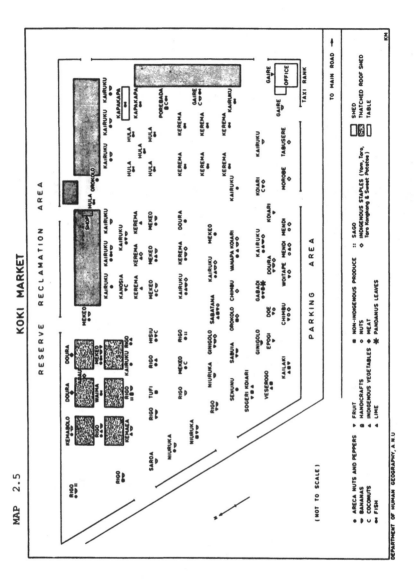

(NOT TO SCALE)

- ● ARECA NUTS AND PEPPERS
- ✿ BANANAS
- C COCONUTS
- ➤ FISH
- ▼ FRUIT
- ❚ HANDICRAFTS
- ▲ INDIGENOUS VEGETABLES
- ▲ LIME
- ■ NON-INDIGENOUS PRODUCE
- ○ NUTS
- ○ MEAT
- ✱ PANDANUS LEAVES
- ∷ SAGO
- ◇ INDIGENOUS STAPLES (Yam, Taro, Tara Kongkong & Sweet Potatoe)

SHED ▮▮ ▯ THATCHED ROOF SHED ▯ TABLE

DEPARTMENT OF HUMAN GEOGRAPHY, A.N.U.

Table 2.1: Urban Population*

	Indigenous		Non-indigenous		Total	
	1966	1971	1966	1971	1966	1971
Kokopo	1,423	1,542	261	290	1,684	1,832
Rabaul	6,925	20,700	3,636	4,078	10,561	24,778
Goroka	3,890	9,238	936	1,518	4,826	10,756
Mt. Hagen	2,764	8,398	551	1,211	3,315	9,609
Lae	13,341	28,494	3,205	6,205	16,546	34,699
Port Moresby	31,983	50,988	9,865	15,256	41,848	66,244

*Source: Papua New Guinea Population Census - July 1971
Preliminary Bulletin 1

33

Table 2.2: Periods of Surveys

		1967	1968	1969
Vunapope			April 6	
Kokopo			April 6	
Rabaul	I:W		January (15 weekdays)	
	I:S		January (4 Saturdays)	
	II:W		April (9 weekdays)	
	II:S		April (2 Saturdays)	
Goroka	I	February (8 days)		
	II	August (8 days)		
Mt. Hagen	I	February (19 days)		
	II	July (8 days)		
Lae	I	August (7 days)		
	II	December (12 days)		
Koki	I		May (14 days)	
	II			February (14 days)

PART TWO:

MARKET TRANSACTIONS

Chapter 3

DEMAND

The discussion of Papua New Guinea market trade
begins here with an examination of buyers behavior.
This is done only to use a convenient point of
entry into the argument. It should not be taken to
indicate that we are dealing here with buyers markets. Quite the contrary; it should become obvious
as the analysis unfolds that at these producer-
seller markets vendors, rather than buyers exert the
decisive influence over produce prices. Yet of
course here too as always trade is determined by the
interaction between supply and demand.

MARKET VISITORS AND BUYERS

The gathering in one spot of large numbers of individual vendors always invites potential customers;
the greater a gathering, the more people are interested to join it, if for no other reason than just
to see for themselves what is going on to attract
people in the first instance to gather together.
Masses often attract greater masses. In Papua New
Guinea this holds true also: at the markets the
number of visitors is a function of the number of
vendors; the more vendors gather to sell their produce the greater is the number of visitors who come
to inspect the market. This is particularly so at
the urban-based market of Port Moresby, where trade
is conducted seven days each week. As already mentioned markets at Lae and Rabaul operate six days
per week; Mt. Hagen and Goroka are open Wednesdays
and Saturdays, and Kokopo and Vunapope have mainly
Saturday markets. Our tally count suggests that
about 50,000 visitors turn up during a week at Koki,
16,000 at Rabaul, 15,000 at Lae, 5,000 at Goroka,
4,000 at Mt. Hagen, 1,200 at Kokopo and 200 at
Vunapope markets (see Table 3.1).

37

Only some of all the market visitors do in fact purchase something. Our observations indicate that no more than 20 percent of all the people who visit Koki, the capital city market, actually purchase something there. Almost 90 percent of the Koki buyers we interviewed said that they had come to the market for the specific purpose of purchasing something (see Chart 3.1). The small proportion of visitors who buy something at Koki and the high proportion of those who do purchase produce there who say that they had come to the market for this very purpose suggests two alternative hypotheses: first, that many of those who do not buy at the market had come there to purchase something and had decided against doing so either because whatever they wanted was not available for sale, or prices were too high or quality too poor, or, second that large numbers of individuals visit the market for reasons other than to purchase goods (e.g., to meet kin or friends), while most of those who come to buy find in fact something they regard worthwhile purchasing. It is of considerable importance to test these hypotheses -- our data does not lend itself to do so -- before deciding on any improvements for Koki; if the latter is true then it might be advisable to try and separate the social from the trading aspects of the market by making available meeting facilities adjacent to the market, if possible. However, if the former is the case, then there is a need for more radical improvements in market supplies.

At Vunapope and Lae markets about 85 percent of visitors make some purchases, whereas the respective percentages for Kokopo are 75, for Goroka and Rabaul 60 and for Mt. Hagen 50. It is easy to explain the high proportion of buyers at Vunapope and Kokopo markets, simply because the total number of visitors there is comparatively small; it is equally easy to understand the greater proportions of individuals who visit the market and do not buy anything at Rabaul, Goroka and Mt. Hagen because of the social aspect of the market-place trade. The comparatively small proportion of those who visit Lae market without buying anything there seems somewhat surprising. It indicates a low social connotation of that particular market. A greater social heterogeneity in the Lae catchment area and a poor infra-structure may account for this phenomenon. The different proportions of visitors who make purchases at the different markets suggest the need for further studies of buyer behavior so as to get a clearer understanding of what motivates individuals to visit local markets.

Peak periods vary between the different markets studied. Koki is busiest at weekends and in the late afternoons when laborers are free to visit the market. During these times crowds throng·through the market, so much so that it becomes difficult to find one's path between the produce laid out on the ground. Similar crowded conditions prevail on Fridays at Lae when about 5,000 individuals visit the market and on Saturdays at Rabaul, when as many as 10,000 turn up. At Mt. Hagen there appear to be about 25 percent more individuals visiting Saturday markets than Wednesday ones, whereas at Goroka there is a fairly even distribution of visitors between these two weekly market days.

The proportion of females among sample buyers varies from its highest of about 66 percent at Vunapope and Kokopo markets to its lowest at Koki, where it is no more than 27 percent. Since most of the investigators were young men who may have been hesitant to interview female buyers, there is a possibility that the sex composition among our interviewees may reflect a sampling bias. However, since this condition applied to all the markets we studied it cannot account for the difference in the proportion of female buyers interviewed at the different markets. Moreover, anyone visiting Koki is always struck by the male predominance not only among sellers but also among the crowd milling round the market. There are two main reasons which can account for the male predominance among visitors and buyers at Koki: first, this reflects the fact that about two-thirds of Port Moresby's population are male and second, that many indigenous men do not like their womenfolk to visit Koki, which they suspect of being a dangerous place. By contrast, at all the other markets where most vendors are female there is also a higher proportion of females among sample buyers (see Chart 3.2).

Unfortunately, our investigators at Goroka, Mt. Hagen and Lae markets failed to record the ethnicity of many of our sample buyers. This data is available for the Gazelle Peninsula as well as Koki markets (see Chart 3.3), from which it emerges that at Rabaul market about 20 percent of the buyers are expatriates, whereas the respective percentage is no more than six at Koki. As already mentioned expatriates in Port Moresby do not like to frequent Koki, whereas their counterparts in Rabaul are keen market followers. Some expatriates send their servants to shop for them at the market, but it is extremely difficult to estimate the numbers of indigenous buyers who purchase for their employers. Since in most cases the individual servants bought goods for themselves too, the answers our assistants recorded cannot be taken as satisfactory and further market studies are needed also to elucidate this particular aspect of purchasing behavior.

There is a remarkable regularity in the answers our sample buyers gave to a number of questions at the different markets we studied. About 80 percent live close to the market, which means they are in most cases urban dwellers. One-third were at the market the previous market day, another 33 percent were there the previous week, 15 percent had been to the market longer ago and the rest had never been before. Almost all buyers interviewed said that they come to the market for the specific purpose of purchasing goods and for no other reason whatsoever (see Chart 3.1). Similarly, almost all buyers purchase for their own consumption and not for resale and 80 percent look around the market before they decide to buy whereas the rest purchase from the first vendor they see who sells what they want to buy. Our questions relating to prices and bargaining proved not really to be meaningful to informants, for the price per bundle of produce is uniform: usually 10 cents or multiples thereof. Price variations manifest themselves in terms of different quantities or qualities of produce sold for the same amount of money. The concept of bargaining seems completely alien to indigenes in Papua New Guinea; only some of the expatriate buyers try to bargain at markets.

The majority of buyers at all the markets surveyed are local indigenes. Only 15 percent of all buyers interviewed at Rabaul market are expatriates. Tolai compose 30 percent of indigenous buyers(1) New Guinean make up 60 percent and Papuans 10 percent. Tolai constitute almost two-thirds of buyers at Vunapope and Kokopo. About 70 percent of buyers at Koki are Papuan and as many as 80 percent of them live within the boundaries of Port Moresby. Expatriate buyers almost invariably use their own vehicles, whereas indigenous buyers use a variety of different means to come to the market.

How Buyers get to the Market

At Koki about 50 percent turn up by bus, 15 percent ride on trucks, 20 percent walk and the remainder come by taxi, bike or canoe. Forty two percent of Koki buyers come from the inner suburbs of Port Moresby, 44 percent from the outer suburbs, four percent from within a distance of five miles and the rest come from further afield. Their average transport costs are about 15 cents. Their modal cost of transport is 23 cents. Cost of transport obviously varies with the distance traveled. Buyers who come from villages within a radius of five miles from Port Moresby pay an average of about 30 cents for their return fares and those who come from further afield pay approximately 50 cents. Those few buyers who travel longer distances to the market and pay the highest fares are miners and quarrymen by occupation.

Lae market buyers display a similar transport pattern as do Koki buyers: about 45 percent walk, 16 percent come by bus, 37 percent use privately owned cars or trucks and the remainder come by plane or canoe. Yet the distance buyers travel to Lae market is much greater than that of their Koki counterparts. It is difficult to decide how much of the expense in traveling to town can justifiably be attributed to purchasing costs at the market. For instance, the maximum return fare any of our Lae sample buyers claimed to have paid is $6. These two buyers had come by plane to Lae for some other purpose and visited the market as an additional attraction only. It seems unreasonable therefore, to treat the $6 as expense incurred in visiting the market. Probably most other Lae buyers who claim to have come from long distances and paid higher fares came also for some other reason and while in town decided to buy something at the market. Some buyers originate from villages more than 100 miles from Lae. The large catchment area for Lae buyers is reflected in their high fares: the modal return fare of those buyers who pay to come to the market being about 95 cents.

Most Highland buyers walk to the market: at Goroka about 85 percent do so and at Mt. Hagen about 70 percent. Three buyers reported that they had spent $8 each on air fares to come to town. Like their Lae counterparts they had come to Goroka for other reasons and then decided to make some market purchases. Therefore, average fares for those Goroka buyers who pay to come to town amount to as much as about $1.50 return. At Mt. Hagen similar transport patterns prevail among market buyers: three of our sample buyers came to town by air and paid $5 each in return fares; average return fares of those who paid to travel to the market amount to about 40 cents per buyer.

The good road network on the Gazelle Peninsula accounts for the fact that about 80 percent of buyers use vehicles to come to the market. Most of these vehicles are owned by groups of people each of

whom stakes a claim to the ownership of the asset.
This helps to explain the fact that about 60 percent
of our Rabaul sample buyers who had come to the market by means of motorized transport, stated that
they had traveled in their own vehicles and therefore had paid no fares. Those who paid to come to
the market spent on an average about 37 cents.
There is hardly any difference in the average fares
paid by buyers who visit Rabaul market during the
week and those who come on Saturdays. Fares are
directly related to distance traveled: buyers who
come from within a radius of five miles pay about 25
cents for their return fares; those who come from
between 10 to 15 miles distance pay about 40 cents.
A similar transport pattern among buyers prevails at
Kokopo market, where 55 percent of those interviewed said that they had come in their own
vehicles. Those buyers who paid to travel to
Kokopo market were charged identical fares per mile
as Rabaul buyers. None of the buyers at Vunapope
market go there specifically to make a purchase;
they all call there only on their way to the
hospital and their expenditure on fares therefore
cannot be counted as part of purchasing expenses.

BUYERS AT URBAN-BASED MARKETS

Koki Buyers: Occupations and Income

During our first survey at Koki informants were
asked about their occupation and fortnightly
income(2). About 75 percent gave details about
their work and of those who did only 35 percent
volunteered income data. The occupational distribution per ethnic category throws into relief the
important role of army personnel and policemen among
Koki buyers. Army and other service personnel
represent the modal occupation (see Table 3.2).
Significantly, two-thirds of Tolai informants at
Koki are engaged in elite occupations; i.e., professional and students, transport and communications,
and army and other services. This is supported by
the fact that 75 percent of Tolai buyers at Koki
earn more than $19 per fortnight as compared with
only 46 percent of New Guineans and 58 percent of
Papuan buyers who do so (see Table 3.3). Unfortunately, at the time of the survey Tolai were the
only tribal group singled out among indigenous Koki
buyers; otherwise all New Guineans and all Papuans
were lumped together under the respective headings.
Yet it would be interesting to know if there are any
other individual tribes equally, or even more,

economically advanced than the Tolai. The large numbers in these overall tribal categories may obscure the occupational pattern as well as the income distribution in any one tribe included among them.

The modal income for most Koki buyer informants lies somewhere within the range of $10 to $19 per fortnight. The same income category represents the mode for all indigenous workers engaged in Papuan urban areas both by Government as well as by private employers. Altogether the income distribution among the Koki sample buyers resembles that among indigenous Government employees: in both cases about 55 percent of workers received more than $19 per fortnight. The range of earnings among Koki buyers is bigger than that among indigenous public and private employees. This is probably due to the fact that among the former expatriates are also included. Indigenous employees of private firms seem to get somewhat lower wages than public servants; i.e., 58 percent earn less than $19 per fortnight (see Table 3.4). It is interesting to note that eight percent of those of the Koki buyers who gave details of their income said that they are earning less than $9 per fortnight, while official statistics indicate that no indigenous employee falls within this income category. It is possible of course that some indigenes may be paid less by their employers than the officially recognized rates. This is another aspect of our market studies which needs further investigation. Altogether it is regrettable that we have available occupational and income data only for one survey at Koki and not for all the markets we studied. It seems essential to know the pattern of market purchases of different occupational and income categories before any realistic estimate of the volume of future urban demand is possible.

The considerably greater difficulties involved in sampling market buyers than sellers accounts for the comparative dearth of reliable data on the purchasing aspect of producer-seller markets, which lend themselves readily for generalized statements. As mentioned earlier (see p. 16) the setting up of most of these markets was encouraged by the Foreign Administration mainly for the purpose of supplying fresh vegetables for expatriates. The role of these markets, however, has been changing and in future they are likely to serve a predominantly indigenous urban population. Population figures alone cannot suffice to estimate the expansion of demand in the future; to do this the occupational and income breakdown as well as respective consumption patterns must also be known.

How Much do Buyers Purchase?

There are many individual vendors at producer-seller markets who each fetch only a limited quantity of goods; similarly, there are many buyers, each of whom buys only a small amount of produce. The average expenditure per buyer is lowest at Vunapope, i.e., 17 cents and highest at Koki where it was $1.77 in May 1968 and $1.51 in February 1969. This considerable difference can readily be accounted for by the fact that purchases outside Vunapope Mission hospital are solely made for the purpose of giving a little pleasure to patients; the buyers are either patients themselves or individuals who visit somebody in hospital. The purchases at Vunapope are thus only marginal acquisitions. In contrast buyers at Koki market purchase staple foods for their consumption and therefore spend about 10 times as much as their Vunapope counterparts (see Table 3.5).

Weekend buyers spend more at Koki market than those who come throughout the week; the highest average expenditure per buyer in May 1968 was $2.51 on a Saturday and in February 1969 $5.39 on a Friday. Expatriates constitute only a small proportion of buyers at Koki market. However, Chinese buyers spend about three times and Europeans about twice the average amount of money spent on daily average purchases. Yet the bulk of purchases are made by indigenous buyers, not only because they constitute the large majority of individuals visiting the market but more important because they turn up at Koki more regularly than do expatriates. Koki is the only source of traditional staple foods for most indigenes residing in Port Moresby; only few of them have access to land in or near the town to cultivate their own supplies or live near enough to their homes to obtain a share of the subsistence output. As already stressed Koki is a seller's market, where prices are high and produce sold is often of low quality.

Profiles of some Koki Buyers

The following summary profiles of Koki buyers clearly indicate the prevailing problems of prices and quality of produce sold.

Hui originates from the Gulf District and came to Port Moresby in 1965 where he now works as medical orderly earning $15 every two weeks; his wife and son live with him in the town. His weekly

44

household expenditure on food is about $5 of which he spends one-third buying fresh fruit and vegetables at Koki market; the remainder he purchases in stores. Hui also buys about $1 worth of areca nuts and other such stimulants at Koki per week. On his twice weekly visits to the market he carefully looks over all the produce offered of the kind in which he is interested. He buys only if he is satisfied with the quality and can afford the price.

Rigo from the Marshall Lagoon who works as shop assistant in Port Moresby earning $20 per fortnight lives with his wife and daughter. They spend about $7 weekly on food of which they buy 40 percent at Koki. Rigo shops at the market every Friday when he usually buys fish, fruit and occasionally also sweet potatoes; he frequently also comes to Koki on Sundays when he buys areca nuts worth about $1.50. His wife does the shop purchases while he buys the things they need from the market. He too stressed his concern over the poor quality and high prices at Koki market; he carefully examines the fruit offered for sale before he decides which lot to buy. Rigo claimed that fish was the only item sold at Koki where he had no complaint about its quality.

Mari from Central District came to Port Moresby with her husband in 1962 since when he has been working as a skilled carpenter earning $30 per fortnight; they have four children. The family spends about $9 on food per week of which $5 worth is usually bought at Koki. Mari lives close to the market and visits it almost daily. She carefully checks the quality of produce offered by different sellers against the set price. She expressed more concern over the poor quality rather than over the high price of foods at Koki market. Mari claimed that about two days every week she leaves the market without having bought a single item because things were of too poor quality. On each of four days in each week she purchases at Koki stuff for about 80 cents and on Friday she buys food as well as areca nuts altogether for about $2. Every other Friday, which is payday, she spends more than during the week when her husband does not get his paypacket.

These profiles which are typical of the many collected among Koki buyers, show the buyers' concern over the quality and price of produce sold at the market. It seems that the quality of produce determines whether a purchase is made at all and the price influences how much is being bought. Unlike developed country trading patterns where it is usually cheaper to buy at open markets than in regular stores, in Port Moresby staple foods are cheaper in stores than at Koki. "The number of calories which can be purchased per unit of money is much greater for the imported starchy foods than the traditional foods most commonly available" (Spinks, 1963:27). Comparative prices of produce are discussed in a later section of this book; here it suffices to note that the higher the income of indigenes who migrated to Port Moresby and now work there, the greater the proportion of their food consumption they purchase at Koki.

The supply conditions prevailing at Koki market in particular and in Port Moresby in general have been a matter of grave concern to the Administration for some time. The Project Planning Team, part of the Department of the Administrator, conducted a 'Fresh Food Study - Port Moresby' first in 1965 and followed it up with another report in 1967, which states that "the total market situation in Port Moresby is one of confusion and inefficiency. Koki market itself is congested, with substandard conditions of food handling prevailing. Although starchy roots and fruits are the natural and preferred staple foods for most Papuans and New Guineans, the high prices force the substitution of rice and low cost grain preparations, except when local foods are used as occasional diets. This results in a smaller demand for local staples than could be expected were they at a lower price, and lack of demand-encouragement to producers" (Yeats, 1967:IV).

Indigenous Versus Expatriate Buyers at Lae Market

Lae, though also an urban-based market, is operated in a much more orderly fashion than Koki. This encourages expatriates living in the town to visit the market themselves or to send one or other of their servants to purchase fresh fruit and vegetables there. Longtime expatriate residents in Lae relate that the character of the market has been changing over the last few years: the proportion of indigenous buyers has increased which is reflected in an increasing quantity of indigenous produce being offered for sale and less importance attached to producing high quality non-indigenous vegetables to meet a small elite demand. The range of food offered for sale at Lae used to be much more tuned in to expatriate demand than it is now. Since the food rationing regulations relating to indigenous laborers have been changed and these employees are now paid cash wages, the demand for food from indigenes has considerably increased.

The importance of expatriate buyers at Lae market has decreased considerably over the years. Fresh vegetables, most of which are by-products of expatriate plantations, are now being sold in shops, which is a source of supply preferred by many Europeans to the goods offered for sale at the market. Moreover, the character of the overall expatriate population in the area has also changed. Until about 1965 the large proportion of expatriates were either administrative personnel on long-term contracts or planters who have lived in Papua New Guinea for years already. In more recent years expatriate administrative staff are there on short-term contracts only; besides the number of tourists is also growing.

Though there are more Europeans and Chinese visiting Lae than Koki market, their modal expenditure is lower at the former than the latter market. The average value of goods purchased at Lae market is about \$1.10 alike for expatriate and indigenous buyers.

All the other markets we studied displayed peak activities on Saturdays; only in Lae Friday is the main market day. Two reasons may be taken to account for this peculiar marketing pattern in Lae. First, urban employees receive their pay on Fridays and many of them visit the market straight after work when they purchase produce; second, sellers at Lae come from further afield than at Hinterland-rooted markets and many of them travel back to their villages on Saturday so as to be able to spend Sundays at home. By contrast, many Koki vendors live too far from Port Moresby to be able to get back home for Sunday.

At Lae, as at most other markets, the average expenditure per buyer varies from day to day; although Fridays are the busiest market days when most sellers turn up with their produce, the average value of goods purchased per buyer is highest on Saturdays. The explanation for this may be that on Fridays much of the large quantities of produce brought for sale is bought by other vendors. It would mean that it is the one main day in the week on which indigenes specializing in the supplies of different types of produce use the market to buy each other's goods(3). This hypothesis gains support from remarks noted by the investigators surveying sellers, who repeatedly pointed out that on Fridays many vendors were leaving their own produce in care of another vendor sitting nearby while they themselves went off to buy something for themselves elsewhere in the market. Intra-market transactions (i.e. vendors buying from other vendors) constitute another area which requires further research. The qualitative as well as the quantitative market data indicate that none of the intra-vendors' transactions are barter; in all of them money is used as the intermediary of exchange.

It seems likely that there is a different pattern of trading prevailing at Lae on Fridays when most vendors bring most produce to the market and many individual buyers, a large proportion of whom may themselves be vendors, each buy goods worth less than $1. This results in larger average gross earnings per vendor and altogether a higher market turnover on Fridays compared with Saturdays when fewer buyers turn up at the market but the value of their average purchases is higher. Saturday is likely to be the day when urban workers visit the market and purchase their weekly requirements of non-perishable produce such as for instance areca nuts. This is shown in a different composition of the average food basket purchased per buyer on Saturdays as compared with other market days: on Saturdays it contains a higher proportion of areca nuts, peppers, sweet potatoes and other items which do not deteriorate as quickly as green vegetables, than on other market days when fresh fruit and vegetables make up more of the value of goods purchased.

BUYERS AT HINTERLAND-ROOTED MARKETS

Market Equilibrium at Mt. Hagen

Mt. Hagen market, which at the time of our survey operated only twice weekly was visited by an average number of about 900 buyers on Wednesdays and about 1,200 on Saturdays. The average value of their purchases per day was $1.35 in February and 74 cents in July 1967. For most weeks of our Mt. Hagen market survey the average expenditure per buyer was higher on Saturdays than on Wednesdays: it was $1.65 on Saturdays and $1.15 on Wednesdays in February 1967; the respective figures for July are 85 cents and 65 cents.

One of the most interesting facts emerging from the Mt. Hagen market study is the great number of sellers compared with buyers. There are only slightly more individuals buying things at the market than there are vendors offering produce for sale. This, however, does not mean that each vendor is also a buyer, but rather that the number of individuals who buy something at the market is small compared with the number of sellers; at Lae market the relationship between numbers of buyers and vendors is about 8:1, at Koki it is 5:1 and at Rabaul 3:1.

The proportion of goods sold of the volume brought to the market is highest at Mt. Hagen of all Papua New Guinea markets we studied. At Mt. Hagen demand and supply appeared to be neatly in equilibrium: about 2,000 vendors attended the market during any one week in 1967, of whom no more than 25 percent had gross earnings exceeding $2 per market day; during the same period about 2,100 buyers purchased goods at the market of whom only 20 percent spent more than $2 each.

Mogl, who belongs to the Moge tribe and comes from Beaprui, a place about five miles from Mt. Hagen, helped to explain how this balance between supply and demand comes about. She related that indigenous growers have their set priorities which determine the quantities each supplies to the market. First of all the production of staple crops, such as sweet potatoes, must cover the household requirements. Second, there must be sufficient available to meet likely temporary food shortages by kinsmen, who may wish to exchange for instance sugarcane for sweet potatoes. Such barter transactions are conducted only within the descent group but never at the market. Third, supplies in excess of these basic needs are taken to the market, where only a small proportion of buyers come from the rural areas surrounding the town. Such rural buyers use the market as a treat rather than to acquire the necessities of life: they either buy such luxury items as areca nuts or if they do buy sweet potatoes, as for instance Mogl did when she was interviewed, they may do so for the same reason as she explained accounted for her own purchases: It was raining in Beaprui and she just did not feel like digging up her own sweet potatoes. She decided to come to the market and to spend on sweet potatoes some of the money she herself had earned by selling this very crop during a previous week.

Mogl's account illustrates that only few growers supplying the needs of indigenous buyers at Mt. Hagen market specialize in one or another particular crop. Significantly, we found fewer different items of indigenous produce sold there than at most of the other markets studied (see Table 3.6). All this seems to indicate a more uniform ecology in the Mt. Hagen Hinterland than prevails for instance on the Gazelle Peninsula. Though Mt. Hagen has a Hinterland-rooted market its existence is demand -- rather than supply -- stimulated. The market's

raison d'etre is to supply fresh food to urban
dwellers who cannot grow their own produce, rather
than to provide an opportunity to indigenous cultivators to purchase each other's specialities.
Indigenous urban demand is not strong enough to
create a sellers market. If local growers buy anything at the market it is likely to be an item which
they themselves produce but for some reason or other
do not have readily available just when wanted. Most
of the buyers are thus urbanites who walk to the
market. Though indigenous staples constitute no
more than about 15 percent of the total value of
produce bought on any one market day, the modal
value of staples bought per buyer was about 50 cents
which exceeded that of all other food categories
purchased. These figures indicate that the majority
of buyers purchase mainly sweet potatoes and the
other few staples, while each of a small number of
buyers spends considerably more on other produce
sold at the market, particularly non-indigenous
produce.

Expatriate clientele is only of marginal importance at Mt. Hagen market; Europeans usually send
their indigenous servants to buy food for the
household at the market; about 80 percent of the
Europeans homes in Mt. Hagen do so. Only 20 percent
are so particular as to go to the market themselves
to select the produce to insure getting firm
tomatoes and fresh crisp beans without strings, etc.
Many expatriates adopted the practice of sending
their domestic servants to the market because they
learned by experience that an indigenous buyer gets
a better deal than does a stranger. Our investigators tried to discover the number of indigenous
buyers who act as purchasing agents for their
employers but failed to elicit this data, probably
because, as already mentioned, most domestic servants buy not only for their employers but also for
themselves when they visit the market; the two
objectives of purchasing produce were thus not
alternatives but rather mutually reinforcing motives.
Since the market material fails to show how many of
the indigenous buyers purchased on behalf of
expatriates it is difficult to estimate the relative
importance of expatriate consumption of locally
produced food in the Mt. Hagen area. However, the
fact that non-indigenous vegetables constitute
about 40 percent of the total value of produce
brought to the market of which no more than 10 percent remained unsold indicates that expatriate
demand was still an important factor in Mt. Hagen
market transactions, even though only few

expatriates personally visited the market. Here it should be noted that expatriates are not the only buyers of non-indigenous produce. Indigenous white-collar urban workers also purchase increasing quantities of recently introduced vegetables and fruit.

In 1967 no more than about half the number of individuals who visited the market actually bought something; the remainder came to the market to accompany their spouses, to meet friends, to look for a wife or girl friend or just to enjoy the fun of the fair. Little seems to have changed in this respect at Mt. Hagen market; Jackson's 1973/4 study reports that "of the indigenous male non-sellers 63 percent are also non-buyers at Mt. Hagen... The majority of men at the market neither buy nor sell, although some non-buyers might be so not by choice, e.g., they were unable to buy the pig they had thought of buying"(p.13).

Female indigenous buyers are usually the wives of urban workers, many of whom come from outside the Highlands. In 1967 the parochial attitude of the Highlanders was reflected in the prevailing animosity with which many of the Mt. Hagen vendors regarded some of the urban workers who migrated from the coast to work in the Highlands and who wanted to buy some of their food requirements at the market. It is interesting to note that by 1973/4 this animosity seems to have declined (Jackson, 1974:13). In the intervening period a growing number of Highlanders migrated to the coast and an increasing number of coastal people have been recruited for work in the Highlands. This broadening of indigenous horizons may have helped to reduce hostilities between people of different regions within Papua New Guinea. The greater ethnic diversification among the urban population can be correlated with an increasing diversification of the goods sold at Mt. Hagen market. In 1967 only food produce supplied by indigenous producers was retailed at Mt. Hagen market. By 1973/4 clothes were also sold there. These clothes vendors "are mainly Tolai wives of urban wage earners" (Jackson,1974:20). The impetus to the development of Mt. Hagen market originated from the establishment of the town; its further expansion is thus closely linked with future urban growth.

Expatriates' Influence at Goroka Market

Goroka is the major town in the Eastern Highlands; its market, though similar in some respects to the one operating at Mt. Hagen, also displays distinctly different features. It is simlar inasmuch as it is also a Hinterland-rooted but urban-stimulated market operating in the Highlands. Yet Goroka market seems to represent a higher level in the morphological development of market place trade than pertains at Mt. Hagen.

Goroka's population in 1966 was about 50 percent bigger than Mt. Hagen's; probably more important than the difference in absolute numbers between the two towns was the greater proportion of expatriates residing in the former (20 percent) as compared with the latter (15 percent). Unlike the balanced numbers of vendors and buyers we found at Mt. Hagen market, there were about twice as many buyers as sellers at Goroka market with numbers being consistently greater on Saturdays than on Wednesdays; about 1,800 buyers turned up on Saturdays and 1,200 on Wednesdays. Average expenditure per buyer was $1.58 in February and fell to 83 cents in August 1967; average value of purchases per buyer was more on Saturdays than on Wednesdays: in February it was $1.92 at the weekend and $1 midweek, the respective figures for August 1967 were $1.23 and 62 cents.

The large majority of buyers walk to Goroka market; the modal transport cost for those buyers who pay to come to the market is slightly more than $1. Saturday markets seem to attract buyers from further afield, which is reflected in a higher average transport cost per fare paying buyer on Saturdays than midweek.

Our records relating to the ethnicity of buyers show that on one Saturday in February 1967 10 percent of the buyers coming to Goroka market were expatriates. Moreover, many expatriates also send their indigenous domestic servants to purchase fresh fruit and vegetables at the market. This makes it difficult to gauge the impact of expatriate demand on indigenous marketing practices. However, since a large proportion of the non-indigenous produce is likely to be bought by expatriates, who are also the main customers for much of the fruit offered for sale, it is possible to estimate that expatriates are responsible for the purchase of about 30 percent of the value of total market turnover. The presence of considerable numbers of expatriates in Goroka, who are keen to purchase fresh foods produced by indigenous growers has certainly contributed to the expansion of the town market. Possibly also important to note in this context is the demonstration effect of expatriates on indigenous consumption as well as production.

Behope, a young man who lives about five miles from Goroka, was selling lettuces and cabbages at the market. He noticed there the sale of indigenously made golf clubs, which were specifically suitable for use in a local version of golf. Behope examined the clubs carefully, counted his day's takings which amounted to $2 and finally decided to treat himself to a set of these golf clubs. Though this particular account does not relate to food purchases it does illustrate neatly the expatriate demonstration effect on indigenous expenditure patterns.

All transactions at Goroka market are conducted by means of cash purchases; no barter takes place. Hatnave, who both sells and buys at Goroka market, explained that he sells produce of which he has a surplus over and above his household consumption needs and he buys whatever particular item he is short of; he never barters or exchanges one type of produce for another at the market. If for instance one of his sweet potato gardens is late in maturing and he needs this staple for his family's consumption he either approaches a member of his own descent group to help out, or if he has some ready cash he buys sweet potatoes at the market to satisfy his temporary needs; if one of his own kinsmen helps out this may be done either by way of gift or he may offer in exchange quantities of some other crop of which he happens to have a surplus just then. Goroka buyers who are also food suppliers thus seem to regard market trade the same way as do their Mt. Hagen counterparts: market purchases are made either to acquire some sundry luxury items such as areca nuts or peanuts, or to meet a temporary deficiency in staple foods. Vendors in Goroka, however, appear to be more market-oriented than those at Mt. Hagen: they fetch a greater variety of different types of produce and seem to try to specialize in supplying higher value per unit weight products than is the case at Mt. Hagen market. The estimated total weight brought weekly to Goroka market is only about two-thirds that fetched to Mt. Hagen market, whereas the estimated value of weekly market turnover is about 50 percent higher for the former than for the latter market (see Table 3.1). The proportion of produce remaining unsold is somewhat higher at Goroka than at Mt. Hagen.

Goroka displays greater diversification in supplies than does Mt. Hagen market: there is a far greater variety of non-indigenous produce sold at Goroka, such as for instance English potatoes, egg-plants, lettuces, celery, tomatoes and so on. By contrast Mt. Hagen sellers, fetch only quantities of the few local staples as well as one or another non-indigenous type produce. This greater diversification of produce sold and greater specialization by vendors at Goroka market does not only relate to non-indigenous produce but is also reflected in a greater number of individual sellers fetching quantities of only one of the local staples. This encourages some of the vendors to buy each others' produce for their own consumption.

Goroka thus seems to be much more of a Hinterland-rooted market than Mt. Hagen; it does not only cater to an urban clientele but also enables local growers to purchase each others' specialities. Yet the large majority of purchases at Goroka market too are made by urbanites, many of whom are migrants from other regions in Papua New Guinea. A large proportion of these migrants originates from New Guinea coastal regions. Their dietary habits differ from Highlanders and they often have to spend considerably more to get hold of their favorite foods in the Highlands than they are accustomed to paying for these items in their home areas. For instance, the Tolai from the Gazelle Peninsula of New Britain, who work in Goroka pay about double the price for cooking bananas and three times the price for areca nuts in the Highlands compared with what they are used to spending at Rabaul market. Some of the coastal staple foods, such as for instance green or dry coconuts are difficult to obtain at Highland markets or not available at all. It is interesting to note in this context that there is a greater mobility of labor than goods within Papua New Guinea which is the opposite to what prevails in most other parts of the world where produce rather than labor is more readily transported from one area to another.

Supply-stimulated Markets on the Gazelle Peninsula

Gazelle Peninsula markets are much more deeply rooted in the rural Hinterland than any of the other markets we studied. The regional ecology is such that it encourages highly localized specialization not only of different types of food, such as hill-grown taro and coastal caught fish, but also different varieties of the same produce, such as the many different varieties of bananas grown on the Gazelle Peninsula. In contrast to many other markets, which have been established and expanded to meet the requirements of a growing urban clientele, Rabaul is basically a supply-stimulated market. Present day Rabaul market is the logical sequel to the pre-European contact trading pattern which prevailed among the Tolai (see p. 13). *Tambu,* the indigenous shell currency facilitated the earlier transactions and is still used as a mediary of exchange at Rabaul market. Though the size of the market, the character of its clientele and the importance of *tambu* transactions has changed considerably since the establishment of Rabaul as a town and because of its subsequent expansion, there is still a large element of continuity noticeable in the Tolai trading pattern. This is reflected in the large number of Tolai, i.e., 28 percent who come to the market for the specific purpose of purchasing something; besides these non-seller buyers there were also many vendors who, like their Lae counterparts, left their wares in the care of neighboring sellers, while they themselves went off to buy from some other seller goods for their own consumption. All these intra-market transactions remained undetected in our survey.

Data collected from Tolai buyers indicate that they purchase about 25 percent of the total value of food sold at Rabaul market; they buy about 30 percent of all the indigenous foods and 40 percent of the poultry. This pattern of Tolai purchases seems to be fairly consistent since it emerged with only slight differences from our studies in January and April 1968. These Tolai buyers, most of whom are themselves food producers, make an important contribution to market demand. Their average value of purchases amounts to about 60 cents on weekdays and $1.20 on Saturdays of which approximately two-thirds is spent on staples.

The modal value of purchases per Tolai is 75 cents on weekdays and Saturdays alike, only on weekdays a larger proportion pays less than that amount whereas on Saturdays the distribution of expenditure per buyer is more heavily weighted above the modal value. No more than one percent of the total value of transactions are conducted by using *tambu* as a media of exchange. Fifteen percent of our Tolai sample buyers bought at least something with shell money. The importance of shell money as a means of payment for market purchases seems to be declining. In 1961 "as much as 25 percent of all intra-Tolai transactions were paid in *tambu* rather than cash" (Epstein, T. S., 1968:149).

IaKaen, a Tolai grower traveled the seven miles together with her two small children from her home to Rabaul on a Saturday in April 1967 for the specific purpose of buying fresh fish and cooking bananas for a feast which was taking place the following day in her village. She explained that she had to come to the market to buy these particular items since her village being inland has no access to fish, nor can they grow there the variety of bananas which cooked together with fish is known to taste most delicious. She traveled in a car driven by her husband who transported sellers with their produce to the market and who therefore did not expect any fare from his wife and children. On arrival at the market at about 8 a.m. she knew immediately where to look for fish sold by the people from Matupit: she bought four fish for $1.50.

She carried her purchases in a big bag woven of coconut leaves suspended from her forehead and hanging down her back; her baby sat on top of the bag strapped in a cloth tied round the woman's neck. She trailed the other child behind. IaKaen had difficulty in making her way through the crowds thronging Rabaul market on Saturdays. She frequently stopped to talk with one or another of her friends who were either selling their produce or like herself had come to buy things. While she herself liked seeing so many people gathered in one place and enjoyed meeting her friends and kin, her children got increasingly more restless. She decided to treat them to some refreshments at the Gazelle cafe where she spent altogether 30 cents. Afterwards she sought out Pilapila vendors whom she knew would sell the particular variety of cooking bananas she wanted; she paid 50 cents for the bananas. Having completed her main purchases she thought it advisable to buy some lime, which is a chewing requisite. Accordingly, she went to one of the Raluana vendors and bought a packet of lime for a *pidik,* a short string of *tambu* numbering 25 shells (worth about five cents). It was by then almost midday and since IaKaen's children were both crying she decided to buy a packet of cooked food (chicken and taro cooked in coconut butter) for 10 cents. They settled down under the trees near the Gazelle Council Chambers and consumed their meal. Subsequently, IaKaen visited a few of the Chinese trade stores opposite the market, where she bought a few items of clothing for her children for $1.50. She then waited until 4 p.m. when her husband was ready to take her back home. Altogether she spent $3.90 and 25 shells.

The distribution of IaKaen's expenditure

between things bought from indigenous suppliers on
the one hand and expatriate stores on the other is
particularly interesting; though her main purpose in
coming to Rabaul was to buy fish and bananas she
spent almost as much in expatriate enterprises as
she did on the market. Her expenditure pattern seems
representative in this respect of most Tolai coming
to purchase specific items at Rabaul market. This
helps to explain the booming business of the Gazelle
cafe (see p.215), as well as the rising turnover in
Chinese trade stores in the town, particularly near
the market site.

The comparative importance of Tolai buyers at
Rabaul market is declining. In 1961 they were
responsible for 42 percent of all market transactions
(Epstein, T.S., 1968:162); by 1968 this proportion
had declined to 25 percent. There has been a shift
of relative strength of demand away from Tolai buyers
to New Guineans, who in 1961 purchased only 11 percent
but in 1968 bought as much as 35 percent of the
total value of purchases. Papuan buyers have also
become relatively more important: in 1961 they were
responsible for only three percent of total purchases, by 1968 their proportionate importance had
increased fivefold. The importance of European
demand declined from 18 percent in 1961 to 15 percent
in 1968; the respective figures for purchases by
Chinese buyers are 26 percent and 10 percent. The
increased importance of indigenous migrants as buyers
at Rabaul market reflects their more than proportionate increase in numbers and also possibly their
improved economic status.

New Guinean buyers at Rabaul market constitute
60 percent of the clientele. They work either in the
town or on nearby plantations. A large proportion of
New Guineans who work in town have their families
living with them; their wives regularly purchase
fresh food at the market. The daily average market
expenditure per New Guinea buyer is about 50 cents on
weekdays and $1 on Saturdays. Many New Guinean urban
workers buy non-indigenous vegetables and fruit;
altogether they purchase about 15 percent of the
total value of non-indigenous produce offered for
sale at Rabaul market. On the basis of his 1961
study of Rabaul buyers Salisbury reported that "they
ate more sweet potatoes and less taro, more salad and
less European greens and fewer native greens, and
more *mau* (eating bananas)." He prophetically stated
that "as their numbers increase, so will the market
for what were in 1961 *European foods*" (1970:213).
This is precisely what appears to have happened by
1968. New Guineans working in Rabaul, particularly

those in white collar occupations, have further
diversified their diet. Non-indigenous vegetables,
and fruit are composing an increasingly larger proportion of their total comsumption. Most New
Guineans living in Rabaul walk to the market; those
who work on plantations usually travel to the market
on a plantation vehicle for which they do not have
to pay. Wayato, a New Guinean from the Lae Hinterland, works in Rabaul for the Public Works Department; in 1968 his fortnightly salary was $20. He
lived with his wife and two young sons on the Public
Works Department compound not very far from Rabaul
market. He visited the market every Saturday when
he bought the various chewing requisites for 40 cents
which usually lasted the whole week; he also purchased sweet potatoes, bananas and coconuts for 10
cents per bundle, as well as lettuce and tomatoes for
another 20 cents; altogether he spent 90 cents on his
purchases on Saturdays. His wife comes to the market
three times weekly and on each visit buys produce
worth about 60 cents. Wayato's weekly market purchases thus amounted to about $2.70 which constituted
about 50 percent of his household's total weekly
expenditure on food. Wayato's account indicates that
the cost of food for urban workers in 1967/8 was considerably lower in Rabaul than in Port Moresby, where
migrant labour had to spend more on food and bought
larger quantities of imported consumption items.
     Papuans visiting Rabaul market are on the whole
urban employees or their wives; they constitute 10
percent of the market clientele. Their average daily
market expenditure was in 1968 70 cents on weekdays
and $1.75 on Saturdays. Most of them live suffi-
ciently near to have easy access to the market.
Madaha is a Papuan woman originating from a village
about 100 miles from Port Moresby. In 1968 she lived
in Rabaul where her husband was employed as a clerk
and earned $30 per fortnight. They have five child-
ren and live in a small house not too far from the
market. Madaha claimed that she visited Rabaul market each day it was open. She emphasized how much
more she enjoyed purchasing fresh food at Rabaul
rather than at Koki market. They had been living in
Port Moresby before her husband was posted to Rabaul
and she was therefore in a good position to compare
the two markets. The only thing she preferred at
Koki to Rabaul market was the ample supply of fresh
fish. Otherwise she regarded Rabaul as a great
improvement compared with Koki market, not only in
terms of quality of produce sold but even more so as
regards prices charged. She pointed out that the
previous year when they were still living in Port

Moresby and her husband was paid there also $30 per fortnight she had a much harder time making ends meet than living in Rabaul. Her household expenditure on food and sundries while living in Port Moresby was about $12 per week of which she spent about $3 at Koki and the rest in trade stores. Since the family moved to Rabaul, Madaha spent no more than $11 per week on food and sundries of which she bought about 60 percent at the market. She reckons that her family was better nourished in Rabaul for less money since she was able to let them have more fresh vegetables and less of the imported rice. Like many of the New Guinean salary earners in Rabaul, Madaha bought some non-indigenous vegetables, such as lettuces, cabbages and tomatoes. She claimed that she had not been able to buy these items while they lived in Port Moresby. Their move to Rabaul has enabled her to provide a more diversified diet for her family. Madaha particularly pointed to the considerable price difference in areca nuts sold at Port Moresby and Rabaul markets. She said that whenever she hears of one of her Papuan friends going back to Port Moresby she tries to send at least some areca nuts to her kin back home. Madaha's account is self explanatory; it neatly illustrates not only the difference between Port Moresby and Rabaul markets but more important is the impact of all this on the household expenditure on food of urban workers and its perceived effect on nutrition.

Many expatriates residing on the Gazelle Peninsula regularly visit Rabaul market, particularly those living in the town itself. A large proportion of expatriates have come to regard Rabaul market as a convenient meeting place on Saturday mornings, when groups of them can be seen chatting under the shelter of the sheds. Fifteen percent of all buyers at Rabaul market are expatriates, which is a fair reflection of the proportion expatriates occupy among the Rabaul buying public. Most of the Rabaul expatriates do their own shopping for fresh food and vegetables at the market; unlike their Highland and Port Moresby counterparts only a few of Rabaul expatriate households delegate market purchasing to their indigenous servants. European and Chinese women are frequently accompanied by their domestic servants who carry their purchases, but they themselves decide what to buy. Europeans compose one half of expatriate buyers at Rabaul market and Chinese the other half. The average daily expenditure per European buyer at Rabaul market was $1 on weekdays and $1.50 on Saturdays; the respective figures for Chinese buyers were $1.20 and $1.98. Most of the expatriates live fairly near to the market and travel there in their own cars. This makes it difficult to assess their transport expenditure when visiting the market. Europeans purchase about one third and Chinese one quarter of all the non-indigenous produce sold at Rabaul market. Chinese also buy considerable quantities of all the small locally produced eggs, which they claim are better suited to their way of cooking than the larger eggs produced under controlled conditions. Europeans only buy the more costly larger eggs which still compare favorably in price with the imported eggs available in the large Rabaul stores. A number of expatriate buyers seek out vendors who sell shells or handicrafts and often take a long time before deciding what to buy. Accordingly, the proportion of the total value of expatriate purchases spent on miscellaneous items is significantly higher on Saturdays as compared with weekdays. Tolai vendors of these items often get to know their customers and try to cater for their individual requirements.

The long and well established Chinese community in Rabaul has introduced Tolai growers to a number of typically Chinese crops such as Chinese cabbage, ginger, etc., which are now available in abundance at Rabaul market and bought in considerable quantities by Chinese buyers. These buyers, however, do not only purchase produce for their household needs, but they also buy about 10 percent of the total value of areca nuts sold at Rabaul market. The Chinese are in fact the only customers in Rabaul who buy goods at the market for resale in their trade stores. Their shrewd business practice of trying to buy produce at the market as cheaply as possible and to resell it in their stores at considerably inflated prices to indigenous clients whose work prevents them from visiting the market themselves in the course of the day, has antagonized many of the Tolai in the area who believe in a 'fair price' for each commodity (Salisbury, 1970: 180).

Apart from the many individual indigenous and non-indigenous buyers at Rabaul market there is also a clientele representing local institutions. It is not difficult to spot these individuals who come to buy large quantities of fresh fruit and vegetables for institutions like residential schools and colleges, mission stations and prisons or private businesses like hotels. Most of them are expatriates who usually walk around the market

60

equipped with long shopping lists through which they keep checking as they are making their purchases; several servants follow them and carry the purchased produce in big bags or baskets on their shoulders. Vendors display more interest in attracting such large scale buyers than the mere individual client. Although there does not seem to exist a more lasting business relationship between individual vendors on the one hand and institutional buyers on the other, the latter have a tendency to concentrate their purchases by repeatedly buying the same variety of produce from vendors representing one village. Several of these buyers explained, when asked about this practice, that they had learned by experience that different villages produce the best quality of different kinds of produce. They stressed that they switch buying a particular commodity from the same village origin only if they discover a better quality supplied from elsewhere. The purchasing behavior of these institutional buyers gives a further indication of the ecological diversity prevailing on the Gazelle Peninsula, which leads to specialized production of different crops or even different varieties of the same crop.

These institutions constitute an element of considerable importance to the total demand for locally produced foods. I was fortunate enough to get hold of the details of the total value and weight of fresh fruit and vegetables (excluding root crops) Malaguna Technical College purchased at Rabaul market during two years, which reveal that average weekly market purchases in 1967 weighed 8.15 cwt. and cost $38.95; in 1968 the weight was slightly less, i.e., 6.70 cwt and the value slightly more, i.e., $39.75.

The College by-passed the market when it purchased staple crops; it contracted with a Tolai "big man" from Napapar about 15 miles from Rabaul for the supply of sweet potatoes and taro kongkong (*xanthosoma*). In 1967 the College purchased a weekly average of 13 cwt. of sweet potatoes at one cent per pound and 7.5 cwt. of *xanthosoma* at 1.25 cents per pound; the following year the prices were unchanged but the quantities bought were smaller, i.e. five cwt. each of sweet potatoes and *xanthosoma*.

This account of Malaguna Technical College's food purchasing pattern reveals several significant facts. Institutions regularly buy their fresh fruit and vegetable requirements at Rabaul market; their buyers usually purchase the same commodity originating from the same village unless they discover a better quality of produce supplied from elsewhere.

They prefer to buy fresh foods under conditions of free competition rather than try to contract for the supply of large quantities at lower than market prices with one or another of the Tolai "big men". Moreover, institutions buy much larger quantities than individuals. In spite of their comparative importance among market buyers the representatives do not behave any differently in their transactions with vendors than do individuals who purchase only small quantities for their own home consumption. The large scale buyers do nothing else but buy greater numbers of bundles of different types of produce compared with individual household buyers. They do not try to bargain by asking the vendor to increase the size of the bundles they are buying. Finally, institutions, such as government schools or prisons usually ask for tenders relating to their requirements of staple crops such as sweet potatoes and *xanthosoma*, and enter into a contract with whoever makes the most attractive offer. In 1968 the average Rabaul price per pound for sweet potatoes was 1.15 cents and for *xanthosoma* it was 1.75 cents, whereas Malaguna Technical College paid one cent per pound for the former crop and 1.25 cents for the latter. These contractual supplies of staple foods seemed attractive not only to the institutions receiving the produce but also to the individual small grower from whom the contractor in turn bought the crop. This arrangement offered an assured sales outlet for large quantities of produce at a price fixed in advance, and saved cultivators the trouble of having to take their staples to Rabaul market where they were unlikely to sell out and therefore had to face taking their unsold stuff back home once more. The "big man" contractors were much in favor of this purchasing agreement for they usually paid the growers no more than two thirds of the price per pound they themselves received from the institution. They argued that the remainder was their reward for collecting the produce and delivering the lot at the gates of the individual institution.

Such contractual purchasing agreements are obviously beneficial both to suppliers and growers. As the system operated in the 1960s though it helped to increase the economic differentiation within Tolai society: a few "big men" all of whom owned and ran large trucks had their contacts with the various larger institutions on the Gazelle Peninsula and managed to clinch contracts for the supply of sweet potatoes and other staples. Their influence as "big men" helped them in purchasing from growers well below the price they were receiving and therefore make a handsome profit. Officials at some government institutions became concerned about the impact their contracts had on enriching the already wealthiest men in the Tolai community, but failed to see a solution to this problem.

The study of Rabaul market presented here points to an alternative and more congenial arrangment whereby institutions wanting to purchase large quantities of sweet potatoes and/or *xanthosoma* rather than ask for tenders from local contractors, publicize by means of public media and/or by informing the Local Government Councillors that a buyer will turn up at Rabaul market about 4 pm on a certain market day. He will be prepared to purchase from individual vendors staple crops at a price fixed in advance, which may be about 25 or 30 percent below the open market price. In view of the fact that in 1968 Rabaul market was supplied with an estimated total of 180 cwt. of sweet potatoes per week of which about one quarter remained unsold and was taken back home by the individual vendors it should be easy to arrange for the various institutions to meet their total requirements of sweet potatoes by buying directly from the vendors before they are due to go back to their villages. Such buying arrangements would eliminate altogether any middlemen activities in the sale and purchase of local staples. It would have the disadvantage of promoting the extremely labor intensive marketing arrangments in existence, which may be compensated by the more even income distribution resulting. A schema for increasing the efficiency of food marketing on the one hand while on the other preventing the development of a too skewed income distribution is discussed at greater length in Chapter 6.

The buying public at Rabaul market displays considerable heterogeneity: different ethnic groups are interested in purchasing different kinds of commodities and spend varying amounts on market purchases. Moreover, not only cash but also shell money is used by Tolai buyers to pay for their purchases. The average expenditure per buyer of the total clientele appears to be about twice as much on Saturdays than on weekdays; it is least on Mondays and increases towards the weekend.

Rabaul is undoubtedly the busiest of all markets on the Gazelle Peninsula; its larger market turnover attracts increasing numbers of vendors, particularly on Saturday. The only other regular market of substantial size in the region is on Saturdays at Kokopo, which is "essentially the same as Rabaul market but lacking certain special features determined by Rabaul's large size" (Salisbury, 1970: 190). In April 1968 it attracted no more than about one tenth of the number of vendors and had no more than eight percent of the turnover at Rabaul market. Yet in terms of change over time the Saturday market at Kokopo has expanded more since 1961 than has Rabaul market. The market turnover on a Saturday in May 1961 was 1,482 shillings which is the equivalent of $148, whereas our April 1968 study indicates a turnover of $613(4). This amounts to an average annual rate of growth of about 45 percent. The average expenditure per Kokopo market buyer was 79 cents on a Saturday in April 1968.

The importance of European demand has considerably declined between 1961 and 1968; in the earlier period more than half the total value of produce sold was bought by Europeans, while during the latter year they bought only 34 percent. The value of non-indigenous produce constituted 37 percent of the total value of goods brought to the market in May 1961 and only four percent in April 1968. Thirteen percent of our Kokopo sample buyers in 1968 were Europeans, whose average expenditure was $2.13. Most of them bought indigenous crops for their employees rather than non-indigenous foods for their own consumption. They prefer to travel the short distance to Rabaul where there is a much greater variety of non-indigenous produce offered for sale, rather than purchase their household requirements at Kokopo.

This emphasis on indigenous staples is indicated in the fact that sweet potatoes made up 14 percent, *xanthosoma* 23 percent and areca nuts 15 percent of the total value of purchases on the day we studied Kokopo market. Altogether indigenous staples constituted more than half the total value of market purchases.

The modal value of market purchases is 50 cents for all Kokopo buyers; 25 percent of European buyers spend more than $2.50 at the market, while none of the other ethnic buyers purchase more than $2 worth of goods. Eighty-two percent of Tolai and all New Guinean buyers spend less than $1 on market purchases.

Plantation laborers bought 10 percent of total value purchased in May 1961 and retained their same proportionate importance in 1968. In the latter year Tolai bought 43 percent of the value of goods purchased; they composed 63 percent of the market clientele, whose average expenditure was 55 cents. Forty five percent of Tolai buyers bought at least one item with shell money; their average shell money

expenditure was worth five cents. Shell money purchases contributed altogether about five percent to
total market turnover. Several vendors at Kokopo
market insisted on being paid in *tambu* and refused to
accept cash. In 1968 *tambu* transactions were propor-
tionately more important at Kokopo than at Rabaul
market. This in fact may help to explain the comparatively more rapid growth of Kokopo than Rabaul
market between 1961 and 1968.

IaParaide, a female Tolai buyer at Kokopo market
lives in Bitareba Rebe about two miles from Kokopo.
When I talked with her as she was leaving the market
she showed me her purchases which consisted of two
bundles each of sweet potatoes and *xanthosoma,* one of
areca nuts and a packet of lime. Altogether she had
spent 55 cents. She explained that she comes to
Kokopo market about once or twice a month; she
travels to Rabaul market only when she intends to buy
larger quantities or more specialized produce. She
used to go more frequently to Rabaul market. However, since increasing numbers of vendors turn up at
Kokopo market she has decided that it is not worth
spending money on fares to Rabaul when she can easily
walk the distance to Kokopo market. She claimed that
there are many more Tolai in the Kokopo Hinterland
who have decided, like herself to give Rabaul market
a miss and instead visit Kokopo.

IaParaide was one of the 43 percent of Kokopo
buyers who originates from villages less than five
miles from Kokopo. Half of our sample buyers walked
to the market; average transport cost per buyer who
traveled to Kokopo market was 12 cents; only seven
percent paid more than 25 cents on fares.
IaPairade's account indicates a trend of decentralization of market place trade on the Gazelle
Peninsula. It will be interesting to observe if this
development is continuing.

Rabaul and Kokopo markets, though most important
in terms of daily turnover and numbers of sellers
attending, are not the only markets on the Gazelle
Peninsula. In line with Tolai precontact trading
patterns there still exist a series of smaller markets, some of which are regular, while most of them
are irregular and occur only when demand warrants
the gathering of vendors. Large mortuary rites or
other ceremonies provide such occasions. For
instance, a number of women from the coastal
settlement of Matupit prepared bundles of cooked
fish and took them for sale at a mortuary rite held
at Rapitok, a village about 20 miles inland. These
female vendors were not only pleased to be able to
sell their wares, but also enjoyed being present at

the big and important ceremony. These sporadic markets are usually demand stimulated. However, there are also such irregular markets on the Gazelle Peninsula which are supply-stimulated, such as for instance the sale of fish by the nearest convenient roadside to passers-by after a catch of fresh fish arrived on the beach. My Gazelle market studies failed to include any of these smaller and irregular markets(5).

Vunapope market outside the Mission hospital is the only smaller market we studied; it has no fixed site or retailing arrangements and is not under the control or jurisdiction of any Local Government Council. One hundred and seventy five buyers spent there an average of 22 cents. Sixty percent of buyers were Tolai, who spent 27 cents each; 36 percent were New Guineans who spent 16 cents each and the remainder were a few Europeans who visited indigenous patients in the hospital and spent 10 cents each.

Two thirds of all the buyers were women, many of them maternity patients, awaiting or recovering from delivery. The existence of a special buying public is reflected in the narrow range of products available for sale at Vunapope. No more than nine different kinds of produce are on offer. The total value of purchases was made up of 27 percent indigemous staples, 14 percent indigenous greens, 38 percent fruit (mainly eating and cooking bananas) and 21 percent sundry items (mainly areca nuts and peanuts). Only 20 percent of the buyers paid fares to come to Vunapope. None of them had come specifically to purchase something, but rather bought on their way to the hospital one or another item from the conveniently placed vendors. Their fares can therefore not realistically be charged as a shopping expense. IaKaen from Raluana got out of a utility, which stopped by the side of Vunapope market; she paid the driver 10 cents and he continued his journey with a few other passengers. She carried a bag full with food, some raw, some cooked, which she was fetching for her sister who she reported was very sick and had been taken to the hospital two days previously. She stopped by the various vendors examining their produce and finally bought a bunch of bananas for 10 cents and a bundle of peanuts for the same amount. She explained that she felt so sorry for her diseased sister that she wanted to give her a special treat. She planned to stay with her a few hours after which she intends to come back to the roadside and catch a ride home on one or other of the passing vehicles for which she will pay another 10 cents. IaKaen represents the typical buyer at Vunapope market. The easy availability of goodies to bring to patients attracts buyers to purchase one or other of the items offered for sale.

Two Tolai women with big bellies, obviously prior to delivery, were sitting near the vendors, dipping long peppers into lime to add to the taste of the areca nuts they were chewing. IaVarpiam from Nodup and IaBung from Malaguna had both been admitted to the hospital the previous day. They were classificatory sisters who had married into the villages of their respective husbands. Knowing of the small market outside the hospital they had decided to walk down the hill to the roadside and treat themselves to chewing requisites. IaVarpiam bought a bunch of areca nuts for 10 cents and IaBung purchased a bundle of peppers for the same amount as well as a small bag of lime for five cents. The two women explained that they knew the hospital authorities did not approve of chewing, which accounted for them sitting around near the market rather than return to their wards. Moreover, they stressed that they enjoyed being near these vendors, a few of them they knew personally and one of them was even a relative of theirs. IaBung recounted that she herself often takes coconuts and indigenous vegetables for sale to Rabaul market, which she said helped her have her own money to spend on whatever she wants. The money she had spent this morning on buying peppers and lime she had earned by selling produce at Rabaul market during the previous few weeks. She knew then that she would have to go into hospital for a few days to have her baby and therefore saved part of what she earned to leave her with some spending for her stay in hospital. Before the two women returned to the hospital they bought a bunch of cooking bananas which they planned to roast for their evening meal as a sort of treat. IaVarpiam and IaBung appear to typify buyers at Vunapope market who are themselves hospital patients. Most of them buy a few sundry items as well as the odd bundle of fruit or staples to add to their hospital diet.

CATEGORIES OF BUYERS

This discussion of demand at seven Papua New Guinea producer-seller markets illustrates its heterogenous nature: there are buyers of different sex and ethnic origin, each buying differing quantities of produce specifically suited to their dietary pattern. In spite of all this heterogeneity in demand it is possible to detect certain regularities in the purchasing pattern. The various types of buyers can be classified into different categories.

Urban Dwellers, who have no opportunity to grow
their own supplies of fresh food. They face the
choice either to frequent the local market and buy
fresh produce there or to shop for appropriate
imported items in the town stores to meet their consumption needs. This category of buyer keenly
examines the quality and price of commodities offered
for sale at the market and compares it with substitute items sold in the stores. Indigenous
employees living in Port Moresby readily fall into
this category of buyers; many of them regard the
purchase of staple root crops at Koki market as a
special treat which they afford themselves on rare
occasions only. They have adjusted to a rice diet.
Indigenous immigrants to Rabaul have responded
positively to the opportunity of buying at the market non-indigenous produce of good quality and at
reasonable prices. They are diversifying their diet
by incorporating increasing proportions of non-
indigenous vegetables and fruit.

Most expatriates in Port Moresby and many at
Lae prefer to buy their vegetables in town stores
rather than to visit the local market. In their
case, comparative quality of produce and the way it
is displayed are more important than prices in determining whether they buy their food supplies at the
market or in the stores.

The growing rate of urbanization is continuously increasing the importance of urban dwellers
as buyers compared with all others who purchase at
local markets. This will decidedly affect the
future development of producer-seller markets in
Papua New Guinea, a theme which is discussed at
greater length in Chapter 6.

Rural Proletarians, who live in the rural sector but
are wage earners, buy most of their food, though
rarely all of it. New Guinea laborers working on
plantations on the Gazelle Peninsula fall into this
category. Many of them grow a limited quantity of
food on land allocated them by the plantation owners.
However, since the abolition of food rations as part
of wages they have to purchase a large proportion of
the food they consume. Like many of the indigenous
urban dwellers they too have adapted to eating lots
of rice, which in many Papua New Guinea areas gives
better calorific value for money than indigenous
staples bought at the market; moreover, it is also
easier to store and cook. A large proportion of
plantation laborers purchase staple crops by-passing

the market; wherever possible they buy straight from the growers neighboring their place of work. These laborers are keen buyers of areca nuts. Those who manage to get to town while the market is open buy large quantities of this sundry item from market vendors, while the others are forced to buy their supplies of areca nuts in the Chinese trade stores at considerably inflated prices.

Wage earners, who work in town but still live in nearby villages and commute to work, can also be qualified as rural proletarians. They frequently live in land-short villages where there is not even enough land available to grow sufficient produce to meet their basic food requirements. Like many of the plantation workers some of these rural commuters arrange to cultivate intensively the small plots of land they have at their disposal in order to provide for themselves at least part of their household consumption needs. Others again, often with the help of their wives, specialize in marketing high value produce to supplement their wage income. The Matupis near Rabaul provide a good example for such behavior; they sell eggs, fish and lime. One of the urban workers from Matupit, for instance, "set his *baubau* during the fishing season which had just come to a close, while a number of the others regularly fished at night with line and bait or gathered megapode eggs at weekends" (Epstein, A.L., 1969:82). About six percent of the average income per Matupi wage earner was derived from the sale of fish, eggs and garden produce (Epstein, A.L., 1969:83). Matupi women are the chief suppliers of megapode eggs (a special Tolai delicacy), fish and lime at Rabaul market; many of them have husbands in regular urban employment. This close link with urban society is reflected in the changed consumption pattern among Matupi households. "Tea with sugar but without milk, and bread usually without butter, form today the standard Matupi breakfast... The urban worker tends to widen his choice. His regular purchases may include meat from the butchery, butter, tinned vegetables, ketchups and relishes, and his wife uses flour and dripping for cooking (Epstein, A. L., 1969:204). These rural commuters constitute only a marginally important section of demand at Rabaul market; they buy some non-indigenous produce and sundry items like areca nuts as well as small quantities of indigenous staple.

Cashcropper-Buyers, who concentrate on cultivating cash crops, such as for instance cocoa, coffee and tea, frequently buy large quantities of sundry items

at local producer-seller markets. Large numbers of
Highland men buying at markets produce considerable
quantities of coffee and many Tolai produce cocoa
and copra. Though these men may specialize in growing particular cash crops, they still participate in
subsistence food production with the aid of their
womenfolk. The daily diet of this category of
buyers is changing only slowly, if at all. Their
basic food requirements are met by subsistence cultivation, yet their cashcropping earns them amounts
of money, which range from about $10 to $100 or more
per month. Much of their cash earnings are invested
in capital assets such as vehicles or copra driers,
part of it is devoted to alcohol or conspicuous consumption by organizing large feasts, while some of
it finds its outlet on the local market in purchases
of sundry items. For instance, the income from their
coffee production enables many Highlanders to pay
the high prices charged at Goroka and Mt. Hagen for
areca nuts, while it facilitates the Tolai purchases
of more high-valued fruit, such as pineapples.
Cashcropper-buyers affect the market by encouraging
the supply of a greater variety of higher-priced
commodities.

Producer-Buyers, are cultivators who not only supply,
but also buy at the market. There are three different types of such producer-buyers. First, there are
those who live in an ecologically diversified rural
Hinterland and use the market as a place where sales
and purchases of the different specialized products
are conducted. Many of the intra-Tolai sales
transactions at Rabaul market are of this kind:
coastal sellers usually fetch fish and lime, while
many of them buy *xanthosoma*, taro or sweet
potatoes; inland vendors, on the other hand, frequently sell corn, sweet potatoes, taro and yam, and
buy fish and lime at the market. The interdependence of different ecological areas is still more
important at Kokopo than at Rabaul market, since the
latter has a much greater urban clientele than the
former. Occasional producer-buyers represent the
second kind under this category and, Mogl, the Mt.
Hagen buyer may be regarded as its prototype (see
p. 49). Such occasional producer-buyers are
motivated to buy at the market not just to get a
commodity they themselves cannot or do not produce,
but rather to compensate for a temporary shortage of
a particular food item which is normally self-
produced. These buyers are only of marginal
importance in terms of quantities of produce bought
at the market, and do not affect the specialization

of production. Luxury producer-buyers constitute
the third kind of buyers under this category. Behope
from Goroka (see p. 53) represents a good example
in this context. He cultivated and sold non-
indigenous produce and with his earnings allowed
himself the luxury of buying a set of golf clubs at
the market. Other such vendors use part or all of
their takings to treat themselves and/or their
families to areca nuts or some other of the non-
essential food items sold at the markets. Unlike
the occasional producer-buyer type the luxury
producer-buyers do encourage increasing specialization, particularly in items which are not really
essential to meet basic food requirements.

Institutional Buyers, are individuals who purchase
large quantities at the market on behalf of major
institutions such as hospitals, colleges and the
like. The example of Malaguna Technical College
on the Gazelle Peninsula of New Britain (see p. 61)
indicates that the scale of these purchases does
not affect prices paid.

Each of these various categories of buyers
exerts a different influence over market supplies
and transactions, as well as having its distinct
impact on the price formation process. These
topics are taken up again in later chapters.

NOTES

1. The number of Tolai buyers interviewed is
likely to be an underrepresentation of the proportion
they constitute of all buyers. This is due to the
fact that buyers were interviewed as they left the
market. Therefore, purchases by Tolai vendors, of
which there must be many, often escaped the
interviewers.
2. These questions were added to the buyers'
schedules at the special request of the Department of
Labour, some of the trainees of which helped in the
study. It is customary for government servants to be
paid fortnightly.
3. The majority of such purchases escaped the
watchful eyes of our investigators, since they interviewed buyers on leaving the market rather than when
purchases were actually being made.
4. The comparative data for 1961 are taken from
Salisbury, 1970, Chapter V.
5. Salisbury gives an interesting account of
one such traditional market at Vunabalbal which was
part of a "celebration in honour of the ancestors of

Vunabalbal clan (*a matamatam)* which was organised by
John ToMarangrang of Vunabalbal village" (1970:198).

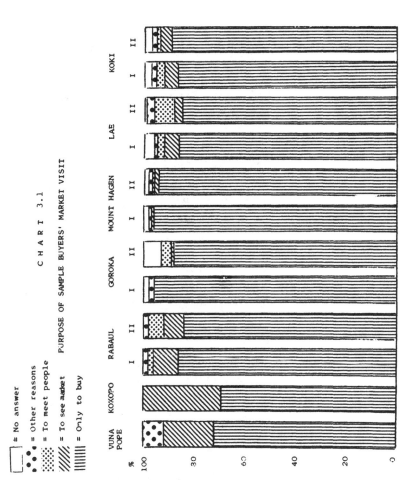

C H A R T 3.1

PURPOSE OF SAMPLE BUYERS' MARKET VISIT

= No answer

= Other reasons

= To meet people

= To see market

= Only to buy

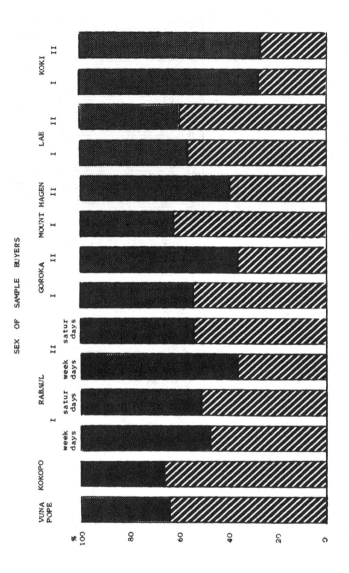

CHART 3.2

SEX OF SAMPLE BUYERS

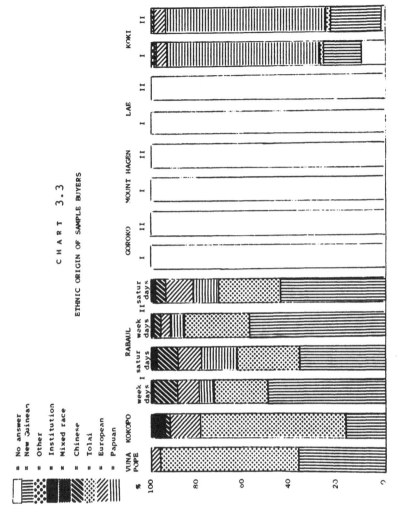

C H A R T 3.3

ETHNIC ORIGIN OF SAMPLE BUYERS

Table 3.1: Papua New Guinea Markets: Estimated Demand and Supply per Week

	Visitors No.	Buyers No.	Sample Buyers No.	Vendors No.	Sample Vendors No.	Turnover $	Weight Supplied Ton
Vunapope (April 1968)	200	175	25	21	15	39	0.75
Kokopo (April 1968)	1,200	875	62	205	35	613	9.25
Rabaul (January 1968)	16,135	10,955	865	3,555	613	10,203	250.00
Rabaul (April 1968)	15,700	10,265	1,120	3,043	558	8,970	212.50
Goroka (February 1967)	6,000	3,025	104	1,798	118	3,563	36.00
Goroka (August 1967)	4,575	2,890	89	1,680	85	3,747	26.50
Mt. Hagen (February 1967)	4,735	2,400	44	2,333	40	3,210	50.00
Mt. Hagen (July 1967)	3,880	1,940	102	1,941	69	2,310	41.00
Lae (August 1967)	14,020	12,554	720	1,466	216	4,413	77.50
Lae (December 1967)	15,600	14,010	548	1,586	216	6,201	90.00
Koki (May 1968)	49,428	12,612	1,553	2,525	507	18,584	150.00
Koki (February 1969)	58,718	7,045	507	1,700	258	9,542	50.00

Table 3.2: Koki Buyers (May 1968): Occupation per Ethnic Category

	No answer %	European %	Chinese %	Mixed Race %	Tolai %	New Guinean %	Papuan %	Other %	Total %
No answer	11	25	22	40	22	26	27	23	25
Professional and students	11	20	4	-	18	9	12	31	12
Administrative	-	3	9	-	-	1	1	-	1
Clerical and sales	11	18	39	34	1	7	9	-	29
Farmers and fishermen	4	1	-	7	-	1	2	-	2
Miners and quarrymen	-	-	-	-	-	-	-	-	-
Transport and communication	7	2	-	7	15	12	8	8	9
Craftsmen and laborers	26	5	9	7	10	15	16	-	16
Army and other services	26	26	17	5	31	28	21	30	2
Miscellaneous	4	-	-	-	3	1	4	8	4
Total	100	100	100	100	100	100	100	100	100
Nos.	27	160	23	15	68	665	2,145	13	3,116

Table 3.3: Koki Buyers (May 1968) : Fortnightly Income per Ethnic Category

Income $	No answer %	European* %	Chinese* %	Mixed Race %	Tolai %	New Guinean %	Papua %	Other %	Total %
1 – 9	-	-	-	-	-	12	7	-	8
10 – 19	34	-	-	-	25	42	35	-	36
20 – 29	11	14	100	50	12	22	24	100	23
30 – 39	22	-	-	-	13	11	18	-	15
40 – 49	33	14	-	-	37	7	12	-	11
50 – 59	-	18	-	25	-	3	3	-	4

60 - 69	1	1	1	13	-	-	-	11	-
70 - 79	-	-	-	-	-	-	-	4	-
80 - 89	1	-	1	1	-	-	-	14	-
90 & over	1	-	-	1	-	25	-	25	-
Total	100	100	100	100	100	100	100	100	100
Nos.	874	1	565	257	8	4	2	28	9

*Many of the expatriate informants were reluctant to disclose their income; therefore data relating to European and Chinese Income cannot be regarded as very reliable.

Table 3.4: Koki Buyers (May 1968) Fortnightly Income per Occupation

Income $	No Answer %	Professional & Students %	Administrative %	Clerical & Sales %	Farmers & Fishermen %	Miners & Quarrymen %
1 - 9	9	9	7	5	-	-
10 - 19	22	33	35	35	42	25
20 - 29	27	10	7	25	33	25
30 - 39	14	18	-	15	17	25
40 - 49	14	16	15	10	-	25
50 - 59	9	5	15	5	-	-
60 - 69	3	5	-	2	-	-
70 - 79	-	-	7	-	-	-
80 - 89	1	1	-	2	-	-
90 & over	1	3	14	1	8	-
Total	100	100	100	100	100	100
Nos.	88	103	14	125	12	4

Table 3.4 (con't)

Income $	Transport & Communications %	Craftsmen & Laborers %	Army & other Services %	Misc. %	Total %	Government* indigenous Employees %	Private Inds.** indigenous Employees %
1 - 9	5	9	9	8	8	-	-
10 - 19	32	36	45	54	36	40	58
20 - 29	36	23	18	30	23	31	26
30 - 39	15	18	11	-	15	17	8
40 - 49	9	11	10	-	11	6	5
50 - 59	2	2	3	8	4	3	1
60 - 69	1	-	2	-	1	3	2
70 - 79	-	-	-	-	-	-	-
80 - 89	-	1	2	-	1	-	-
90 & over	-	-	-	-	1	-	-
Total	100	100	100	100	100	100	100
Nos.	110	220	185	13	874	6,096	8,235

Source * - D.o.L., 1968:33

** - D.o.L., 1968:35

Table 3.5: Average Expenditure per Buyer
at Papua New Guinea Markets

		Purchases $	Transport Charges $
Vunapope		0.17	-
Kokopo		0.70	0.12
Rabaul	I:W	0.76	0.10
	I:S	1.45	0.18
	II:W	0.62	0.10
	II:S	1.14	0.15
Goroka	I	1.58	2.55(?)
	II	0.83	0.27
Mt. Hagen	I	1.35	0.06
	II	0.74	0.23
Lae	I	1.02	0.31
	II	1.17	0.23
Koki	I	1.77	0.14
	II	1.51	0.15

(?) Inflated by airfares to Goroka

Table 3:6: Numbers of Different Items
Sold at Papua New Guinea Markets

		No.
Vunapope		8
Kokopo		26
Rabaul	I:W	72
	I:S	64
	II:W	48
	II:S	53
Goroka	I	67
	II	45
Mt. Hagen	I	46
	II	35
Lae	I	55
	II	69
Koki	I	48
	II	52

Chapter 4

SUPPLY

The various categories of buyers discussed in the
previous chapter are likely to feature at most developing country markets. There is therefore nothing
distinct about the demand side. Pacific markets are
different from most others only in terms of their
supply characterisitcs (Brookfield, 1969). Papua New
Guinea markets in particular are dominated by
producer-sellers. The large bulk of goods they offer
for sale thus consists of locally grown staple foods,
fresh fruit and vegetables, eggs, chicken and fish as
well as sundry native stimulants. Manufactured
articles, imported goods and export crops are traded
through channels other than the market place. The
markets discussed here are thus radically different
from those of many other parts of the world, where
middlemen predominate (Bauer, 1954; Belshaw, 1965;
Bohannon and Dalton, 1962; Cassidy, 1974; Dewey,
1962; Szanton, 1972).

Most market material available so far relates to
the more frequently occuring retail markets. This
accounts for the many generalizations in the literature on markets which claim the inevitable development of a hierarchy of market centers (Bromley, 1971:
127). Some announce categorically that "market
centers are only the basic building blocks of a much
more complex hierarchy of central places, capable of
knitting the entire spatial economic structure
together in a functional sense" (Johnson, 1970:418),
while others regard the market as the most important
central place institution. Skinner (1964) showed
that the Chinese market system can be understood in
terms of hierarchical structures of centers with
hexagonal trade areas. He "perhaps gave too much
emphasis to the formal, geometrical aspects .... and
neglected the more basic and universally applicable
concepts of the maximum and minimum range of goods"
(Bromley, 1971:128).

In the context of these theoretical statements the question arises where Pacific markets fit into the scheme of market place trade. Are they an earlier form of market arrangements that must inevitably change as the country develops or do they represent a different kind of market structure altogether? I suggest that the answer can be found only by a detailed examination of producer-seller markets and viewing them as symbolic of the social structure of which they are part. Accordingly, this chapter presents a detailed account of the economic and social aspects of sellers at Papua New Guinea producer-seller markets.

CHARACTERISTICS OF SUPPLIERS

Women constitute a large proportion of market vendors in Papua New Guinea, particularly at Hinterland-rooted markets (see Chart 4.1). It accords with the customary division of labor between the sexes in traditional societies, which allocates to women the tasks of planting, tending, harvesting, cooking and distributing staple crops. Except for the initial clearing of the bush, which is done by men, all other cultivation activities fall within the domain of women. Many young new Guinea men regard it below their dignity to carry food produce to the market and offer it there for sale.

In the Highlands the saying goes that *'Lapoon man olesem ol i save tinktink long moni, tasol, maski tinktink long meri. Ol yang man ol i save tinktink long ol meri pren bilong ol, ol i sem long stanap long market long salim kaikai, ol i save raun na lukim pren belong em'*. ('Old men are concerned only with money and do not care about women. Young men are all concerned about their girlfriends and would feel ashamed to be seen by them selling food produce at the market'). Market trade is regarded as women's work, because it is directly connected with the cultivation and distribution of food. This sex specialization of economic functions seems to be widely accepted not only by New Guinea men but also women. For instance Kiripanu, who is and elderly widow living in the vicinity of Goroka where she frequently sells sweet potatoes at the market emphatically stated that she would never ask her grown sons to help her carry her produce to the market. Her sons prepare the ground for new gardens; they cultivate and sell coffee and sometimes take cut firewood for sale at Goroka market. Kiripanu does not not want her sons to carry food to the market for they are not boys any more, they are men now and therefore must not be seen carrying sweet potatoes.

Women, together with a sprinkling of elderly men, make up most of the sales force at Hinterland-rooted markets.

There are other factors besides the male-female role differentiation, which help to account for the predominance of women among market vendors in Papua New Guinea. For instance, the Tolai suppliers of Gazelle Peninsula markets practise viri-local residence. This means that each Tolai girl moves on marriage to her husband's home parish. It results in a widespread inter-parish network of kinship and friendship relations between women from different areas, many of whom look forward to their regular meetings at the market site. These cross-cutting ties among women vendors from different parts of the Gazelle Peninsula are also reflected in some of their sales arrangements whereby many of them deposit part of their produce with friends or kin for them to sell while they themselves try to sell the rest of their stuff. "For instance, I saw one woman placing her small baskets of tomatoes in the care of another seller, who was also displaying for sale her own tomatoes. The first one was from Volavolo on the northwest coast of the Gazelle Peninsula and the second was from Tinganagalip about 10 miles southwest of Rabaul and about 16 miles from Volavolo. When I enquired how the two women had got to know each other, they explained that they were affines; the first one was born and had grown up in Raluana, a coastal parish about five miles south of Rabaul; she had married into Tinganangalip, while the second one was from Tinganangalip and had married into Volavolo. It never occured to the Tinganagalip vendor, who looked after her own tomatoes as well as those belonging to her Volavolo friend, to induce buyers to purchase her own produce in preference to that brought by her affine, nor did she try to increase the size or improve the appearance of her own small baskets of tomatoes to attract buyers to purchase her own rather than those belonging to the other vendor" (Epstein, T.S. 1968:144).

Such sales practice is fostered on the Gazelle Peninsula by the tribal homogeniety of market vendors; it is therefore rare, or even non-existent in other parts of Papua New Guinea where sellers belonging to many different tribes come together at the market place.

Koki market differs significantly from all the other markets we studied in the sex composition of its vendors; about two thirds of Koki vendors are men. This difference can be readily accounted for by the fact that supplies travel much longer distances to Port Moresby; therefore, sellers fetch more produce on one journey and stay longer in town than is the case anywhere else in Papua New Guinea. In contrast to the Hinterland-rooted markets where the large proportion of sellers originates from within a market radius of 20 miles, at the urban-based markets vendors come from much further afield (see Chart 4.2), about two thirds of Koki vendors travel more than 50 miles to get to the market. Significantly, about 80 percent of Koki and Lae vendors who stayed more than one day in town were men.

There are certain moral considerations affecting the tendency of women to return to their own homes at night; if women have to stay in town overnight they are usually chaperoned by one or two of their close male kin on their expedition. Very rarely, if ever, do female vendors venture to remain away from their homes for more than one day without male protection. The difficult terrain in the Highlands and in the Lae Hinterland, which is reflected in a poor system of communications, results in many market vendors having to walk long hours before they reach the nearest road where they can catch some motorized means of transport, or before they get to the market itself. The difficulties involved in getting to the market often encourage women from one village or supply region to arrange for a few of them to set off walking together on a marketing expedition; they usually take along with them a number of young girls, who carry the produce in headloads, as well as one or two male protectors. These marketing parties set off and return jointly and frequently stay together at the market as well as at night in the home of one of their friends now residing in the town. This type of group marketing attendance seems to be particularly prevalent among vendors supplying Lae market.

The compact Hinterland of Gazelle Peninsula markets with its outstanding road network and tribal homogeneity enables sellers to return home at night after attending one or another of the markets during the day. It is this fact which possibly accounts for the almost total absence of male vendors at Vunapope, Kokopo and Rabaul markets.

In spite of the difficult terrain and the resulting poor communications most market vendors we interviewed traveled at least part of the way to the market in a motorized vehicle (see Chart 4.3); only in the Highlands as many as half of the vendors walk to the market, which reflects the lack of feeder roads in the region. By way of contrast all Rabaul sample sellers drive to the market. Each Saturday morning almost all Tolai owned trucks, jeeps and utilities, of which there were at least 500 in 1968, as well as many non-native owned vehicles hired by Tolai, converge on Rabaul -- many of them make several trips -- to bring women with their produce to the market. There is, for instance, an almost regular taxi service plowing between Matupit, a coastal parish about two miles outside Rabaul, and the market site, fetching vendors; the return trip costs 20 cents. The traffic jams in the vicinity of Rabaul certainly indicate that on Saturdays on the Gazelle Peninsula all roads lead to the market.

Vendors at other Papua New Guinea markets use more heterogenous means of transport. As already mentioned a considerable proportion of Highland vendors walk to the market; three percent of the Lae sample sellers and about 15 percent of the Koki vendors come by sea transport. There exist even some exceptional arrangements whereby produce arrives by air. For instance, there is one group of people from the Pindiu area in the Lae Hinterland who sometimes charter a small plane on Fridays to fly oranges, beans, carrots, potatoes, onions, bananas, sweet potatoes and taro to Lae, where the consignments are picked up by the Pindiu people residing in Lae, who sell the produce at the market and bank the proceeds. Pindiu is about 50 miles from Lae but inaccessible by road.

The low frequency with which individual vendors attend markets (see Charts 4.4 and 4.5) suggests that a large proportion of them are target operators and means that they have a specific purpose in mind for which they want to utilize the money realized from market sales. This hypothesis gains support from the fact that the majority of vendors spend almost immediately most of the money received from the sale of their produce on purchases of imported food and clothing in the town shops (see Chart 4.6). Chinese trade stores have been established near most of Papua New Guinea market sites in response to this growing demand for imported goods, such as rice, tinned fish, items of clothing, household chattel, etc. The idea of saving at least part of the receipts from market trading for later investment in more costly assets, such as houses and cars does not seem very prominent among New Guinea market vendors; of all the markets we surveyed only at Koki do more than 25 percent of sample sellers intend to save for a car or house (see Chart 4.6). Only a small proportion of vendors hand their takings over to their spouses, particularly on Gazelle Peninsula markets the number of sellers who do so appear to be very few(1). One of the most frequent miscellaneous uses of sales receipts mentioned by our sample vendors is their aim to contribute to church activites or pay school fees for one or other of their children.

Most of the produce vendors bring for sale are indigenous staple food items of which a considerable proportion remains unsold; a lot of it they take back for their own consumption (see Chart 4.7). Only at Koki market do a considerable number of sellers turn up day after day until they have sold all they brought along. Since many of the items offered for sale are perishable and their quality deteriorates quickly in the hot climate of Port Moresby there is a striking difference in the appearance of the food sold at Koki on the one hand and at all the other markets we surveyed at the other. At Koki we can see for instance bananas for sale with black patches on their skin, which denotes the fact that they are no more fresh; such a sight would be inconceivable at any other Papua New Guinea market, particularly on the Gazelle Peninsula. Yet hardly any of the produce brought for sale to Koki is ever thrown away; some of it is given by vendors as a gift to their urban hosts who provide them with board and lodging during their stay in town.

At Rabaul market a considerable proportion of the unsold produce thrown away consists of European vegetables, such as lettuce and Chinese cabbage, which deteriorate quickly and which are not consumed by indigenes. Many Tolai women vendors prefer to throw away their unsold lettuces rather than yield to the bargaining attempts by Chinese buyers to sell for instance two bundles of lettuces for the price of one. Some of them, on the other hand, agree to reduce prices of European vegetables at the end of the day to cut their losses of unsold produce. The price formation process is discussed in a later section of this book; here it only needs to be stressed that different types of vendors display different attitudes towards selling produce which is part of their staple diet and therefore represents surplus production on the one hand, and pure cash crops such as lettuce on the other.

MARKET TRAFFIC

Motorized transport is a fairly recent innovation for Papua New Guinea market vendors. The first vehicles came within their reach when the Army began to pull out of New Guinea after the war and auctioned cheaply many different kinds of trucks. An indigene could then acquire a truck in reasonably good condition for less than £20, which was well within the means of many of them at the time. A large proportion of these first vehicles acquired by indigenes were jointly owned by many individuals. Each of them contributed towards its purchase amounts differing from one shilling to £10. Like land, these trucks came to be vested in the kin group and managed by its elders. Many of these early vehicles were acquired for prestige purposes rather than as economic asset. There was no organized management or bookkeeping associated with these novel transport ventures and many passengers traveled free, particularly those who had contributed money towards the purchase of the vehicle, however small an amount, and regard themselves as co-owners in the enterprise. This practice soon ran into difficulties for there was often no money for repairs when trucks needed it. This accounts for the large number of trucks abandoned by the roadside for lack of repair facilities.

The best among the first indigenous drivers who appeared on the Mumeng road in the Lae Hinterland was a man from the Sepik District. He had acquired an old Army truck which he treated with great concern -- never traveling faster than about 15 miles per hour, and which he used as a successful business venture transporting passengers and produce fairly regularly to and from Lae. Subsequently, he bought a new truck and serviced Markham Road passengers. Truck transport to Lae market developed dramatically only since about 1964; prior to that only a few indigenes in the Lae Hinterland owned vehicles, but most of the market vendors walked to the market and carried their produce bodily. Some of the Lae buyers claim that the produce sold at the market then was in much better condition than it is now. The present system of market transport may easily account for this. Indigenous trucks coming from further afield, for instance Bulolo, stop in almost every village on the way, picking up passengers and produce and often also dogs and pigs. These trucks do not only transport vendors with their produce to the market, but also operate as bus service for individuals wishing to travel to places on the road. Therefore, it often happens that trucks are so crowded that passengers squat on top of bags filled with goods for sale at the market. This obviously does not help to improve the quality of the produce.

The opening of the Highlands highway at the beginning of the 1960s represents a watershed in the regional communication system. Prior to it air transport was the only link between the coast and the Highlands. At one time the number of aircraft flying into Mt. Hagen even exceeded 1,800 per month; these were regular chartered aircrafts of different types and sizes. For instance, the Mt. Hagen Shell agent alone required daily the use of three planes. Significantly, since the establishment of the Highlands highway all fuel is transported there by road. Trucks bring regular supplies from the coast to the Highlands, but appear to have difficulties in securing the necessary backloads, except when coffee needs to be sent out of the country. However, since climatic conditions in Lae are said to have an adverse effect on the moisture content and/or color of coffee beans, growers prefer to store this produce in the Highlands. Therefore, coffee is transported to Lae only sporadically. This fact adds to the backloading problem and seems to warrant greater efforts to encourage the transport of other Highland produce to Lae. Expatriates in Lae already claim that the Highlands highway, which considerably reduced freight on vegetables brought from Goroka, has played a major part in reducing vegetable prices at Lae market. Similarly, increased supplies of areca nuts reaching Goroka from Lae have helped to reduce the price differential between the two markets.

Roads and motorized transport encourage increased and more regular market supplies from a widening area. Many Highland vendors emphatically state that they bring their produce to the market only if transport is available to fetch them. A large proportion of them are dependent on vehicles owned by expatriate plantations in the area. Growers are usually told in advance when transport to the market is due to leave and make their plans accordingly. If the trip is canceled for one reason or another growers wait until alternative transport comes available, rather than walk.

The shortage of transport facilities in part of the Goroka Hinterland has resulted in a decentralization of market place trading; smaller and dispersed trading sites are developing where transactions are almost solely conducted between indigenous vendors and indigenous buyers. Prices on these markets seem to be lower than the absence of fares and freight would warrant in comparison with the larger markets in towns. This means that it is in the interest of vendors to sell at the higher priced urban markets and motorized transport is a necessary prerequisite to do so. Even if the vehicles as such may be run at a loss, the vendors who use them for taking their produce to the larger urban markets certainly benefit from them. This may account for what at first sight appears as an irrational and uneconomic indigenous investment in trucks.

The honeymoon with cheap ex-Army vehicles did not last very long in New Guinea, because of the initial lack of indigenous know-how in operating motorized transport. Wherever there were available trained indigenous drivers and/or mechanics the early transport ventures lasted longer. On the Gazelle Peninsula, for instance, where there were numbers of Tolai men, who had worked as drivers on expatriate plantations prior to the last war, a considerable number of Army surplus vehicles were still running at the beginning of the 1960s. Only very few of the pre-war Highland plantation laborers belonged to the workers' elite of skilled men. This accounts for the fact that their first transport ventures soon landed in difficulties. Fortunately for them, in the meantime they were able to accumulate money from the sale of coffee and other cash crops. In line with customary arrangements groups of people pooled their resources and jointly invested in trucks, many of which were new. Individual contributions varied from a few shillings to a few hundred pounds; the men who contributed most took control over running the trucks. In order to protect these new and much more costly assests from rapid deterioration, a number of Highland kin groups owning trucks have entered into contracts with an expatriate transport business based in Goroka, according to which their trucks are efficiently serviced and supervised and fixed amounts received for long distance trips -- for instance, truck owners receive $300 for every trip their truck makes to Lae. This arrangement appears to be beneficial all round: it gives the expatriate entrepeneur an opportunity to earn profits; it yields regular cash returns to the truck owners and reduces the depreciation rate on their assets; and lastly and possibly most important it helps train indigenes in the running of transport ventures. This arrangement resembles the operation of some radio cab companies in some of the large cities in the developed countries, where a man driving his own taxi joins the company by paying the firm a commission on his turnover in return for being part of a wider radio communication network. He thus retains his own business identity while at the same time being able to benefit from economies of scale by being a member of a larger company of taxi drivers. It should be posssible to devise a trucking system for New Guinea vehicle owners, whereby they too could have the best of both worlds; i.e., operate their vehicles separately but join together with others in having their

trucks properly serviced and their accounts efficiently kept.

The excess demand for transport facilities in
relation to the available means of transport mitigates against competition between different truck
owners. Fares and freight charges seem to be fairly
uniform, varying only with distance. The average
fare per person seems to be about five cents per
mile for journeys of less than three miles; three
cents per mile for three miles and up to 15 miles;
and two cents per mile for longer distances.

As part of our market studies we also surveyed
the vehicles servicing the markets. The large number of different kinds of vehicles arriving at
Rabaul and Koki markets -- more than one per minute
(see Table 4.1) -- made it impossible for us to distinguish between those which had brought only sellers
and those which fetched potential buyers; nor were
we able to establish how many of the vehicles made
more than one journey to the market per day.

At Goroka and Mt, Hagen markets most vehicles
fetching vendors made at least two journeys: 72
trucks accounted for the 123 vehicles fetching vendors to Goroka market in March 1967. In the same
month 26 trucks accounted for 41 vehicles fetching
vendors to Mt. Hagen market. The average number of
persons arriving per truck was then about 11 in
Goroka and Mt. Hagen. The depth study of market
traffic fetching vendors to Lae market, which was
conducted on five days between Tuesday August 29,
1967 and Saturday September 2, 1967, indicates that
few sellers, i.e., an average of about seven per
truck were carried, but each brought more produce
than did the individual Highland vendor. This is
reflected in the considerable difference in the
average daily earnings between vendors at Highland
and Lae markets.

The number of vehicles servicing the different
markets appears to be a function of carrying capacity per vehicle, the overall market turnover and
the distance from which supplies are brought for
sale; the greater the turnover the larger the number
of vehicles arriving at the market site; on the
other hand, the greater the distance they travel the
fewer the journeys each can make.

The large number of small utilities which service Rabaul market and the limited distance they
have to travel to get there together with the comparatively big overall turnover easily account for
the large number of vehicles arriving daily at
Rabaul market. Tolai transport entrepreneurs
learned by experience that it is difficult for them

to run profitably large and costly trucks. According-ly they substituted smaller and cheaper Japanese utilities for the bigger and more costly vehicles. This trend is reflected in the fact that in 1961 for every utility two large trucks arrived at the market (Salisbury, 1961:1), whereas by 1968 the relation-ship had become reversed: there were almost twice as many utilities as trucks servicing Rabaul and Kokopo markets.

The more distant areas supplying Koki market and the underdeveloped road network in the Port Moresby Hinterland necessitates sea and even air travel for a considerable proportion of vendors. Moreover, because of the distance vendors have to travel to reach Koki many of them bring such large quantities of produce so that they have to stay several days in the town before they sell out and return to their home villages. A large proportion of the road borne supplies reaching Koki originates from Rigo, about 60 miles from Port Moresby. Ward estimates that in 1967 an average of 57 tons of village produce were moved weekly from Rigo to Port Moresby (1970:38). Of the 47 Rigo based vehicles she surveyed only 32 percent were individually owned while the rest were collectively controled.

This brief analysis of market traffic seems to indicate that the state of the market Hinterland road network, as well as rationalization of trans-port arrangements are two very important factors which jointly affect the volume of supplies pro-ducers are prepared to sell at urban markets in Papua New Guinea.

MARKET ATTENDANCE

The dominant feature of producer-seller markets is the large number of individual vendors, each trans-porting and selling his/her own produce at the mar-ket. The lack of regular market attendance by indi-vidual vendors and the comparatively small quanti-ties each fetches for sale reflects the fact that selling their produce is only of marginal importance to their whole livelihood.

Since the Local Councils that are responsible for Papua New Guinea markets charge a fee, records of tickets sold are available. These records clearly indicate the trend of increasing numbers attending urban markets. Here it should be noted though, that the number of vendors is likely to have increased more than the records of tickets sold indicate, simply because the proportion of sellers who escape having to pay their market fees increases with the total size of the market. For instance, our counts at Rabaul market showed three times as many vendors than had bought tickets during the period of our market study. The discrepancy between numbers of vendors attending and tickets sold is particularly great on Saturdays, when there are about 2,500 sellers at Rabaul market; it is less on weekdays when on average no more than about 250 vendors come to the market. On weekdays it is much easier for the official collecting the money to insure that each vendor pays her fee than it is on Saturdays, when large crowds throng the market and it is extremely difficult to keep track of all the sellers, many of whom keep moving around within the market. Some vendors purposely try to escape having to pay their fees and disappear when they see the approaching official; others operate a "ticket pool", whereby two or three tickets may be shared by as many as ten vendors. They do this by passing the tickets around and displaying them wherever the official happens to be approaching; usually small children are sent to keep an eye on the official's movements as well as to act as messengers in conveying the tickets between different vendors. I was able to spot these practices at Rabaul market, simply because I was familiar with Tolai practices, was known to many vendors and understood their vernacular. Unfortunately, I failed to have these advantages at Koki. However, it is reasonable to assume that the efficiency of policing ticket sales is everywhere inversely related to the size of the market and that there are vendors at all the markets who try to avoid having to pay their fees. In view of this, it should be realised that the number of vendors attending Koki market must have increased considerably more than the tickets sold indicate (see Graph 4.1).

Even though the records of market tickets sold may understate numbers of sellers in attendance, they are likely to represent more reliably the daily and monthly fluctuations in numbers of vendors coming to the market. This then poses the question, why do more vendors bring their produce to the market in some months than in others. One reason which seems immediately obvious is the climatic variations in the market Hinterland which affect the supply of cash crops as well as the surplus of subsistence produce. Rainfall obviously affects the maturation of crops particularly in their early stages of growth. Therefore, it is necessary to allow for a time lag between rainfall in the Hinterland and sale of produce at the urban market. The Koki supply area covers a considerable distance and produces such a great variety of different crops that it is difficult to decide the average period of crop maturation.

By comparing the graphs showing the seasonal fluctuations on the one hand in rainfall and on the other in market attendance it emerged that a time lag of seven months showed a neat fit (see Graph 4.2). I subsequently checked with agricultural officers working in the area how appropriate it is to think of a seven months crop maturity period and learned that it does apply readily to taro and yam, but not to sweet potatoes, which take only six months to grow.

A similar exercise of trying to determine the time lag that would offer a reasonable fit between fluctuations in Hinterland rainfall and market attendance for Goroka, Lae and Mt. Hagen suggests six months for Lae, seven months for Goroka and eight months for Mt. Hagen (see Graphs 4.3, 4.4 and 4.5).

It needs to be stressed here that these correlations are only suggestive; much more agronomic and climatological research has to be done before a definite causal connection can be claimed between rainfall in the supply areas and market attendance. In this context it is interesting to note though that on the Gazelle Peninsula where there are no such distinct seasonal variations in any one year, market attendance seems to be also more even, displaying less fluctuations throughout the year than at any of the other Papua New Guinea markets.

There are of course also other than economic and ecological reasons which motivate vendors to take their produce to the market (see Chart 4.8); some want to visit the town and take produce to the market for the sole purpose of recouping the expenditure on their fares; others go to sell at the market simply because this is a social occasion which they enjoy; again others are pure target vendors, that is to say they are motivated to sell because they have in mind a certain object they wish to buy. For instance, the large number of vendors at Koki in July need not only be the result of high rainfalls in the Hinterland seven months before but may also be connected with the need for cash to pay Local Government taxes, which are being collected in July. Another but similar incentive may be the need to accumulate shell money. For instance, if a Tolai woman has a son of marriageable age, she is expected to contribute to his bridewealth. Therefore, women vendors in such circumstances try to sell more at

the market; they accept only shell money and refuse
to be paid in cash (see p.136).

PRODUCE SUPPLIED

The number of different items sold at Papua New
Guinea markets is striking particularly in view of
the fact that almost all represent one or other type
of crop grown locally. A few vendors offer their
domestic artifacts or handicrafts for sale, but
there are no manufactured articles displayed at any
of the markets. Indigenous growers do not only produce many different kinds of food but also many
varieties of one and the same crop. For instance,
"some seventy named banana varieties are known to
the Tolai... Each variety is distinguished by
appearance and taste, and many are planted for their
suitability for some particular purpose, for example,
as a 'breakfast' food, or for feeding to young
babies or old people" (Epstein, A.L., 1969:70).
This great variety makes it difficult to compare
prices of produce. Our investigators recorded the
specific name of all the individual varieties sold
but when it came to coding we were compelled to
reduce the number of items. For instance, we put
all bananas under two categories, namely 'eating and
cooking'. Even so we coded more than 50 different
types for most of the markets we studied (see Chart
4.9) except for Vunapope, which catered only for
hospital patients and their visitors where the
variety of items sold is limited. In order to
facilitate the analysis of our data we further cat-
ergorized the many different items sold under nine
headings: non-indigenous vegetables such as cabbage,
cucumber, tomatoes, etc.; indigenous staples, where
we included sweet potatoes, taro, etc.; indigenous
greens, such as leaf vegetables, etc.; fruit, such
as bananas, oranges, etc.; sundries, including areca
nuts, lime, etc.; meat and eggs; fish; handicrafts,
such as baskets, mats, etc.; and miscellaneous,
covering firewood, beads, etc. The proportion of
the total value of produce offered for sale which
falls within each of these categories reflects the
ecology of the market supply area and producers'
response to market incentives.

Non-indigenous vegetables: Since the last war the
Australian Administration has encouraged indigenous
growers to produce non-indigenous vegetables wherever this was possible to insure supplies of fresh
food for expatriates as well as to increase indigenous cash income. The Department of Agriculture

began to distribute seeds free of charge to indigenous growers after the last war. Besides this official encouragement for local producers to cultivate non-indigenous crops, individual Chinese and Europeans living in Papua New Guinea also introduced a number of vegetables previously unknown to indigenous producers. The considerable quantities of non-indigenous produce offered for sale at some of the markets indicates the success of these earlier attempts. This category of produce contributes about 40 percent of the total value of produce brought to Highland markets and comparatively little of it remains unsold (see Tables 4.2 and 4.3). At Lae non-indigenous vegetables constitute about 33 percent of produce at the market of which about one-third remains unsold on any one day. However, many Lae vendors try to sell their unsold produce at the market again the next day. Rabaul market too displays considerable quantities of non-indigenous vegetables: on weekdays this category of produce constitutes 12 percent and on Saturdays about 20 percent of the total volume of goods offered for sale. Vunapope and Kokopo markets specialize almost exclusively in customary local food items; almost two-thirds of the buyers at these markets are themselves Tolai, the tribe inhabiting most of the supply area. The comparatively small amount of non-indigenous items sold at Kokopo market is produced by vendors who live close to the town. The few Europeans and Chinese who visit the market buy mainly for their plantation or domestic labor. As already mentioned, they prefer to purchase the fresh fruit and vegetables for their own consumption at the much larger market in Rabaul, particularly on Saturdays. Less than 20 percent of the non-indigenous produce brought to Rabaul market remains unsold on any one market day.

The number of expatriates and their fresh food requirements are fairly stable. This means that "anyone trying to go into larger scale production of European foods is very likely to flood the market and be left with most of his goods on his hands" (Salisbury, 1970:194). For instance, one of the growers outside Goroka tried to specialize in cabbages. He planted a large area with this crop all of which matured at the same time. On one day he thus harvested 1,500 cabbages, took them to the market and sold only a few of them. At the end of the day he tried to give away free the many cabbages he had left over, but indigenes do not eat cabbages and therefore, refused his free gift. He ultimately threw away the whole lot and vouched never to

99

produce any novel crop again. This incident illustrates the great risk indigenous growers run if they undertake production of non-indigenous crops on a larger scale and explains the marginality of the market of such produce in relation to staple foods. The individual producer-seller, who tries to specialize in non-indigenous produce runs the risk of failing to sell a large proportion of it, whereas a vendor who diversifies her produce and grows only a small quantity of tomatoes, lettuce, etc., has a much greater chance of selling more of the stuff she fetches to the market.

The absence of wholesale trading and the lack of an efficient intra-country system of communications effectively isolates the different markets from each other. Each market is fully dependent on its own Hinterland for its supplies. The few commerical attempts which have so far been made to try and transport goods produced in one area for sale to another area have failed miserably. Yet some individual Chinese seem to buy fresh vegetables regularly at Rabaul market, pack them in crates and dispatch them by air to their friends and kin residing in Port Moresby. The fact that such commercially minded business men as the Chinese shopkeepers in Rabaul are prepared to regard it as a reasonable proposition to air freight vegetables from Rabaul to Port Moresby seems to indicate that such transactions may be profitably conducted on a larger scale.

Comparative market prices and intra-country marketing is discussed in later sections. Here it suffices to stress the domination of market supplies by the immediate market Hinterland producers. This emerges clearly from our study of Koki market which shows that non-indigenous produce there contributes less than five percent to the total value of produce brought to the market on any one day. Port Moresby has the greatest number of expatriates of all Papua New Guinea towns, yet most of them refuse even to visit Koki let alone purchase some of the poor quality and unhygienically displayed produce. As already mentioned at Rabaul market Chinese and European buyers seem to enjoy choosing fresh vegetables and fruit from among the abundant and high quality supplies whereas Koki is the market most of them try to avoid. There appear to be several reasons for the failure of Koki market to cater for the considerable volume of expatriate demand. Most important here is the character of the market Hinterland. It does not lend itself readily to the cultivation of non-indigenous produce -- even indigenous staples are difficult to grow there -- unless

novel techniques of cultivation are employed. However, using modern production methods it does not
seem to be impossible to grow lettuces, tomatoes,
etc., within the vicinity of Port Moresby.

Australian and American troops managed to produce large quantities of vegetables in the area
during the war. "The Australian farm near Port
Moresby had 160 acres of land under cultivation by
early 1944. In 1943 an average of 5,000 daily rations of vegetables was supplied to Australian forces
in the area... The farm was said to have produced an
average of 15,300 pounds of vegetables to an acre in
1943. Crops included cabbage, silverbeets, French
beans, snake beans, Chinese cabbage, tomatoes, cucumbers, radishes, lettuces, pumpkins, marrows, squash,
sweet potatoes, yams, sweet corn, carrots, pineapples, papayas, bananas, citrus fruit, avocados,
water melons, rock melons, and cantaloupe... In the
dry season (May to November) irrigation pumps supplied more than 4 million gallons of water a week
from a nearby stream... Crops were sprayed to prevent
loss to insects and fungi, and commercial fertilizer
was used as needed. It was estimated that the cost
of vegetable production amounted to 3d per pound ...
The American farm on the Lakoki River north of Port
Moresby was begun early in 1943 on a 70 acre tract
and by October that year some 15 acres were under
cultivation. By early 1944 the farm had been
expanded to 250 acres. Planting was done frequently
to assure a regular supply of vegetables, and sprays
were installed to supplement the natural rainfall.
Lettuces, Chinese cabbage and silverbeets produce
about 30,000 pounds to an acre a year, and squash,
radishes, water melons, carrots and eggplant about
20,000 pounds... Production on the American farm in
1944 exceeded the requirements of the American
forces remaining in the Port Moresby area, and on
one occasion it was necessary to dump 100,000 pounds
of lettuces into the harbour because the refriger-
ated storage space was full. Shipments of fresh
vegetables were made by air to Milne Bay, Finschhafen
and Oro Bay" (Bowman, 1946:431). On the basis of
the wartime evidence some experts claim that "there
would seem to be no difficulty in providing settlers
in the lowland valleys with almost every kind of
food they are accustomed to eat without alienating
large tracts of fertile soil in the Highlands.
During early 1944 it was the hope of the 5th Air
Force Headquarters to supply 40,000 air corps troops
stationed at Nazdab with fresh vegetables and fruits
from a few small (10 to 15 acre) farms on the plateau at Bena Bena, Goroka, Kerowagi and Mt. Hagen,

supplemented in parts by surplus products from native gardens in the vicinity of these four outposts. That this goal was never achieved was due to uncertain flying weather, lack of sufficient American transport planes and agricultural machinery when and where they were most needed" (Bowman, 1948: 51). These accounts clearly indicate that all that is required to increase the food production in the Port Moresby area is efficient organization and appropriate inputs. Extension work on irrigation, application of fertilizer and insecticides should not be beyond the abilities of the Department of Agriculture. The other alternative to improving Port Moresby's supply of fresh foods is to promote a better intra-country distribution system.

Papua New Guinea Administration files contain many statements and memoranda referring to the need of improving the supply and marketing of food produce. A statement by the Business Advisory Officer, dated 21 June 1966, begins by deploring that "far too much money is spent on importing vegetables which can be produced within the Territory. This money would be far better channelled internally with a boost to the local economy and income and a reduction in the import bill... One prominent aspect of vegetable marketing which is common in most countries, that is seasonal glut periods with low prices, is almost completely absent from the market picture in Port Moresby. This is a typical picture of an under-supply/excess-demand situation which would normally attract more producers until the situation is reversed. There is certainly evidence of new producers being attracted, but none of the increased volume is forcing prices down." Another memorandum claims that "the attempt to encourage Native People to farm in the Lakoki River area has generally failed. A few relatively affluent Hannuabadans, etc., have weekend farms there but there are few permanent settlers. The amount of food produced in the Lakoki area by these people has not significantly affected the local food situation" (D.N. Fenbury, 20.11.1967). The accounts seem to indicate the need for extension services to train indigenous growers in using modern cultivation techniques, as well as helping them acquire the means to do so, such as for instance irrigation pumps, sprinkler irrigation etc., etc.

Some expatriate shop owners regard the producer-seller markets as their source of wholesale supplies, that is to say they buy fresh food at the market at current rates and resell at considerably inflated prices in their stores to expatriate buyers who do not like to visit the market themselves.

A number of Lae shop owners have been reported to follow this practice. Some expatriate plantation owners have tried to go into market gardening and set up their own retail outlets in the towns. Though these expatriate ventures insured regular high quality supplies most of them failed because their large scale production was as risky as that of indigenes. Moreover, they could not compete in price with local producers. Native growers, however, do not seem to be able to produce good quality lettuces, which seems to be the result of lack of applying the necessary sulphate of ammonia.

The rapidly growing towns in Papua New Guinea require increasing supplies of food at reasonable prices to keep the urban cost of living from rising too quickly. The country is extremely fortunate in terms of availability of cultivable land compared with other developing countries such as for instance India where the population is already pressing hard on landed resources and any further extension of area under cultivation is almost impossible. Thus in Papua New Guinea all that seems to be needed to cope with increasing food requirements is to plan agricultural productivity accordingly and to improve the intra-country system of distribution.

Indigenous staples: The customary diet differs considerably between parts of Papua New Guinea; in the Highlands, for instance, sweet potatoes are the staple food, while in some coastal regions bananas and taro, cooked in coconut juice seems to be preferred. The obligation of employers to provide their laborers with food rations resulted in the initial stages in attempts by expatriates to buy indigenous staples in bulk. Many of them soon discovered that it was cheaper and easier to feed their laborers with imported rice rather than to depend on fluctuating sweet potato supplies from indigenous growers; some tried to arrange for the cultivation of sweet potatoes on their own lands so as to be able to feed their laborers with home produced crops. Those planters who produced an excess over their own needs had no difficulty in selling their surplus to institutions such as hospitals or prisons where there is always a great demand for bulk supplies of staple foods.

As a result many of the expatriate plantation owners in the Highlands have given careful thought to the possibility of producing sweet potatoes as a cash crop and concluded that it might be more profitable even than growing coffee. Machine planted sweet potatoes yield about five to seven tons per acre and the crop is worth about $40 to $50 per ton. One European planter, for instance, planted 80 acres of sweet potatoes in 1967 which brought him a gross return of $24,000. He lost interest in coffee growing and switched altogether over to mechanized production of sweet potatoes. He reckoned that there is such a big and rapidly growing demand for sweet potatoes that it is likely to exceed supply at current prices for years to come.

Indigenous growers hesitate for several reasons to venture into large scale production of sweet potatoes. First, they know by experience that sweet potatoes take a lot of nourishment out of the soil and therefore no more than two crops can be planted on any one plot before it has to be fallowed; second, though many of them know about manure they doubt the efficacy of fertilizer in insuring indefinite periods of cultivation of one and the same area; moreover, they know that fertilizers are costly and therefore too expensive to use; also indigenous growers lack the necessary capital and know how to practise mechanized cultivation; and lastly, bulk production needs different sales outlets rather than individual market place transactions.

This last consideration is very important. Its relevance is evidenced by the fact that indigenous staples constitute less than 20 percent of the value of produce brought for sale at most Papua New Guinea markets except on the Gazelle Peninsula where it makes up about one third. A large proportion -- at some markets over 90 percent -- of indigenous staples brought for sale are sold on any one market day, while prices remain fairly fixed in the short run. This indicates that market supplies and demand for indigenous staples are fairly well in equilibrium, except for Gazelle markets where demand falls persistently short of supplies. Yet as already mentioned, vendors are not really worried about having failed to sell part of the indigenous staples they brought to the market for they can always take them back home again and use for their own household consumption.

Indigenous greens, such as spinach (Abelmoschu Manihot) deteriorate much more quickly than do the staple root crops. This accounts for the fact that indigenous greens constitute no more than about 15 percent of the total value of produce offered for sale at the markets, except for Vunapope where the special demand pattern results in indigenous greens constituting almost 40 percent of market turnover.

Indigenous greens are usually cultivated by women on plots not too far away from their homes. They harvest the crop for their household consumption if and when needed. Hardly any female farmers plant indigenous greens for the specific purpose of selling at the market. The usual pattern of indigenous greens' sales is that when a grower has decided to take some of her produce to the market and finds after she has assembled all she wants to sell that it lacks variety, she cuts some bundles of indigenous greens and adds them to the lot. She hopes in this way to attract more buyers to purchase some of her produce. Indigenous greens, like non-indigenous vegetables, constitute thus only a marginal addition to the produce brought for sale by most of the individual vendors. In all our market studies we did not come across a single vendor who specialized exclusively in the sale of indigenous greens; we encountered a few sellers who specialized in selling non-indigenous vegetables.

Fruit is bought at markets not only by indigenous but also by expatriate buyers. It contributes about 15 percent to the total value of goods fetched to the markets of which a large part is made up of different varieties of cooking and eating bananas. Whereas bananas are a luxury for expatriates, for many indigenes they are very much an essential ingredient of their daily diet. This is reflected in the different demand patterns for bananas displayed by expatriates and indigenous buyers. Expatriates seek bananas without blemished skins, which they judge to be high quality and for which they are prepared to pay higher prices; in contrast, indigenous buyers cannot afford to pay such high prices, on the other hand they are less concerned with the outward appearance of bananas. This explains why vendors at Koki are able to sell at current prices bananas with almost black skin. No expatriate buyer would ever be prepared to even look at the sort of bananas many indigenes are readily prepared to buy. This should not be taken to indicate lack of judgement on the part of indigenous buyers, it simply illustrates different criteria for choice as well as the existence of a sellers' market at Koki where demand for bananas and other foods greatly exceeds supplies.

Many indigenous buyers visit Koki after their day's work is over and shortly before the market closes just in order to purchase cooking bananas for their evening meal. They have little choice but to buy whatever is available. Banana vendors are aware of this and take advantage of it. I observed many vendors displaying their better quality stock in the morning when more discriminating buyers visit the market, while putting out for sale in the afternoon bananas they had not been able to sell the previous day. There is obviously a risk involved in this sales practice, for there is a limit to the number of days the same bunches of bananas can be displayed at the market. However, with demand as it is at Koki the risk is not too high; moreover, vendors can always consume, or give away as presents to their urban hosts, bananas that have deteriorated so much that they have become unsuitable for market sale. At Koki about one third of fruit brought for sale remains unsold on any one day. However, in the course of our Koki market study we did not encounter a single vendor who failed to sell almost all the produce brought for sale; all that is required there is the preparedness to sell produce on several successive days. Similar arrangements operate at Lae market also, where about one third of the fruit brought for sale on any one day remains unsold, but individual sellers attend the market a few days in succession and in most cases manage to sell most of their fruit.

On Highland and Gazelle Peninsula markets, where the same vendors hardly ever turn up one day after another, the proportion of produce sold on any one day is significantly higher than at Koki and Lae, where individual vendors attend markets more regularly.

Sundries, in particular areca nuts, peppers and lime, constitute a considerable proportion of total produce brought for sale, particularly at Rabaul market, where these items account for almost half the total value of produce brought for sale on weekdays; about one third remains unsold. Though the bulk of the sundries purchases is made by indigenous buyers, as already mentioned (see p. 60), some Chinese shopkeepers purchase areca nuts at the market and resell them in their stores; for instance, one can buy a bunch of 50 or 60 areca nuts for 10 cents at the market and resell these nuts in small lots of six or eight for 10 cents in trade stores to laborers who work throughout the day and therefore are unable to shop at the market. These laborers frequent Chinese stores in the evenings and regard the purchase of areca nuts as a treat and do not seem to mind paying much more than the market price. Chinese shopkeepers resell areca nuts purchased at the market not only in their Rabaul stores but also frequently send supplies by sea to some of their satellite shops on the Duke of York Islands and New Ireland.

Areca nuts, peppers and lime together represent a stimulant. Accordingly, demand appears to be highly price inelastic. Just as drug addicts are prepared to pay almost any price to get hold of their stimulant, similarly indigenes do not appear to mind how much they have to pay in order to acquire areca nuts.

In the Highlands areca nuts were hardly known until the beginning of the 1960s. Occasionally a policeman transferred from the coast to the Highlands brought a bag of areca nuts with him. The story is related in the Highlands of one such bag of areca nuts having been confiscated by one of the expatriate administrative officials in Mt. Hagen in 1960 because he thought it was illegal to import areca nuts to the Highlands. It was soon discovered, however, that the confiscation itself was illegal rather than the import of areca nuts. This incident illustrates how little was known until recently about areca nuts in the Highlands. The opening of the highway connecting the Highlands with the coast facilitated road transport of areca nuts, which immediately began to flow into the Highlands.

The custom of chewing areca nuts quickly spread among the Highlanders. Nowadays, areca nuts are sold in fairly large quantities at the major Highland markets, as well as along the roads leading to Goroka and Mt. Hagen. Almost every truck going from the Markham valley or Lae to the Highlands fetches some areca nuts and coconuts. Truck drivers regard this trade as an attractive additional income. They frequently buy two dollars worth of areca nuts at Lae market and resell them in the Highlands for six to eight dollars.

Sundries represent 10 percent of the total value of produce displayed for sale at Goroka market and about 15 percent at Mt. Hagen market; at Goroka about 85 percent of sundries are sold and at Mt. Hagen market almost all are sold. By 1973 Mt. Hagen market had introduced "a separately fenced area for the sale of betel nut and its accoutrements. However, chewing the nut is forbidden in the market" (Jackson, 1974: 3). The fact that areca nut chewing can still be prohibited at Mt. Hagen market reflects the recent innovation of this custom in the Highlands. In contrast there has been no official attempt to regulate the chewing of areca nuts at coastal markets. Even if this had been tried it would have been extremely difficult to police such a bylaw, simply because chewing areca nuts is a deeply rooted and widely spread custom in these regions. Being a narcotic possibly acccounts for the rapid spread of the areca nut in areas where it was previously unknown.

Areca nuts and their accoutrements contribute almost 20 percent to the total value of produce brought for sale to Lae market, of which a quarter remains unsold. Lae Market Trustees realized the potential expansion of areca nuts' sales and discusssed in June 1966 posssible improvements in marketing this commodity. An amount of $236 was earmarked for the erection of a stall for the sole purpose of selling areca nuts.

The influx of large numbers of indigenous immigrants to Port Moresby has resulted in a rapidly growing demand for areca nuts at Koki market, where this commodity represents about 20 percent of the total value of produce on display; about a quarter of it remains unsold on any one day. However, as mentioned already Koki like Lae vendors attend the market a few days in succession and usually manage to sell almost all the produce they brought to town for sale. Most of the areca nuts sold at Koki are brought by Mekeo vendors who travel more than 100 miles by sea to take their produce to Port Moresby. Individual vendors fetch an average of about $50 worth of goods and remain in the town about nine days before they sell out and return home again. The average price of one pound of areca nuts at Koki is about four times what is charged at Rabaul and roughly double the Lae market price. Immigrant labor in Port Moresby is prepared to pay almost any price for areca nuts. The supply of areca nuts for Koki seems to be effectively isolated from other regions where this commodity is produced, so much so that Mekeo vendors have a monopoly over it. This enables them to keep the price much higher than it is at other markets.

The distribution of areca nuts by some Chinese traders in Rabaul and Lae as well as by some indigenous truck drivers who transport this commodity from the coast to the Highlands represents an embryonic stage in the development of wholesale trading. Yet it should be noted that almost all these trading ventures still secure their supplies by purchasing areca nuts at the market at the current retail price rather than bypass the retail outlet and buy from the grower directly at the place of production. It is the isolation of each market from the others that facilitates discriminatory pricing and enables a few *colporteurs* to corner the market in cartel like fashion and thereby make a handsome profit.

Meat and eggs: The sale of pork is rare at Gazelle Peninsula markets. In the 1960s extension services began to encourage local farmers to breed pigs for market sales, which subsequently may have resulted in pork sales at the markets. A few indigenes usually fetch some skinny chickens and a few dozen small eggs to Rabaul markets on Saturdays, most of which are purchased by Chinese. The price of chicken sold at the market compares unfavorably with that charged for better quality poultry imported from Australia and sold in the urban supermarkets. Accordingly, few Europeans buy chicken at Rabaul market.

Only one or two Tolai men bring regularly to the market a few dozen fresh large eggs which, as they explained to me, are the result of their following meticulously the extension officer's advice on how to feed their chickens. Europeans have come to know these vendors and therefore their eggs are usually bought up within a short time of their reaching the market. The larger eggs sell at higher prices, but European buyers are prepared to pay more for quality and size of produce. Chinese buyers explained that they prefer the taste of the small indigenous chicken and eggs to that of imported equivalents. Indigenous buyers never purchase chicken eggs and hardly ever buy chickens. The only eggs Tolai are interested in buying are the eggs of the megapode, which are regarded as a special delicacy and sold raw or cooked at the market. These megapode eggs are found only in the sands in the vicinity of Matupit crater between May and October and gathering them is "an arduous and hazardous business" (Epstein, A.L., 1969:73). This accounts for the small quantity of these eggs offered at Rabaul market, particularly during our studies which were conducted during the megapode off season. Meat and eggs together account for only one percent of the total value of produce brought to Rabaul market on Saturdays, of which almost everything is sold.

At all the other markets we studied meat and eggs contributed about three percent to the total value of produce brought for sale, except during our first survey of Goroka market when this category of produce contributed as much as 12 percent. The data gives no indication why this unusually large quantity of pork should have been brought to Goroka market in February 1967; I can only guess that it may have something to do with the local pig cycles. It is interesting to note though that almost two thirds remained unsold. Pork constitutes the large bulk of meat sold at Papua New Guinea markets other

than those on the Gazelle Peninsula. The proportion
of pork sold varies from 33 percent at Goroka to 100
percent at Mt. Hagen market. Some of the unsold raw
pork at Koki is smoked and brought back for sale as
smoked meat. The quality of raw meat deteriorates
quickly in the tropical climate. Therefore, unless
freezing, canning or smoking facilities are available meat has to be consumed quickly before it loses
its freshness. Freezing and canning facilities are
as yet not available to indigenous meat producers
and only a few enterprising indigenes have started
smoking meat. This accounts for the fact that only
small quantities of pork are brought to the markets
for sale. In the Highlands most of the pork consumption is not channelled through the markets but
rather through the institution of pig feasts.

Fish: The lack of preservation and/or processing
facilities affects fish just as much as meat. It
accounts for the total absence of fish sales at
Highland markets. At Koki there is a freezer shop
where frozen fish is sold, but none of it is locally
caught fish; all of it originates from Australia.
The reason for this appears to be the necessity of
fishing vessels to be equipped either with freezing
facilities or large quantities of ice. Indigenous
fishermen as yet lack the working capital to invest
in freezing plants for their boats and "the use of
ice by Port Moresby fishermen has not usually been
successful because they use the ice sparingly and
keep the fish too long before selling. It would not
be satisfactory simply to put fish on ice after the
market closes" (D.o.F., 1963:1), though it may
safely be put into deep freeze.
     Fish constitutes about 15 percent to the total
value of produce brought to Koki, of which about 80
percent is sold fresh daily. Most of the fish sold
at Koki is supplied by Hula fishermen who have their
houseboats tied up in Koki Bay and who often fish
for considerable periods before returning to base.
The quantity of fresh fish at Koki varies greatly
from day to day and between the different seasons.
In May 1968 there were on average about 475 lbs
of fresh fish brought daily to Koki; the respective
total for February 1968 was 210 lbs. The fishing
grounds are usually within a radius of ten miles
from Koki and fishermen show much skill in making
regular landings under various weather conditions
between 3 and 5 pm daily. Potential fish buyers
eagerly await the landing of boats in the afternoon.
Fish are displayed hanging from poles, and buyers
crowd round as soon as the poles are put up.

Indigenous buyers usually buy small fish the price
per pound of which is considerably higher than that
of larger fish. The few expatriates who are prepared to visit Koki usually come to buy fresh fish.
They can afford to buy the larger fish weighing several pounds each and therefore get better bargains
than indigenous fish buyers.

The sale of fish at Koki appears to have been a
matter of considerable concern for some time. Recom-
mendations were made, which, if implemented, would
help to increase the quantity, improve the quality
and reduce the price of fish sold at Koki. "The
Division of Fisheries, some years ago, planned the
introduction of small built vessels to improve supplies and marketing at Koki, but finance was never
made available" (D.o.F., 1963:2). Like in so many
other instances of this kind here too the helpful
suggestions and the good intentions relating to one
particular aspect of economic development have been
in existence for many years; alas, lack of necessary
administrative finance prevented the materialization
of positive results. Therefore, the Koki fish trade
has remained in its unsatisfactory condition.

The greatly fluctuating quantities of fish
supplies and the lack of preservation facilities
make the sale of fish a risky enterprise; on some
days there is a glut of fish and large proportions
of the supplies may remain unsold, while on others
only few fish are available at the market, which are
bought up quickly. If fish could be canned locally,
this would not only greatly reduce the risk in the
fish trade and encourage increased supplies, but it
would also reduce the need to import all the large
quantity of tinned mackerels, which have been bought
annually from Japan. The demand for tinned mackerels is so great in Papua New Guinea that Japanese
exporters regard Papua New Guinea as their single
best customer of this product. The value of annually imported tinned fish increased by 38 percent
between 1961/2 and 1963/4; in the latter year it was
£196,000, i.e., $392,000 (P.P.T., 1965:79) which is
equivalent to about 40 percent of the total annual
turnover at Koki market in 1967/8. The fact that
Japanese trawlers have sought fishing rights in
Territorial waters can be taken as evidence for the
existence of ample fish in the area. The availi-
bility of fresh fish in local waters on the one hand
and the sizable demand for tinned fish within the
country suggest the need to investigate the possibilities of establishing fish canneries at convenient points along the coast.

Fishing is conducted at most of the coastal

areas. However, of all the urban markets we studied
only Koki is situated right at the shore and facilitates therefore the sale of fish at the market. On
the Gazelle Peninsula much of the fish trade by-
passes the market and is conducted either at the
shore or offered for sale to passing transport on
one or another of the nearby main roads. This
accounts for the comparatively small sales volume of
fresh fish at Rabaul market; it amounts to no more
than about four percent of the total value of produce brought to the market and about 20 percent
remains unsold. A considerable proportion of the
fresh fish caught is bought by women, who cook it
together with taro or bananas in coconut juice and
sell this delicacy in bundles at the market. "When
fishing is in progress numbers of women are also
present, gathered together a little further back
along the beach. As soon as the catch is landed,
they come forward to purchase fish, which they then
cook and prepare for sale at the market or various
settlements around Rabaul" (Epstein, A.L., 1969:77).
The supply at the market of these bundles of delicious cooked food lures many men to the market, who
buy them as a special treat. Cooked food bundles
always sell quickly.

The roaring trade done by the Gazelle cafe (see
p.215), which is situated by the side of Rabaul market and which is frequented by many market vendors
and visitors, indicates that there is a great demand
for cooked food. Thus there should be a possiblity
to substitute the sale of cooked imported foods,
such as for instance fried potatoes, by cooked but
locally produced food.

Altogether there seems to be ample scope for a
considerable expansion in the volume of the fish
trade, provided the necessary processing and appropriate markets can be arranged.

Handicrafts: The distribution of traditional items
of arts takes place only rarely by market place
transactions. The organizers of feasts usually commission the making of masks and dance decorations
specifically for the occasion and reward the craftsmen directly in the customarily accepted manner; on
the Gazelle Peninsula, for instance, shell money is
the means of payment. The sale of handicrafts is
therefore only of marginal importance to market
place trading. Accordingly, this category of produce contributes no more than three percent to the
total value of goods brought to any of the markets
we studied and the proportion of it sold varies from
39 percent at Koki to a sellout at Goroka and

Mt. Hagen.

The type of handicraft sold varies between the different markets in line with the different demand patterns. At Rabaul market most of the domestic industry products brought to the market are items of interest to tourists, such as for instance, carved fish, seed and bead necklaces, shells and so on. Whenever there is a tourist ship in port, vendors of these items have a reasonable chance to sell their wares; otherwise, they manage to make only the odd sale to one or another of the expatriates who is interested in acquiring a special item. For instance expatriate collectors of shells, carefully peruse the shells offered for sale and pick out whatever catches their attention.

Handicrafts sold at Highland markets cater more for an indigenous rather than expatriate clientele. Highlanders like to decorate themselves with beaded necklaces and bracelets. These are made by village women who sell some of their handiwork at the market. *Bilums,* string bags, are another item frequently sold at Highland markets. Highland women use these *bilums* to carry their head loads of produce not only to the market but also from their gardens to their homes. These *bilums* too are made by village women who sell some of them at the market.

Lae market seems to cater both for indigenous as well as expatriate demand for handicrafts. Here one can find for sale a mixture of the handicrafts sold at Rabaul and at Highland markets, of which altogether about one third remains unsold.

The aversion of expatriates to visit Koki -- even tourists are only rarely taken to the market -- accounts for the virtual absence of novel domestically produced handicrafts on sale there. At a number of stores in Port Moresby such goods are regularly sold. At Koki itself the occasional *bilum* or bead ornaments are bought by indigenous buyers.

This discussion of the different categories of market supplies indicates the mutual interaction between the Hinterland ecology on the one hand and demand on the other in determining the pattern of trade at producer-seller markets. Moreover, it shows that the volume of production and market place trade is severly restricted by lack of suitable storage facilities as well as appropriate distribution and processing arrangements.

VENDORS AT DIFFERENT MARKETS

Almost all Papua New Guinea vendors sell goods they themselves not only produce but also personally arrange to transport to the market place. This individual involvement in the marketing of produce severly limits the volume and variety of goods each seller can offer for sale. Producer-seller marketing is a highly labor intensive activity. Most Papua New Guinea vendors do not appear to regard as an item of cost the time spent on cultivating and/or displaying their produce. Many of them are content as long as their gross earnings cover their fares and market fees. Moreover, there are even some sellers who may be called trippers, i.e., they are not concerned even if their earnings fall short of their expenses. They treat this deficit as the price they are prepared to pay for the sheer pleasure of the outing. These trippers are not concerned with prices as are more profit conscious vendors. They fetch smaller quantities for sale. Their existence thus obviously depreciates average gross and net earnings per seller. Accordingly, there exists a direct correlation between the proportion of vendors who are trippers and average receipts per seller.

Highland markets have the lowest per seller daily average gross and net earnings (see Table 4.4) which suggests a predominance of trippers at Mt. Hagen and Goroka. Altogether the composition of vendors in terms of their different types appears to account for the sales patterns prevailing at the various Papua New Guinea markets. This is indicated in the following in-depth discussion of the individual markets studied.

Koki: Target Sellers and Profiteers

There are hardly any trippers at Koki. Vendors there come either to raise money for a specific purpose and are therefore target sellers, or they are mainly profit motivated.

Koki vendors come from far afield, particularly during the dry season when some of them travel up to 160 miles by canoe to sell their taro and other produce in Port Moresby. Seventy five percent of Koki vendors travel more than 35 miles to get to the market. Their average transport costs are thus considerably higher -- i.e., $3.23 in May 1968 and $3.87 in February 1969 -- than their Mt. Hagen counterparts -- i.e., five cents in March and three cent in July 1967 -- most of whom originate from nearer the market where a large proportion come on foot. Except for the Hula vendors at Koki market who supply much of the fish and live on houseboats, most other Koki vendors have their homes too far away to make the return trip to Port Moresby in a day and therefore stay longer in town. The fact that most Koki vendors bring considerable quantities of produce to town and attend the market daily until they manage to sell out, makes it difficult to calculate their individual net earnings from selling for any one day. Of all the produce offered for sale at Koki market during any one day, 37 percent remained unsold during May 1968 and 25 percent during February 1969. On the assumption that sellers stayed in town four days in May and five days in February -- more of them came from further afield during the latter period -- their average daily transport costs amounts to 76 cents in May 1968 and 81 cents in February 1969. Accordingly, in May 1968 daily average net earnings were $6.45 and net returns for their marketing ventures amounted to $25.80; the relevant figures for February 1969 were $4.69 and $23.45 (see Table 4.5). These calculations, however, do not take into account the expenses vendors may incur by staying in town for a few days, nor the time spent displaying their wares.

The number of sellers attending Koki market varies from day to day and so does their daily average sales return. In fact there appears to be a positive correlation between these two variables with the numbers of sellers being the determining one (see Graphs 4.6 and 4.7). This correlation may be the result either of a high proportion of intra-market transactions, i.e., the more vendors gather at the market the more purchases are being made and/or of a strong positive correlation between the number of vendors on the one hand and the number of visitors and buyers on the other. Our graphs indicate that such a correlation does exist.

As mentioned already we found it impossible to estimate the number of buyers as a result of our counts at market gates, nor did we manage to collect details of purchases made by vendors at the market. The case studies we collected of several vendors at Koki market and my personal observations of ongoing trade there during the period of our survey suggest that only a few transactions were conducted among vendors themselves; while larger numbers of sellers usually coincided with larger crowds at the market. Weekends are the busiest market days, particularly those when Papua New Guinea public servants receive their fortnightly pay. Pay days occurred half way through both our Koki market studies, which accounts for the peak attendance of sellers and their higher than usual average daily earnings during those weekends. On Sundays vendors arrive later at Koki than on weekdays; on inquiry it emerged that many of them attend church services before settling down to selling their wares at the market. The Hula fishermen are altogether conspicuous in their absence on Sundays when it is said they go to church and do not fish.

The Mekeo from the Kairuku area are a powerful group at Koki market. They have taken over a large area which is one of the best protected from the rain and sun. Other tribal groups complained but were not able to dislodge them. Mekeo vendors have a virtual monopoly in the sale of areca nuts; they stay longest in town and thereby make their marketing ventures more profitable compared with other tribal vendors. Their homes are about 80 miles from Port Moresby where they fetch mainly areca nuts but also some other produce in sufficiently large quantities to make them stay in town several days before they sell out.

Most produce from the Mekeo-Kairuku area comes to Koki by water transport. "There are two types of water transport used: a) canoe transport direct to the Koki anchorage and b) by coastal boats off loading cargo in Fairfax harbour, from where produce is trucked to Koki. Sherwin quotes total fares from the region as anything from $8.50 to about $30, generally between $20 and $30. These high transport costs and long periods from garden to market, conducive to spoilage, have largely forced the Mekeo into specialized areca nut trade. Certainly, compared to their relative importance as suppliers of foods to Koki in 1965, the Mekeo are now minor suppliers to the market" (Yeats, 1967:13). The Mekeo-Kairuku vendors have an obvious comparative advantage in selling areca nuts at Koki and have therefore wisely specialized in supplying this item. The average vendor from this area brought about $50 worth of goods to Koki market in May 1968, stayed eight days in town, spent about $7 on transport and 80 cents on market fees yielding an approximate net return for his market trip of $40 (see Table 4.5).

Maia, who comes from beyond Kairuku related that he started in 1965 to plant areca nuts, bananas and coconuts for the specific purpose of selling produce at Koki market. He pays $5 for his return fare and usually another $5 for fetching his produce on the motor boat. He claims that freight charges vary between different skippers while fares are uniform. He takes stuff to Koki market three or four times a year and stays eight to ten days in town. Maia has a brother who works and lives in Port Moresby with whom he can stay without paying for it, though he usually takes some food offerings along. Maia stated that he regards his market venture as a failure if he earns no more than $3 per day, as worthwhile if he gets $5 daily and as a success if he collects $8 to $10 per day. His gross income from market sales in 1967, when he came three times to Koki market amounted to $200, which he regarded as a reasonable return. He likes these trips to Port Moresby where he can enjoy the pleasures of urban life.

The Chimbu, who supply Koki market originate from the Highlands but are presently employed as plantation labor in the Sogeri Hills, about 30 miles from Port Moresby. They are keen farmers and grow considerable quantities of sweet potatoes on land which the plantation allocates to them. They usually arrive at Koki on Fridays with truckloads of sweet potatoes and sell out by Sunday when they return to their plantation work. The average Chimbu brought about $40 worth of sweet potatoes to Koki in May 1968, paid about $2 for his transport and market fees and netted $38 on his market venture. It is interesting to note in this context the greater market orientation displayed by Chimbu men working on plantations compared with their fellow tribesmen still living in the Highlands. At Goroka market where the Chimbu constitute a considerable proportion of vendors, less than one third are men and very few, if any of the male vendors sell sweet potatoes. As mentioned earlier, Highlanders regard the cultivation and distribution of food crops as a job for women only. In contrast to this traditional attitude still prevalent in the Highlands, Chimbu men who have taken up plantation labor, are keen growers and suppliers of sweet potatoes in the Port Moresby area. Many of them sell sweet potatoes in town so as to be able to buy particular items there; for instance, a transistor radio.

The Hula fishermen, many of whom live on house-boats near Koki, fish from their own canoes and bring their catch straight to the market; they incur no transport cost and can return to their homes each night. The average daily net takings per Hula vendor were during February 1969 less than half those during May 1968. This considerable variation is due to climatic conditions. Rough weather during February made fishing difficult, if not impossible, whereas in May conditions for fishing were much more favorable.

The average gross turnover per Koki vendor is directly related to the distance of the home village, so is the value of total produce brought to the market (see Table 4.6). Sellers, who originate from villages more than 100 miles from Koki market, fetch goods more than twice the value than their counterparts coming from within a radius of 35 miles. It seems imperative for individual sellers coming long distances to the market to fetch larger quantities of produce for sale not only to cover their own more costly fares but also to benefit from freight economies of scale: the freight for a large bag of goods is hardly more than for a small bag. Therefore it is more economical to fetch larger rather than smaller quantities of produce for sale. This however, may necessitate sellers spending a few days in town to sell out before returning to their villages, which many seem to regard as an attraction rather than as an unwelcome chore. Many long distance sellers take their total consignment on arrival in Port Moresby to wherever they have arranged to put up; then they ration these supplies over how many days they planned to stay in town and each day take to the market only part of their total produce. By trial and error they have gained a good idea of demand conditions operating at Koki market; they know that the greater the value of supplies each fetches to the market the higher the proportion of produce remaining unsold.

There is thus a direct correlation between the supply distance, being the determining variable on the one hand, and the average value of supplies per seller and the proportion of unsold produce per day, on the other. Koki has the widest supply catchment area of all Papua New Guinea markets. The rapidly growing urban population attracts increasing supplies to the market. Yet the frequency of market visits by individual vendors at Koki is not much different from any of the other Papua New Guinea markets: about two thirds of Koki sample vendors venture to sell their produce only occasionally throughout the year. In the course of the February 1969 survey a special effort was made to interview sellers who were apparently acting as agents for growers in the villages. Seven examples were found. In every case sellers were sent produce by close relatives. Selling was conducted on an *ad hoc* basis with the seller having a job in Port Moresby or possibly receiving produce from his village during the course of a visit to the town. No examples were found of an agent selling produce as a full time occupation over a long period of time.

In spite of the obviously greater market orientation displayed by Koki market vendors compared with their counterparts in other Papua New Guinea areas, there is no evidence to be found of the development of a retail distribution system for indigenous produce. The absence of retail arrangements at Koki market which after all serves the capital, the largest urban settlement in Papua New Guinea can be taken as a sign that producer-seller markets, rather than wholesale-retail trade, still provides the outlet for indigenous produce sales in the whole of the country.

Lae: Marginalists and Profiteers

Lae market serves the second biggest town in Papua New Guinea and is similar in character to Koki. Yet while it shares many features with Koki, which are typical of Port Moresby's urban-based market, it also resembles in many aspects the Hinterland-rooted markets we studied in the Highlands and on the Gazelle Peninsula. Lae market thus appears to be in the transition phase from a Hinterland-rooted market as for instance that of Rabaul, to a fully urban-based one like Koki.

The tribal heterogenity among vendors at Lae market is such that our investigators found it impossible to record the tribal identity of individual informants. At Koki we identified a few dominant tribes and introduced larger tribal categories, as for instance Papuan or New Guinean to cope with this problem. Such procedure proved impossible at Lae market.

Lae being situated in the Morobe Bay at the east coast of Papua New Guinea attracts supplies mainly from areas to its west: about half the Lae sample sellers originated from southwest and a third from northwest of the town. Lae vendors come from further afield than their counterparts at the Hinterland-rooted markets we studied; yet they travel shorter distances than Koki vendors. The market is open six days per week and provides much better sales facilities than Koki which is open each day of the week. Most of the Lae produce is displayed on tables under the shelter of corrugated roofed sheds. Friday is the busiest market day in the week at Lae, when many more vendors turn up to sell their produce than on any other day. During our August 1967 study average gross earnings per seller were also highest on Friday whereas during December 1967 vendors made most money on Thursdays (see Graph 4.8 and 4.9). The extraordinarily high average gross earnings per seller on the second Thursday of our December 1967 study reflects the holding of a mortuary feast by workers in Lae for which they bought large quantities of food at the market.

Male vendors travel longer distances to Lae market than their female counterparts: 29 percent of male and only 17 percent of female vendors originate from villages more than 30 miles from the town. The average transport cost per male vendor is thus almost twice as much as female vendors pay (see Table 4.7); men also fetch a higher average value of produce for sale than do women. They supply more than women sellers of the non-indigenous vegetables and fruit sold at the market, which are high value and low volume products. Men are not prepared to carry heavy loads over as long distances as women do. If their village is some way off the nearest road they often get their womenfolk to carry by headload the produce to the spot where they can pick up transport to the town. Many village women carry weighty consignments in large bags resting on their forehead and hanging down their backs, to the nearest road from where their menfolk take them by vehicle to Lae market while the women return to their village homes.

The proportion of the value of goods brought which is sold is higher for women than for men market vendors at Lae. Male vendors marketing activities are more risky than females: 40 percent of male, but only 26 percent of female sellers spend more than their daily gross earnings on transport. However, many more male than female vendors stay overnight in town and sell again at the market the following day. Their transport costs should therefore be apportioned over the total length of their marketing trips, as was done for Koki vendors. We assumed that most vendors stay two days in Lae on each of their market trips and therefore halved their average transport costs. Some male sellers stay longer in town, whereas some female ones return to their villages after a day at the market; it seems much more difficult for women to make satisfactory arrangements to spend nights in Lae than it is for men to find a place to sleep. Besides their fares vendors also have to pay 20 cents marketing fees each. Marketing expenses constitute about 15 percent of their average gross earnings.

All this data provides indicators for the difference in marketing patterns between male and female vendors at Lae market. Men are more market oriented than women; they sell more of the crops, like non-indigenous vegetables, which are grown for the specific purpose of sale, while women mostly bring the surplus of their own staple foods they themselves produced. The main incentive for women to sell at Lae market seems to be the opportunity of being able to satisfy their current need: they want to buy goods in the town shops and possibly also some food at the market. Nasa, one of the female vendors at Lae market remarked that while she does not make big money by selling, it is a convenient way to supplement the family income with her cash earnings. Often her takings fall short of her expectations and she has to take back home some of the yams, indigenous leaf vegetables and other staple foods she brings to the market. Whenever she has earned a few dollars she purchases in the town shops some tinned food, rice and possibly a few items of clothing for her children.

Men are more motivated to take produce for sale so as to be able to buy a share in a vehicle or save to build a European style house for themselves in their home village. Thus female market vendors mostly spend their earnings from the sale of produce to satisfy their current needs, whereas male vendors seem to be keener to invest in durable assets. This difference in motivation may account for the difference in marketing behavior displayed by male and female vendors at Lae market.

Mt. Hagen: Target Sellers and Trippers

In 1967 Mt. Hagen market served only a small population. Trade was then done only two days per week: Wednesdays and Saturdays. Mt. Hagen's population has been increasing at an annual rate of about 40 percent and market place transactions have grown accordingly. It "is rapidly attaining the status of a daily market (including Sundays) as one might expect of a rapidly growing town" (Jackson, 1974:12). Yet the total number of sellers attending the market during any one week has not increased very much over the last few years; what has happened is a reorganization of the trading pattern: the number of sellers turning up on Wednesdays and Saturdays has grown only slightly, whereas on remaining days in the week more and more sellers congregate, which is particularly true for Sundays when large crowds are attracted to the market place. "It is by this means that the rapid growth in demand from urban dwellers is being satisfied" (Jackson, 1974:12).

During our study of Mt. Hagen market the average weekly attendance of sellers was about 2,500 in March and 2,000 in July. The proportion of men among the sellers was highest at Mt. Hagen as compared with all the other Hinterland-rooted markets we studied; it was 50 percent in March and 43 percent in July 1967. Since then the proportion of female sellers has considerably increased; in 1973 it was 77 percent. "The reason for this decline in male interest in most areas of marketing appear to be numerous, but chief amongst them is the simple economic fact that they

121

have ready access to other sources of cash, especially through coffee growing which is more easily acquired than is the case with market sales. Women usually have no such avenue open to them and have increasingly utilized the market place to acquire cash" (Jackson, 1974:13). To this needs to be added the fact that daily average gross earnings per seller at Mt. Hagen market are so low that they can hardly be a great incentive for money oriented individuals to spend their time selling produce. Mt. Hagen vendors have the lowest daily average gross earnings of all the Papua New Guinea sellers we studied: $1.35 in March 1967 and $1.19 in July 1967. They sell over 90 percent of the produce they fetch to the market, which means that the value of produce brought to the market by individual sellers is also low compared with other Papua New Guinea markets. About half the sellers walk to the market; the proportion of sellers who walk is directly correlated with the volume of produce each fetches to the market and is inversely related to the distance they have come to reach the market. Less than 20 percent of Mt. Hagen vendors come from villages more than 10 miles away. As mentioned earlier, the small supply area and the high proportion of sellers who walk to the market is reflected in a low average cost of transport per seller; i.e., no more than 10 cents.

The low average transport cost for Mt. Hagen as compared with Lae sellers accounts for the much smaller proportion among the former who have negative market earnings than among the latter.

Male vendors fetch a lower average of produce and pay higher fares and thus have lower gross and net earnings than their female counterparts at Mt. Hagen market. Accordingly, the proportion of male vendors whose one day market venture yields them no positive monetary returns, is higher -- i.e., eight percent -- than among females -- i.e., five percent.

Mt. Hagen market vendors appear to have much lower earning targets than sellers at Koki (see p. 117). Kup, an indigenous grower originating from the Mt. Hagen Hinterland, put it explicitly that he regarded one dollar as a good reward for a day at the market, although he realized that some vendors earn more than that. He was quick to point out that he himself had managed to earn as much as $24 in one day when he fetched a truckload of sweet potatoes to the market. The marketing of sweet potatoes seems to involve least risk; almost all sweet potatoes brought to the market find buyers. However, sweet potatoes are bulkier and fetch a lower price per

pound than for instance peanuts. Yoga, another
Mt. Hagen vendor, explained that if he brings a lot
of produce to the market he can earn about $2; if he
fetches only a small quantity his takings are usually
no more than 50 cents. He attends the market about
two or three times per month and rarely earns more
than 50 cents on any one day; if he makes as much as
80 cents he is happy with his marketing venture.
When he was interviewed at the market he had brought
along produce worth 70 cents just so that he may
meet some of his friends and talk with them about
getting himself a wife.

Gras, who lives in Keltika a village about five
miles from Mt. Hagen always comes to town on foot.
She outlined the difficult considerations which
determine what kind and quantity of produce she
takes to the market. She knows from experience that
if she takes nothing else but sweet potatoes she can
carry only one *bilum* and sell them for about 50 to 60
cents. She usually is pretty certain that she sells
all the sweet potatoes she brings along. If she
also takes along peanuts she has to carry two *bilums*
and if she manages to sell out she can earn altogether about $2, but she can never be sure that she
will be able to get rid of all her peanuts. If she
has any peanuts left she has to decide either to
carry them back home, which she finds tedious, or to
give or throw them away in town. Peanuts are a less
bulky and more costly commodity than sweet potatoes,
but at Mt. Hagen at least 35 percent of peanuts
brought remain unsold. By contrast sweet potatoes
are part of the staple diet, whereas peanuts fall
into the category of sundry commodities as do areca
nuts for instance; more than 95 percent of sweet
potatoes brought are sold. Gras attends the market
about once or twice every month. The frequency of
her market visits depends on the quantity of crop
she manages to produce and the home demand for it.
Whenever she has a surplus of sweet potatoes and
wants to buy something for herself or one of her
children she decides to sell at the market.

Unlike Gras, who seems convinced that staple
foods are the best items to try and sell at the market, Balga specializes exclusively in supplying non-
indigenous vegetables, such as lettuces and tomatoes.
He travels by truck the 12 miles from his home village for which he pays 50 cents return fare; he
fetches produce worth about $3 or $4. He rarely
manages to sell out and seems quite happy if he sells
as much as 90 percent of all that he brought. He
claims to have established a reputation among buyers
for supplying top quality non-indigenous produce.

He gives this as the reason for the success of his marketing ventures. He attends about 15 to 20 market days per year, depending on the output of the different introduced crops he cultivates. He is aware of the fact that demand for non-indigenous crops is strictly limited and therefore carefully tries to grow sufficient to enable him to sell most of his produce when he takes it to the market. His wife cultivates sweet potatoes and like Gras sells them at the market. He categorically stated that he and his wife have strictly segregated accounts; it is entirely left to each of them to decide how much to take to the market and sell and what to do with the money earned without the other's interference. Sometimes his wife asks him to save her money for her, which he then does as requested and lets her have it back whenever she wants it. The strict separation of funds operating between Balga and his wife does not seem to apply uniformly to all marital partnerships among Western Highlanders. For intance, Kwiperu related that she always gives all the money that remains from her market earnings, after she has made a few purchases, to her husband to look after, so that she would not lose it. Her husband is a councilor who plans to buy a vehicle using the money of his 'line'. Kwiperu does not think of the money she gives her husband as a loan, but rather expects to get her money's worth in terms of free rides on the vehicle once it has been bought. She first began to sell at the market in order to get some cash for buying food and clothes in the town stores. It was only subsequently that her husband conceived the idea of saving for a truck and she readily agreed to let him have her contributions.

In spite of the considerable increase in demand for foods since 1967 as a result of the rapidly growing population of Mt. Hagen the daily average earnings per market vendor has hardly increased. Jackson's 1973/4 survey reports that "the great majority of sellers sell between $1 to $2 worth of produce; pay a 10 cent entry fee and pay between 20 and 50 cents for transport, gaining a net income of 70 cents to $1.40 per trip" (1974:16). Our case studies of Mt. Hagen vendors point to some of the reasons which may account for the low earnings per seller at the market.

As long as many individual sellers walk long distances to the market and carry their wares bodily the quantity of goods each can fetch remains strictly limited. A female seller is unlikely to be able to take more than two or three *bilums* of produce to the market weighing altogether about one hundred pounds, if she has to carry the stuff every step of the way. This is particularly relevant to the staple crops such as sweet potatoes and yams which are bulky with a comparatively low per unit weight price. In fact almost half of all the sweet potatoes sold at Mt. Hagen market originate from villages less than six miles from the town.

The demand for non-indigenous foods such as lettuce and tomatoes is limited and cultivating these crops is more difficult than growing traditional staples. This obviously discourages individual growers from supplying large quantities of these more risky goods.

Moreover, the success of diversifiying supplies to meet the changing pattern of indigenous demand, depends on the general level of indigenous incomes. In 1967 peanuts were still regarded as a luxury item of consumption and therefore demand was less steady for this crop than for instance for sweet potatoes. There are signs though that increasing indigenous incomes are reflected in the purchase at the market place of increasing quantities of sundry luxury items such as areca nuts, peanuts and the like. The positive correlation between numbers of vendors and their average daily income at Mt. Hagen market (see Graphs 4.10 and 4.11) suggests a high proportion of intra-market transactions, unlike at Koki market where this does not seem to be the case.

The different factors affecting supply and demand are thus jointly responsible for the persistence of the sales pattern prevailing at Mt. Hagen market, whereby large numbers of vendors gather each fetching only a small quantity of produce which is bought by large numbers of individual buyers each spending only a small amount on market purchases.

Goroka: Trippers and Marginalists

Goroka is the main urban center in the Eastern Highlands; its market operated in 1967 only on Wednesdays and Saturdays and catered for a somewhat larger town population than its Western Highland counterpart. Saturdays attract about twice as many vendors than Wednesdays. At Goroka there is hardly any correlation between the number of sellers and their average earnings (see Graph 4.12 and 4.13). More vendors turn up regularly on Saturdays than on Wednesdays; average earnings per seller seem to fluctuate' in an unpredictable fashion. Total turnover on a market day is determined by the number of people who visit the market and their purchases. At Koki market larger numbers of vendors seem to be accompanied by larger crowds visiting the market and at Mt. Hagen more sellers result in more intra-market transactions; at Goroka neither of these phenomena seem to occur. Possibly this is due to the fact that people from the large rural Hinterland swell in an irregular and unpredictable fashion the ranks of Goroka market visitors, among whom there are many rural proletarians (see p. 68). Also there are a number of smaller markets which have been set up in the region and which obviously affect the turn-over and attendance at Goroka market, but unfortunately we lack data on them.

Many of the Goroka vendors are trippers, while others are marginalists, who take produce for sale whenever they have a surplus over their household requirements.

An average number of about 3,000 vendors per week brought some produce to Goroka market, whose daily average gross earnings were $1.99 in February 1967; the respective figures for August 1967 are 2,900 and $2.23. By contrast with Mt. Hagen at Goroka male vendors earn more than females ones. Until mid 1967, vendors at Goroka market were charged a *per capita* fee of five cents each. The Native Local Government Council introduced a graduated market entrance fee in June 1967 varying with the different kinds and quantities vendors fetch for sale. Those fetching small quantities only continue to pay five cents; large quantities warrant a fee of 10 cents; vendors of large quantities of costly commodities, such as areca nuts or chicken are charged 20 cents and those selling pigs have to pay 30 cents. Throughout February 1967 when we conducted our first study of Goroka market there was no difference in the market fees paid by male and female vendors. By July 1967 the new system of market fees had come into operation and male vendors, most of whom fetched more costly produce, paid an average of 10 cents while female ones continued to pay only five cents each. Male vendors paid more in transport costs than female ones during both our surveys in 1967.

The fact that male vendors tend to fetch more non-indigenous produce, thereby running a greater risk of being left with large unsold quantities, together with their higher transport costs is reflected in the higher proportion among them -- i.e., 13 percent -- whose marketing venture involves them in a loss, than among female ones -- i.e., five percent.

The beginnings of specialization which we found at Mt. Hagen market whereby female vendors fetch mainly staple foods which have a low per unit weight price, while male vendors tend to concentrate on selling more valuable goods, appears to be more pronounced at Goroka market. There is a greater variety of goods sold at Goroka market, but each vendor sells fewer different kinds of produce than at Mt. Hagen. Patik, a young man coming from 10 miles away sold celery, lettuces and tomatoes at Goroka. He claims that there is now a generational specialization among vendors: the older folk grow only the staple crops such as sweet potatoes, sugar cane and the like and sell the surplus remaining after they meet their household requirements. The "smart young people" venture into cultivating different types of fruit and vegetables, specifically as cash crops. By lunchtime Patik had sold about 90 percent of what he had brought. His gross takings were $4.50. Since sales had been slack for the last hour or so he decided to call it a day. He threw away the unsold lettuces and celery and proceeded to the nearest trade store where he spent 50 cents on cigarettes, a drink of lemonade and other small items. He had paid 30 cents for his fare and freight coming to the market as well as 10 cents in entrance fees and expected to pay another 10 cents for his return journey. Patik took home $3.50 which, he explained, he wanted to save for buying a share in a truck.

Unfortunately, our investigators were unable to collect data on the age of vendors, yet impressionistic views of Highland vendors support Patik's statement: at Goroka a larger proportion of male vendors are young men and more of them tend to specialize in selling the more costly introduced types of produce than female vendors at Goroka market or vendors altogether at Mt. Hagen market.

In an environment such as exists in Goroka where demand for introduced foods is limited, greater specialization in produce brought for sale is accompanied by a greater risk in being left with all or a large proportion of it unsold. This is indicated in Table 4.2 which shows that of all the produce brought to Goroka market one third remained unsold in February and 15 percent in August 1967; about two thirds of the value of fruit as well as meat and eggs offered for sale in February 1967 remained unsold. By contrast almost all the indigenous staples brought to the market during the same period were sold.   .

The lower daily average gross earnings per female than per male vendor do not necessarily reflect a sexual differentiation in the marketing pattern at Goroka. Several of our case studies indicate that men arrange for their womenfolk to sell

sweet potatoes on their behalf at the market.
Worae's account provides a good example in this context. His home is about eight miles from Goroka.
The day we interviewed him he claimed was representative of his market ventures which he undertakes
about three times a month. He had come to Goroka
with his wife and two of his brothers' wives. Each
of the three women carried two *bilums* of sweet potatoes from his gardens. They set off walking to the
road from where they picked up a truck that took
them to the market. Worae paid the driver $1.20 for
fares and freight for all of them. Moreover, he paid
five cents each for the three women to enter the market, and gave them altogether 90 cents to spend on
smokes or anything else they may wish to buy for
themselves. On arrival at the market each of the
women took about one third of all the sweet potatoes
they had brought along and settled down to offering
it for sale. Worae's wife placed herself apart from
the other two women who sat next to each other. The
three of them managed to sell most of Worae's sweet
potatoes within a couple of hours, for which they
received altogether $4.50; they only had a small
quantity left over when Worae came to collect them
and they set off walking back home; his wife carried
the unsold produce. The women handed Worae all the
money they had been given in payment for the sweet
potatoes they sold. His net receipt for the market
venture was $2.25 and he regarded this as a good
day's income. The three women acknowledged with a
grin that they too were satisfied with their outing;
they had enjoyed being at the market place, seeing
all these many people and listening to the gossip as
well as being able to buy a little something with the
30 cents Worae had given each of them.

Worae explained the *raison d'etre* for this sex
division of labor whereby he organizes the trip to
the market and women do the actual selling: approximately two years previously, when he remarried, he
started extending his sweet potato cultivation as an
additional source of income, since coffee prices
began to fall. He established new gardens together
with his wife: he prepared the land, dug the
trenches and fenced the gardens in, while his wife
planted and harvested the sweet potatoes. He
regarded it as women's work to dig up the sweet
potato crop and sell it at the market. To offset
this specialized task of his wife, i.e., sweet potato
cultivation, he accepted coffee growing, harvesting
and selling as man's work and saw to that himself.

Such cases like that of Worae, which indicate
important aspects of producer-seller markets would

not have emerged from our quantitative market studies; if the three women had been part of our sample vendors our interviewers would have kept a record separately for each of them and these female vendors would never have been linked together with a male grower who did not even appear at the market himself. Profiles such as Worae's are thus a useful device by which to illustrate certain phenomena in marketing practices which would otherwise remain hidden.

Other case studies of Goroka market sellers indicate that such informal arrangements as existed between Worae and the three women who sold his sweet potatoes at the market seem to be restricted to close kin. Nasa, for instance, takes her mother's sweet potatoes together with her own when she ventures to sell at the market. She does not retain any of the money earned from her mother's produce, nor does her mother give her any. Instead her mother rewards her by giving her yams and bananas. Nasa emphatically declared that she would never dream of selling anyone else's produce except that of her own mother or sister. Likewise Koni related that he sometimes agrees to take some of his brother's non-indigenous produce, such as lettuce and celery to the market when he himself takes his own crops for sale. He, like Nasa, stressed that he had never taken anyone else's produce for sale, not even that of his closest friends.

These accounts indicate that rationalization of marketing practices at Highland producer-seller markets is limited to the informal relationships between close kin. These informal sales agency arrangements appear to be the rare exception. The general rule is still that individual producers each fetch their surplus food crops for sale at the market. Though there is an obvious trend towards more intentional cash cropping, the large majority of Goroka vendors did not cultivate the crops with the objective in mind of selling the yield at the market, but rather planted their subsistence foods and sold the surplus if and when it occurred. The growers first concern is to provide sufficient food to meet their household needs. For instance Atau, a Gorokan vendor, related that he plants only one garden at a time and when he does so he does not divide it into areas for home consumption on the one hand and for sale on the other, though he does try to make a garden large enough so that he may have some ·surplus produce for sale.

Goroka vendors appear to be somewhat more market oriented than their Mt. Hagen counterparts, yet their market attendance still seems to be more supply than

demand stimulated. Most of them come to the market
not because they planted crops for sale to meet market demand, but rather because they have some surplus
staples which they are prepared to sell in order to
earn a bit of cash for one or another specific purpose.

Gazelle Peninsula: Trippers, Buyer-sellers and Profiteers

The overall framework of marketing practices in Papua
New Guinea also readily accommodates Gazelle
Peninsula markets. Many of the dominant features we
already noted for the other markets also apply on the
Gazelle Peninsula: large numbers of individual small
producers irregularly fetch their own crops which
they price in terms of multiples of 10 cents; there
is no bargaining and a striking absence of efforts to
force a sale. Yet there are also considerable differences between market place trade on the Gazelle
Peninsula and that in other regions. As already
mentioned the Tolai, who are the people residing on
the Gazelle Peninsula have a tradition of market
place trade which pre-dates European contact and
which is the natural consequence of the ecological
diversification existing in the area. The use of
shell money facilitated these necessary transactions
whereby coastal dwellers sold their goods to people
residing futher inland and in turn bought the
latter's produce. This customary specialization is
reflected in the continuing importance of intra-Tolai
trade conducted at Rabaul and Kokopo market.

On the Gazelle Peninsula seasonal variations are
less pronounced than in the Port Moresby region. It
is possible that our studies were not conducted
during the appropriate periods, and therefore do not
illustrate seasonal variations. However, rainfall
statistics collected at Rabaul airport indicate the
absence of pronounced seasons. Therefore, it is
likely that the greater similarity between the findings of the two seasons studied at Rabaul as compared
with Koki market reflect a greater uniformity in
climatic conditions throughout the year in the market
Hinterland. The number of sellers during one week in
April was 85 percent of that attending during January
1968; the relationship of the total weight of produce
brought to the market was also 85 percent and that of
the turnover was 80 percent (see Table 3.1).

The tradition of market trade accompanied by
fertile soils is probably the major factor accounting
for the greater number of sellers and larger volume
of supplies at Rabaul as compared with Koki market.

For Gazelle Peninsula markets the supply area varies
directly with the volume of demand. Vunapope and
Kokopo markets are attended by sellers who come from
within a radius of 15 miles; their average transport
costs amount to 35 cents in each case. About one
third of all Rabaul vendors come from villages more
than 15 miles away; the maximum distance any one vendor travels to Rabaul market is 42 miles and there is
a good network of roads servicing the whole of the
Tolai region. Transport charges for Rabaul vendors
range between 10 cents and $1.90, average charges
amounting to about 51 cents on weekdays and 72 cents
on Saturdays (see Table 4.4), which is slightly less
than what they were in 1961 (Epstein, T.S., 1968:156).
The lower average fares are possibly the result of
rationlization of market traffic; as already mentioned there has been a switch from large trucks to
smaller and less costly utilities servicing the market.

None of our Rabaul market sample vendors walked
to the market, all of them came by one or another
type of motorized transport. Yet about one third of
them did not have to pay for fares or freight. They
traveled in vehicles owned either by their husbands'
or their own close kin and therefore got free rides.
Altogether the cost of transport bears only little
relation to the quantity of produce brought; rather
it varies with the distance traveled. Identical
amounts are charged for outward and homeward journeys. Each vendor at Rabaul market is expected to
pay a 20 cents fee, though as already mentioned many
of them escape the collector and do not pay their
dues. The potential average marketing costs per
vendor -- i.e., transport charges and fee -- constitute as much as 30 percent on weekdays of gross earnings and about 10 percent on Saturdays. It would
therefore be more efficient for a number or producers
to appoint one as their sales agent or for a few
enterprising individuals to travel round the countryside buying up supplies on the spot and retailing
them at the market. Such change in marketing practice could drastically reduce the number of sellers
at the market and free considerable manpower for
productive activities. "If manpower or capital is
used in marketing, when it would yield a higher real
return in some other employment, the community is by
so much the poorer for the misuse of its resources"
(Galbraith, 1955:1). Yet Tolai women seem to enjoy
these outings to the market so much so that some of
them are prepared to incur a loss by not being able
to cover their expenses. "They are satisficers
rather than maximisers" (Brookfield, 1969:154).

Moreover, there are only few alternative income earning opportunities. Thus the opportunity cost of their market attendance is practically zero.

The narrow supply belt surrounding Rabaul enables sellers to come to the market just for the day and return home at night. In spite of this easy access to the market, vendors do not attend regularly: two thirds of the vendors bring their produce only occasionally to the market; only one percent attends the market daily and 32 percent weekly. Almost all sellers on Gazelle Peninsula markets are Tolai women. A few enterprising men from the New Guinea mainland, who work on plantations in the vicinity of Rabaul, grow some fruit and non-indigenous vegetables or run a small poultry farm and, like their Chimbu counterparts working on Sogeri plantations (see p.117), they sell their produce at the market on Saturdays. A few European poultry farmers occasionally use the market as a venue for selling their chickens and eggs mainly to expatriate customers. They engage one or two of their indigenous farm helpers as sellers at the market.

The relative importance of non-indigenous vegetables had declined over the years at Rabaul market. In June 1961 they constituted 36 percent on weekdays and 40 percent on Saturdays of the total value of produce brought (Epstein, T.S., 1968:158). By 1968 the proportions had declined to 10 and 15 percent, respectively. Non-indigenous produce is nicely displayed on tables; sellers come equipped with buckets in which they keep water to sprinkle over the vegetables in order to keep them fresh throughout the market day. In January 1968, which was a peak period in the supply of non-indigenous vegetables, about half of all vendors on weekdays and Saturdays alike brought some non-indigenous produce. April 1968 was a slack season for the supply of non-indigenous crops, yet even then about one third of all Rabaul vendors fetched some non-indigenous produce for sale. Some of them displayed it together with their staple crops, while most had arrangements with one or another of their kin who concentrated on selling non-indigenous produce whereby their odd bundles would be added to those of the specialized vendor. Often this involved a reciprocal agreement whereby those vendors who mainly sold staple crops would in turn accept the responsibility of displaying the few bundles brought by growers who mainly specialized in selling non-indigenous produce. IaTuraram from Rapitok, a village 15 miles from Rabaul had such an informal arrangement with IaPilai from Navuneram, a village about 10 miles from the market. IaTuraram and

Iapilai are classificatory sisters who come from
Vunadadir, a place about halfway between Rapitok and
Navuneram. They moved to their present residences on
marriage and have lived there ever since. IaTuraram
is now widowed and lives with the two younger of her
four children in the hamlet of her husband's classificatory brother who helps in the preparation of her
gardens. She explained that she always cultivates
sufficient food for her own household consumption as
well as to have a surplus for sale. She has done so
for many years and failed to remember exactly when
she started taking her own produce to Rabaul market;
she thought it must have been soon after she married
into Rapitok. She frequents the market about two or
three Saturdays each month and takes areca nuts,
bananas, corn, galip nuts, sugar cane, sweet potatoes,
taro, yams and *xanthosoma* for sale. Besides these
staples she also grows a limited quantity of tomatoes
which she takes to the market whenever they are ripe.
Of the indigenous foods she always selects the best
to take for sale and leaves the inferior ones for
home consumption, whereas she takes all her tomato
crop to the market since they themselves never eat
tomatoes. Her return fare to Rabaul usually costs
$1. The first thing she does on arrival at the mar-
ket is to seek out IaPilai to put in her care the few
bundles of tomatoes she brought along. IaPilai
coming from Navuneram, which is nearer to Rabaul than
Rapitok, usually gets to the market before IaTuraram
and by the time the latter arrives has already laid
out her lettuces, cucumbers, tomatoes and other non-
indigenous produce in attractive fashion, sprinkled
with water to keep fresh. IaPilai readily accepts
the responsibility of selling IaTuraram's tomatoes
and in turn hands over to her classificatory sister
the few bundles of sweet potatoes she had brought
along for sale. The day we interviewed these two
vendors IaTuraram had brought 50 lots of indigenous
produce and three bundles of tomatoes which she
hoped to sell for $5.30 altogther. IaPilai fetched
75 bundles of non-indigenous produce for which she
expected to get $7.50 as well as five lots of sweet
potatoes for 10 cents each. IaTuraram settled down
under a tree near other vendors coming from Rapitok
and displayed her own stuff together with IaPilai's
sweet potatoes, while IaPilai having taken up her
position in one of the sheds, offered her non-
indigenous produce for sale together with IaTuraram's
tomatoes. At midday both women left their wares in
the care of neighboring sellers and together treated
themselves to a bundle of fish and bananas cooked in
coconut juice which they bought for 10 cents from a

vendor coming from a coastal settlment. IaTuraram
also bought fish for 30 cents from the same seller.
Afterwards they went to the Gazelle cafe where they
bought a bottle of lemonade for another 10 cents.
Before they returned to their respective places at
the market IaPilai bought a small bag of lime for
20 *tambu* from another coastal vendor and offered it
as spice to IaTuraram as they were indulging in
areca nuts and peppers the latter had brought along
in her handbag. By 4 pm when their respective cars
were waiting to take them back home IaTuraram had $1
worth of produce still unsold as well as one of
IaPilai's five bundles of sweet potatoes, which she
returned to her classificatory sister, when she
handed her 40 cents for what she had sold. IaPilai
had sold out but received only $7 altogether as she
had decided to reorder her bundles and increase
their size as the day wore on and she began to fear
that she would be left with a lot of unsold produce.
She had also sold IaTuraram"s three lots of tomatoes
but had gotten only 20 cents for the lot. She passed
the money over to her. IaTurarum's gross takings
were $4.70 of which she spent $1 on fares, 30 cents
on fish, 10 cents on refreshments and 20 cents for
market fees; she was thus left with $3.10 which she
regarded as a fair day's income. Before she boarded
her transport back home taking with her the unsold
produce left over, she called at one of the Chinese
trade stores across from the market and bought sticks
of tobacco, sugar, tinned mackerels and a dress for
her daughter spending altogher $2.40. IaTuraram
took back home no more than 70 cents, but she
explained with a broad grin on her face that she had
thoroughly enjoyed her outing to Rabaul and was look-
ing forward to meeting IaPilai again the following
Saturday.

IaPilai had to pay 70 cents for her return fare
and another 20 cents for her market ticket as well
as 10 cents out of her $7.40 gross takings for
refreshments. Moreover, she brought lime for 20
shells. She was thus left with $6.40 less the cash
equivalent for 20 shells which is about four cents.
Like IaTuraram she too purchased groceries, tobacco
and clothes in one of the Chinese trade stores and
spent altogether $3.50. She stressed that she felt
she had had a good day at the market and explained
that by experience she had learnt to start increasing
after midday the size of the bundles of non-
indigenous produce that remain by then still unsold.

This account of two female vendors who sell
their produce at Rabaul market illustrates several
important features of Tolai marketing practices. It

134

shows the network of social relations that results from the Tolai matrilineal kinship system coupled with patrivirilocal marriage, and reflects the influence of all this on the specialization in trading of different categories of produce. Moreover, it indicates the attitudes different vendors display to pricing indigenous crops: IaTuraram did not attempt to reduce the price of her wares by increasing the size of each bundle and was quite happy to take back home the unsold quantities which her household consumes. By contrast IaPilai, who seemed to be a seasoned vendor of non-indigenous produce keenly observed the pace at which she managed to sell her stuff and shrewdly reduced prices of what remained unsold after lunch thereby suceeding in selling out. As she was explaining her attitudes to me she pointed to the heap of wilted lettuces and squashed tomatoes piled up in the corner of the market and said triumphantly "this is what I try to avoid; rather than have to throw away much of my goods I prefer to sell them at reduced prices!"

IaTurarum's and IaPilai's account, moreover, illustrates the continued use of *tambu* as a means of exchange at Rabaul market. Some Tolai vendors prefer to sell their goods for *tambu* rather than for cash. The purchasing power parity varies for different items; for the majority of produce sold both for cash and *tambu* one fathom (about 350 shells) equals $1. This is the exchange rate I employed in evaluating sales for shell money. As already mentioned the significance of shell money as a means of market transactions has greatly declined since 1961, when it accounted for 10 percent of the total value of produce sold. By 1968 it had been reduced to one percent. Yet even in 1968 there were about 10 vendors each weekday and 50 on Saturdays who sold their goods for *tambu*, a number of whom even refused to accept cash as payment. Most of these '*tambu* vendors' sold areca nuts, peppers and lime in small lots for 10 or 20 shells each. Tolai men and women who visit the market either as vendors or potential buyers each carry a bag containing shell money as small change. If they want to give themselves or their friends a treat, as many of them do, they purchase small lots of areca nuts, peppers and lime with pieces of 10 or 20 shells. As 10 cents is the smallest cash coin used at Rabaul market *tambu* has the advantage of offering a unit of smaller denomination. Until individual cent coins become common currency in Rabaul market transactions, it is likely that shell money will continue to be used as a medium of exchange quite apart from its persisting importance in the social sphere, such as bridewealth and mortuary rites. Though of course these two different kinds of transactions using *tambu* are inter-dependent. It is only as long as *tambu* will con-tinue to keep its important role in Tolai society, that it will be accepted in payment by market ven-dors. In 1968 this was obviously still the case.

IaBokoro who comes from Matupit, a coastal settlement not far from the market, sells lime there; she usually takes along bigger packets of lime which she sells for 10 cents each as well as a lot of small ones which she sells for six, 10, or 20 shells depending on size. For the last few months she has been going to the market three times per week because she wants to earn as much *tambu* as possible. Sometimes she also fetches fresh fish or bundles of cooked food which she tries to sell for *tambu*. She sells for money only after she failed to attract shell money buyers. She had accumulated about 10 fathoms *tambu* in this way and aimed at earning five more to contribute 15 fathoms altogether to her eldest son's bridewealth on his forthcoming marriage. She frequently takes her little girl with her and they travel by car for which she pays 10 cents. She always takes sufficient food with her so that she need not buy anything to eat while at the market, but she pays the 20 cent market fee.

On the day we interviewed her she had brought along bigger packets worth $2 and small ones of the value of altogether 300 shells; she managed to sell 10 of the bigger packets for $1 and smaller ones for 126 shells. She was well satisfied with her day's trade, except that she said she would have liked to sell more of the smaller packets for shell money.

IaBokoro's case illustrates the incentive which motivates women vendors to attend the market regu-larly and more important still to prefer to sell their wares for shell money rather than cash. In terms of gross earnings 'tambu vendors' averaged 63 cents; their earnings ranged up to $3. In terms of cash equivalent many of these 'tambu vendors' can barely cover their expenses. Yet if a woman wants to contribute to her son's bridewealth, as IaBokoro for instance does, she is prepared to invest cash and get *tambu* in return. There is never an outright exchange between cash and *tambu* and arbitrage is too risky in view of the high proportion of unsold pro-duce each day.

Vendors who sell for cash usually earn a lot more than those who sell for *tambu*; their average daily gross earnings were $3.79 in January and $2.81 in April 1968. On Saturdays average takings per

seller are considerably higher than on weekdays; in
January 1968 average turnover per seller on Saturdays
was more than double that on weekdays, while it was
one third as large again in April (see Table 4.4).
Non-Tolai vendors have considerably higher daily
earnings than local people: New Guineans net $7.30
and Europeans as much as $108.30. Tolai daily gross
income from market sales per vendor ranges up to $20
but only 15 percent get more than $8.50. The value
of Rabaul market trade increased between 1961 and
1968 at an average annual growth rate of about six
percent. The average weekly gross income per vendor
was $1.47 on weekdays and $2.60 on Saturdays in June
1961 (Epstein, T.S., 1968: 156); by January 1968 the
respective totals had risen to $2.28 and $4.82
(see Table 4.4). Numbers of sellers also increased
over this period: in 1961 an average number of 150
vendors came to the market on weekdays and 2,112 on
Saturdays (Epstein, T.S., 1968:156); the respective
figures for January 1968 are 225 and 2,453. April
1968 produced slacker market trade than the previous
January, but even then total market turnover was 35
percent more than in June 1961.

     At Rabaul, as at Koki, Lae and Mt. Hagen markets
there is a positive correlation between the number of
vendors and their average earnings (see Graphs 4.14
and 4.15). The reasons for this are more obvious in
relation to Rabaul market than for any other of the
Papua New Guinea markets we studied. Larger numbers
of sellers also represent larger numbers of buyers;
most Tolai vendors purchase something at the market,
if nothing else they buy peanuts, areca nuts or lime.
Moreover, the large number of vendors on Saturdays
attracts crowds of visitors to the market, many of
whom then become actual buyers. The impact of varying volumes of supply and demand on prices is discusssed in a subsequent section. In this context it
is important to mention only the fact that although
all the markets we studied were situated in towns
where one might have justifiably expected a steady
demand determined by the size of the urban population
and therefore an inverse correlation between the
numbers of vendors and their average gross earnings,
this was in fact not so. Much of our data shows a
positive relationship between these two variables.
The two reasons mentioned above help to explain this
somewhat strange phenomenon.

     The average value of goods brought per seller to
Rabaul market is almost twice as high on Saturdays as
it is on weekdays: on weekdays it varies directly
with the distance of the vendors' home villages, so
do average net earnings (see Table 4.8). For

Saturdays, there is no such obvious correlation. Weekday vendors may be more business oriented than their Saturday counterparts, many of whom obviously come for the fun of the excursion rather than for the distinct purpose of earning cash or *tambu*. Another explanation possible may be that weekday marketing is still more risky than Saturday trade since the proportion or produce remaining unsold is higher; therefore weekday vendors are more cost conscious and those who have to pay higher transport charges fetch more goods to insure that they will at least cover their expenses. On Saturdays there is a smaller risk of not selling out than there is during the week: 50 percent of vendors sell all their goods as compared with only 40 percent on weekdays. In January 39 percent of all produce brought to Rabaul market remained unsold on weekdays, and only 21 percent on Saturdays (see Table 4.2); the respective figures for April 1968 are 25 and 21 percent. During the former period 32 percent of all vendors on weekdays managed to sell out and 49 percent of those on Saturday, whereas the appropriate figures for the latter period are 49 and 54 percent.

ToEsli, a Tolai from Vunagalip, about 15 miles inland from Rabaul, who in 1968 was in his early 50s outlined for us the history of his involvement in food marketing. As a young boy he learnt to read and write by means of missionary eduction. Subsequently, he became a cook for a European family living in Rabaul where he worked until his employers were forced to leave New Britain when the Japanese invaded the Gazelle Peninsula. He then returned to his home village where he settled down to clearing the bush on some of his clan lands and cultivated bananas, sweet potatoes, taro and yams. His output by far exceeded his consumption needs and it was then that he began his marketing ventures; "marketing food is one of our traditional activities" were his own words on the subject. ToEsli related that Tolai market place trade continued to function during the earlier part of the period of Japanese occupation. Tolai growers reverted to their precontact type of a chain of smaller markets rather than to concentrate marketing all their produce in one or two places, the practice which had developed under Australian rule. This intra-Tolai marketing continued until the occupying forces became desperate for food and exactions by Japanese became the order of the day. "Both the Japanese and their Indian prisoners encouraged rice growing, and by 1945 rice covered much of the available plantation land" (Salisbury, 1970:54). The occupying troops and their prisoners were not

accustomed to eating Tolai staple crops and therefore insisted as long as they could that rice must be
grown to feed them. The Japanese authorities collected the rice from growers without rewarding them
for it. Some of the Tolai who refused to work for
the Japanese had their heads chopped off (Epstein,
T.S., 1968:60). "The 100,000 Japanese troops appear
to have fathered no half-caste children, and occasional bartering of *sake* for fresh food seems to
have been the only contact between villagers and
Japanese troops" (Salisbury, 1970:53).

ToEsli related that he tried to have as little
as possible to do with the Japanese during their
occupation. He admitted though that he had learned
from them the art of distilling alcohol from
bananas and rice. He remembers that he got drunk
for the first time in his life during the war when
he was about 30 years old. By that time he had got
married and produced two children. He claimed that
he sold his surplus produce to other Tolai for *tambu*
and in turn bought with shell money goods from his
fellow tribesmen which he needed and of which they
had a surplus right throughout the years of Japanese
occupation. At first this trade was conducted openly
at market sites, while subsequently, when the
Japanese on New Britain had been cut off from Japan
and had become ruthless in their demand for local
foods, intra-Tolai trade became a clandestine
activity. During this period of secret trading many
coastal Tolai used to come to Vunagalip to try and
purchase some of the staple root crops grown there.
In turn they brought with them packets of lime and
other coastal produce which they sold to inland
Tolai. This shortage of food supplies, according to
ToEsli, was a novel experience for many a Tolai.
Vunagalip people were comparatively fortunate; they
hardly suffered from bombing attacks and lived far
away inland so as not to be under the constant sur-
veillance of the Japanese troops. ToEsli admitted
that he managed to accumulate a lot of shell money
during this period of secret trading. Accounts from
other sources verify ToEsli's story of food shortages during the Japanese occupation and the drift of
tambu from less to more fortunate Tolai communities.
Salisbury relates that "one quarter of the prewar
Vunamami population was dead, from sickness and hunger or as a result of bombings" (1970:54) and
Epstein, A.L. states for Matupit, a coastal settlement that "much of the *tambu* was actually destroyed
by the Japanese, but great quantities were also used
up on clandestine trips to purchase food from more
fortunately situated Tolai communities" (1969:32)

The return to the Gazelle Peninsula of the
Australian authorities after the war once more
revived the Tolai economy and market trade was
quickly resumed. Since the war ToEsli's wife IaTiula
has largely taken over the sale of their produce at
Rabaul market. She is a regular supplier of produce
and carefully chooses the best of her crops to take
to Rabaul. ToEsli explained that during the war he
did not want to let his wife be responsible for
decisions relating to cultivation or marketing of
produce, because this involved dangerous activities.
Since the war when conditions returned to normal, he
has been happy to hand over to his wife much of the
responsibilities he had taken on because of the war.
According to Tolai custom she is now responsible to
arrange for the growing of food crops and for selling
the surplus at the market. IaTiula attends the market three Saturdays and four weekdays per month. She
pays $1 for transport charges and 20 cents for selling
at the market. On the Saturday we interviewed her
she had brought areca nuts, bananas, corn and taro
altogether worth $6; she managed to sell goods worth
$4.30 and took the unsold stuff back home with her.
She complained that she had had a bad day at the
market, but was quick to point out that her family
is always happy when she returns home with the unsold
produce. Since she always takes only the best
quality of everything with her, they look forward to
consuming whatever she does not manage to sell.
IaTiula regards $5 as a fair day's market earnings
and is thrilled if she manages to earn $6 or more per
day. She related that whenever she has had a good
day at the market she goes to one or another of the
Chinese trade stores and buys some groceries and
other things. On a bad day, such as she had when we
talked with her, she went straight back home without
spending any money in the town shops. Her marketing
expenses constituted almost 30 percent of her gross
earnings and she was left with $3.10. She said that
she regularly hands her husband at least $2 after
each of her marketing expeditions since they were
saving up to buy a share in a vehicle.

ToEsli's and his wife's account of their marketing involvement illustrates several features typical
of Tolai marketing practices. If we believe his
tale, and I have found no evidence to contradict it,
the reference to intra-Tolai trading right throughout the period of Japanese occupation is particularly
interesting. It indicates the economic interdependence of the Tolai region and contrasts it with the
Port Moresby Hinterland where no such traditional
trading arrangements existed. Koki market was

established as a result of urban demand, whereas Tolai markets reflect a regionally integrated food economy. Moreover, *tambu* facilitated this intra-Tolai trade and insured its continuation when the character of cash changed from Australian tender to Japanese war currency. Inland Tolai settlements like Vungalip were able to accumulate *tambu* during the war, while coastal dwellers like the Matupit disposed of most of theirs.

The protective role of Tolai men came into play during the war when men like ToElsi took over some of the activities customarily performed by their women-folk. Similarly, a riot at Rabaul market in 1961, which resulted when a Sepik worker molested a Tolai woman and was assaulted by the agrieved husband, altered the balance of male and female sellers. "Instead of the pre-riot pattern of thirty to forty male sellers among about three hundred women in and around the European shed, with a flow of men coming at about two thirty in the afternoon to collect the proceeds from the sales, after the riot there were about eighty male vendors, nearly half the total number inside the shed" (Salisbury, 1970:203) (2).

IaTiula's specialization in selling only staple foods coincides with the more widespread practice according to which villages more than 10 miles from Rabaul sell only small quantities of non-indigenous produce, the bulk of which comes from a radius of between five and ten miles from the market.

Kokopo and Vunapope are both much smaller markets than the one in Rabaul. The relationship between these three markets in terms of numbers of sellers attending is one of geometric progression with Vunapope being the smallest, Kokopo about 10 times its size and Rabaul more than 100 times (see Table 3.1). The market at Vunapope was in 1962 served by as many as twenty or thirty women sellers and Kokopo market by 160 vendors(3). During our market studies in 1968 we found 21 vendors at Vunapope and 205 at Kokopo market. The average value of produce brought per seller to Kokopo market appears to have almost trebled between 1962 and 1968; Salisbury calculates the total value of produce brought as 1,972s (which equals $197.20) of which 490s ($49) remained unsold on May 13, 1961, which for 160 vendors amounts to an average of $1.23 worth of produce brought and 92 cents sold per seller.

The corresponding figures for 1968 are $3.35 and $2.99, respectively. The proportion of the value of produce remaining unsold declined from 24 percent in 1962 to 11 percent in 1968. Kokopo appears to have developed increasingly into a market catering for indigenous demand rather than supplying expatriate needs: in 1961 non-indigenous produce constituted 37 percent of the total value of goods brought to the market, whereas by 1968 this proportion had drastically declined to four percent. Vendors obviously learned by bitter experience that it is much more risky to cultivate non-indigenous produce than local staples for sale. Salisbury noted that in 1961 the volume of European goods remaining unsold "increases dramatically as the number of sellers increases, whereas the amount of native produce unsold remains more or less steady, or even decreases as the proportion of the total goods in a larger market" (1970: 194). He estimates that about 25 percent of European foodstuffs remained unsold on May 13, 1961 at Kokopo market. In April 1968 only three percent of the value of non-indigenous produce brought to the market remained unsold. These two comparative studies over time of Kokopo market indicate that vendors seemed shrewdly to adjust to the small and decreasing demand for European foodstuffs and ventured into increasing supplies of local staples for which there has been a growing demand stemming mostly from workers on nearby plantations as well as from Tolai themselves. In 1961 about 15 percent of native vegetables brought to the market remained unsold; in 1968 no more than five percent of indigenous staples was left over by the end of the market day. Salisbury makes no mention of the sale of cooked food in 1961; during our study seven years later there were about half a dozen vendors who brought mainly cooked food but also some bananas and indigenous greens.

IaKilala coming from Ngatur, about eight miles from Kokopo told us that she prepares bundles of bananas and chicken or taro and chicken cooked in coconut juice about two or three times each month and sells the lot on Saturdays at Kokopo market. She cultivates all the bananas, coconuts and taro and rears the chickens she uses for her food preparations. On the day we interviewed her she had brought 32 bundles of cooked food for which she charged 10 cents each. By lunchtime she had sold out. Many plantation laborers sought her out having sampled her food before and liked it. IaKilala seemed to have a joking relationship with several of them and exchanged some sentences in pidgin English with them. She explained to us that it was through her contact with these New Guinea laborers, who spoke no Tolai, that she had begun to learn some pidgin English and that she enjoyed her bit of fun with them. She told us that she had been selling cooked food for over two years. She had got the idea of doing so when

she noticed some coastal Tolai women selling such
bundles at Rabaul market. When she first began
cooking food for sale she ventured to Rabaul but did
not think that her market trips were successful.
First of all she had to travel 18 miles to Rabaul, a
much longer distance than to Kokopo, and pay about
$1 in fares; and second, she had to compete with
sellers from several other villages, who offered
cooked food for sale, most of which contains fish,
which many buyers regard as a special delicacy. This
experience induced IaKilala to try selling at Kokopo
market, which she found a better proposition. She
prefers the more intimate atmosphere of Kokopo market
where fewer vendors and buyers turn up than at Rabaul
and where she has a chance to get to know at least
some of her buyers. Moreover, she pays only 40 cents
for her return fare and pays the same market fee as
at Rabaul. On the day we interviewed her, which
IaKilala claimed represented a typical market day for
her, her gross earnings amounted to $3.20 and her net
takings to $2.60. She was pleased with her market
venture and stated that her gross earnings depended
on the number of bundles she manages to prepare for
sale, since she invariably sells whatever quantity
she fetches. She stated that there are usually
another two or three women from her village who sell
cooked food at Kokopo, but none of them specializes
exclusively in this; they rather fetch in addition
a variety of other indigenous raw produce.

IaKilala'a account shows the advantages some
sellers derive from decentralized marketing at Kokopo
rather than to attend Rabaul market and face the
competition from many more vendors. It is particularly interesting to note that IaKilala, who concentrated in selling one specialized type of commodity,
found this so. Many other vendors at Kokopo, who
sell mainly staple crops still attend also Rabaul
market and go there with frequencies ranging from
once every two months to twice every month. The
proportion of vendors who sell out is 57 percent at
Kokopo which is higher than at Rabaul market and
makes trading at the former market rather less risky
and less costly for those growers who live closer to
that town than to Rabaul.

Vunapope is the smallest of the markets we
studied; 21 vendors offered their produce for sale to
about 200 visitors of whom 175 actually bought something. The average gross income per vendor was on a
Saturday in April 1968 $1.86 and net takings were
$1.51. The total market turnover per Saturday at
Vunapope was then only about six percent of that at
Kokopo market. The estimated relationship between

the total weight of produce sold at these two markets was eight percent. As mentioned already Vunapope market caters for a specific hospital clientele and the goods sold there are accordingly limited in range. Only indigenous type produce is sold; i.e, bundles of cooked food, staple root crops, bananas, peanuts, areca nuts and their accoutrements and other such like goods. 15 percent of the total value of produce brought to Vunapope market remains unsold and 60 percent of the vendors take some of their produce back home with them, the rest sell out. One third of the vendors regularly attend Vunapope markets each Saturday, the remainder come only occasionally.

IaEn, one of the vendors at Vunapope originates from Vunatagia, about five miles away. When we met her she explained that she has been regularly attending Vunapope market for the past few Saturdays, prior to which she used to sell at the nearby Kokopo market. She had switched to Vunapope because her sister was admitted to the hospital and she thought it better to combine her marketing with visiting her sister. If her sister was well enough and allowed out of the hospital she would come to the roadside market and join IaEn there, who would give her some of the stuff she had brought along; otherwise IaEn usually left the market about 3 or 4 pm after which she went to visit her sister in the hospital and gave her all the produce she had not been able to sell. On the day we talked with IaEn she had brought along 10 bundles of cooked food, as well as five each of peanuts, areca nuts and peppers, which she offered for sale at 10 cents per bundle. She had arrived by a small utility car and paid 10 cents for her fare. By about 3 pm IaEn had sold everything except two bundles each of cooked food and peanuts. She decided to pack up and take her unsold goods to her sister with whom she planned to stay about one hour before returning home to Vunatagia. She expected to pay another 10 cents for her return trip. Her gross takings thus amounted to $2.10 out of which she had to pay 20 cents for transport, which left her with $1.90 net earnings. She emphasized that she did not regard her fare as part of her marketing expense, since she would have come to Vunapope in any case to visit her sister in the hospital. She remarked that it was in fact better for her to attend Vunapope rather than Kokopo market for at the former no fees are charged whereas each vendor has to pay 20 cents at the latter. This tempted her to continue selling at Vunapope even after her sister will have been released from the hospital. She thought she may alternate between the two markets, for she said she misses her regular New Guinea plantation worker customers at Kokopo with whom she has established a joking relationship. On the other hand she also now enjoys selling at Vunapope where she has made friends among the small group of female vendors.

IaEn's case probably typifies many of the Vunapope vendors; her initial attraction to sell at Vunapope was not the market outlet in itself but rather the possibility of combining marketing with visits to her sick sister. Her experience at Vunapope was such that it encouraged her to continue selling there even after the initial motive will have disappeared, i.e., after her sister has returned home once more. Vunapope is thus likely to continue to grow slightly, but the strictly limited demand presents an obstacle to its further expansion. In a sense it is only an annexe to the hospital rather than a site specifically set up for the purpose of trading transactions where vendors go to sell and buyers to purchase goods.

CATEGORIES OF VENDORS

The outline of market supply, like that of demand, has indicated the heterogeneity of the trade conducted at producer-seller markets in Papua New Guinea. At each market we studied numerous vendors sell a great variety of different types of produce; at some of the markets, as for instance on the Gazelle Peninsula, there is considerable ethnic homogenity among vendors and buyers whereas at others, as at Koki many different tribes are represented. Gazelle Peninsula markets are dominated by female vendors whereas at Koki male sellers predominate. This great variety in vendors' characteristics as well as in the produce they sell makes it difficult to discover some order within what may appear chaotic marketing arrangements. Yet on closer examination certain regularities emerge. Foremost in this context is the fact that market trade constitutes only a small part of the total income of most or all vendors. Each has alternative cash earning opportunities of which he/she avails him/herself with varying aptitude. They can earn cash by wage labor and/or perennial cash cropping of export crops, and/or business ventures. Producer-sellers can therefore afford to forego the chance of maximizing their returns from market sales and rather aim at maximum satisfaction. This marginal importance of market trade as regards vendors' cash or total income is the one most significant variable influencing market transactions. Within this overall framework of market place trade, which is only of marginal importance to the individuals involved, five different categories of vendors emerge.

Trippers are sellers who attend the market for the fun of it and/or for its social aspects. They come irregularly and when they do they fetch only small quantities of indigenous staples or sundries the total value of which only slightly exceeds their transport costs. They are satisfied if they do no more than break even and they do not mind having to take some of their unsold produce back home with them again.

Trippers do not usually cultivate crops for the specific purpose of selling them, but rather try to harvest a surplus over and above their own immediate consumption needs whenever they decide they want to attend the market. Their main motivation in coming to the market is thus not so much to sell produce to earn cash or shell money, but rather to be able to participate in the large social gatherings which occur at market sites. They are at the extreme end of the progression of vendors ranging from satisficers to profiteers; they personify what Brookfield calls "satisficers" (1969:154). Many vendors at Papua New Guinea markets are trippers; the greater the proportion they constitute of the total number of sellers, the smaller the average net earnings per seller, and the greater the percentage of vendors who make no gains or even incur losses.

Marginalists are sellers who are mainly subsistence farmers but who frequently produce a small surplus exceeding their consumption needs, which they then take to the market for sale. Their trading activities are supply stimulated, though of course they are pleased with their earnings. Like trippers, most marginalists also sell irregularly and when they do fetch only small quantities of indigenous produce; they cheerfully return home with whatever of it is left over at the end of the market day.

A large proportion of Highland vendors appear to fall into this category of marginalists. This is indicated by our survey data and supported by our case studies. Marginalists are also satisficers, but not quite to the same extent as trippers. Neither trippers nor marginalists try to anticipate market demand by growing crops specifically intended for sale, nor do they plan their market trip long in advance; their decisions to take produce to the market are frequently made spontaneously. Their

146

supplies meet some of the urban demand for fresh foods.

Buyer-sellers are vendors who sell and buy at the market. Rabaul market represents a good example of a site where many such buyer-sellers trade. The *raison d'etre* of such trade is not so much urban demand but rather the ecological diversification of the market Hinterland which promotes an exchange economy, which in turn was facilitated by the use of shell money among the Tolai.

The presence of the buyer-seller phenomenon is not necessarily the result only of such area specialization in production as exists among the Tolai, but occurs at most markets. The Mt. Hagen buyer who frequently sells her sweet potatoes at the market but also periodically buys some of this same crop for herself, for instance when rain makes it unpalatable for her to dig up her sweet potatoes for her own household needs (see p. 49), provides an example of buyer-seller transactions different from those conducted at Rabaul market. Most buyer-sellers are motivated to grow a surplus of whatever they can cultivate to be able to buy goods they themselves cannot produce or at a certain time lack.

They attend the market at fairly regular intervals and usually fetch larger quantities of produce than trippers and marginalists. The considerable proportion of the total trade conducted between cultivators at Papua New Guinea markets indicates the importance of this particular category of buyer-sellers. Obviously not all the produce brought for sale by them is bought by other indigenous suppliers; a large part of it is purchased by urban dwellers. Yet the existence of such buyer-sellers at Highland markets augurs well for the development of specialization among growers in terms of different kinds of produce and/or in supplying the same produce during different periods in the year. The intra-cultivator trade conducted at Rabaul involves specialization in different kinds of produce whereas at Mt. Hagen it indicates specialization in timing of planting and harvesting. Though buyer-sellers are also satisficers to a certain degree, their production and trading is much more market oriented than that of trippers and marginalists, while at the same time personal relations between buyers and sellers are also more important for them.

Target Operators are vendors, who are motivated to produce for the market in order to satisfy a particular need, such as for instance to earn money to buy a specific article in one of the town shops or to pay school fees for a child or such like reason. Target operators plan more carefully to produce for the market than buyer-sellers, and they also fetch larger quantities of more valuable produce. They are the ones who bring indigenous as well as some non-indigenous produce for sale. They attend the market at irregular intervals and if necessary are prepared to stay longer in town to sell out and reach their target.

Many of the vendors at Koki and Mt. Hagen are such target sellers; they constitute a higher proportion among male than among female vendors. They are more concerned with maximizing their sales proceeds rather than with the social aspect of their marketing venture, yet their major incentive is to achieve one or another of their ambitions; the more costly their targets the greater their marketing efforts. For instance, some men who want to invest in a vehicle or pay for the repairs of their broken down transport become regular suppliers of produce until they manage to put sufficient cash together to reach their objective, after which they relax their sales drive. IaBokoro features another type of target operator (see p. 136); she aimed at accumulating shell money for her son's bridewealth and therefore regularly sold the type of produce which is bought with *tambu*.

Profiteers are vendors who are keen to maximize their returns; they produce specially for the market, many of them supply non-indigenous produce. In doing so they run the risk of being left with unsold produce which they themselves cannot consume; on the other hand if they manage to sell all or most of their wares their returns are higher than those who supply indigenous staples. There are not many profiteers among Papua New Guinea market vendors. IaPilai (see p.134) ranks in this category; significantly, her net earnings from selling non-indigenous produce were about 85 percent more than IaTuraram's who as a buyer-seller had fetched mainly local staples to the market. IaPilai displayed remarkable shrewdness in knowing at what point in the market day it was advisable to lower prices if left with unsold non-indigenous produce. Her skill was rewarded by her sell out. By way of contrast IaTuraram was left with unsold produce amounting to almost 20 percent of the total value she brought to Rabaul. She made no attempt to lower the price and thereby attract buyers to purchase her goods and was not unduly perturbed about having to return home with the left over produce. While IaPilai can be classified as a profiteer, IaTuraram is much more of a target seller: she brought for sale some of the produce which grows best in the region from which she originates, and in turn bought fish from the market, an article unobtainable in her inland village; she spent most of her sale proceeds on purchases in one of the town stores, and altogether enjoyed her outing.

Many of the vendors at Koki rank as profiteers. They fetch larger quantities of more valuable produce and remain in town until they have sold out, even if this involves staying in town more than one week. They travel longer distances than Highland or Gazelle Peninsula vendors and their marketing ventures thus involve much more careful and long-term planning, which appears to make them more profit oriented.

These five categories of vendors are useful for analytical purposes. They are not meant to be mutually exclusive. In fact they can be viewed as a series of overlapping circles, i.e., some features of several of the different categories may coexist in many vendors. For instance, some profiteers may enjoy the social aspect of the market, like trippers, as well as have a special object in mind which motivates their market trade, like target operators. Bohannan and Dalton in their analysis of African markets distinguish between three groups of communities according to their different techniques of facilitating exchanges: "first one in which there are no market places... second... in which market places exist and the market principle operates, but only peripherally;...finally,... in which market places may be (and usually are) present, but in which the primary source of subsistence goods for buyers and of income for sellers and producers is the market in the sense of transactional principle" (1962: 4). Papua New Guinea producer-sellers' markets do not seem to fit readily into any one of these three groups: they are certainly not marketless, nor can they be included under the third type, for there are hardly any market vendors who depend primarily on the market for a livelihood. Besides Papua New Guinea producer-vendors usually are, or at least can be, self-sufficient in food supplies. Papua New Guinea marketing bears some resemblance to peripheral market societies, yet displays many distinct features which marks it off from this group; most important here is the fact that a large proportion of buyers are urban dwellers who depend for their food supplies largely on the market. Thus it would seem that the demand aspects of Papua New Guinea marketing resemble

149

Bohannan and Dalton's *market societies,* whereas supply
coincides more readily with *peripheral market societies.*
Yet this categorization is not really helpful in the
discussion of Papua New Guinea producer-seller markets. It is possible that our understanding of the
operation of Hinterland-based markets serving smaller
towns in Africa and other parts of the developing
world may be improved if categories identical or
similar to the ones I suggest here were used as
analytical tools to supplement the analysis by
Bohannan and Dalton for African markets.

The categories of vendors and buyers developed
on the basis of our market studies are used in the
following chapters as a means to analyse the price
formation process and the role of food marketing in
Papua New Guinea.

NOTES

1.   This contradicts R.F. Salisbury's statement
referring to Tolai women selling European vegetables
at Rabaul market that 'in the early afternoon each
woman's husband can usually be seen arriving and
demanding from her the day's proceeds" (1970:180).
2.   Salisbury (1970) claims that Tolai women
selling non-indigenous produce do so only on behalf
of their husbands. "For a woman to profit from what
she herself has made is permissable but unusual"
(1970:180). He claims that I failed to observe this
practice in 1961. But even my more detailed market
studies conducted in 1968 re-affirm that most Tolai
women who sell both indigenous and non-indigenous
produce do so independently of their husbands.
Salisbury argues that the easy substitution after the
riot of male for female non-indigenous produce
sellers proves that Tolai men have long had a monopoly over this kind of trade. His analysis of Tolai
marketing which outlines a specialization by women
in reciprocal trade transactions and men in profit
oriented trade (1970:180) would have gained support
had he been able to recount that the proportion of
male vendors selling staple food remained unchanged
after the riot. Salisbury is silent on this important point. Administrative officers who were in
Rabaul at the time of the riot told me that many Tolai
men took over from their womenfolk the marketing of
indigenous and non-indigenous produce alike, simply
because they did not want to expose them to unneces-
sary dangers. This accords with ToElsi's protecting
his wife during the war like many other Tolai men
are reported to have done. In 1968 the proportion of

male vendors selling non-indigenous produce was minimal.

3. The 1961/2 data used here as a basis for comparison is derived from Salisbury. 1970:Chapter 5.

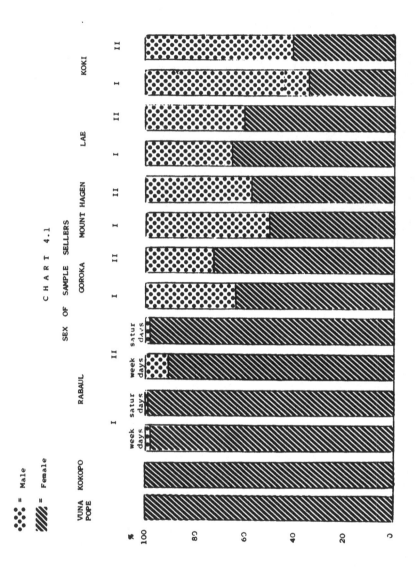

CHART 4.1

SEX OF SAMPLE SELLERS

= Male
= Female

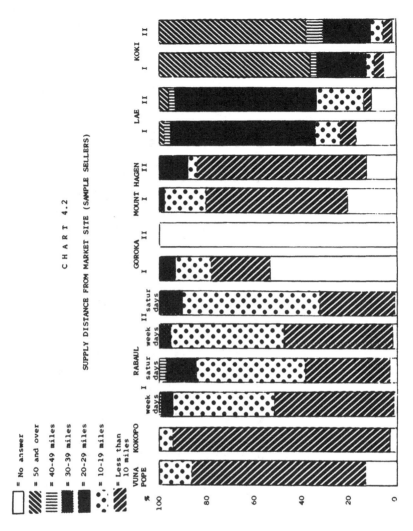

C H A R T 4.2

SUPPLY DISTANCE FROM MARKET SITE (SAMPLE SELLERS)

☐ = No answer
▨ = 50 and over
▤ = 40-49 miles
■ = 30-39 miles
▩ = 20-29 miles
⋰ = 10-19 miles
▨ = Less than 10 miles

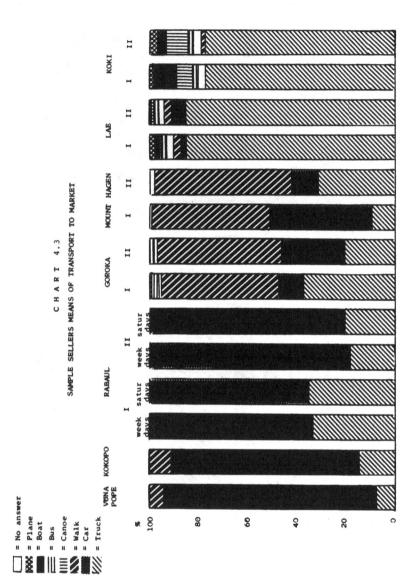

C H A R T   4.3

SAMPLE SELLERS MEANS OF TRANSPORT TO MARKET

☐ = No answer
▨ = Plane
■ = Boat
☰ = Bus
⦀ = Canoe
⬚ = Walk
■ = Car
▨ = Truck

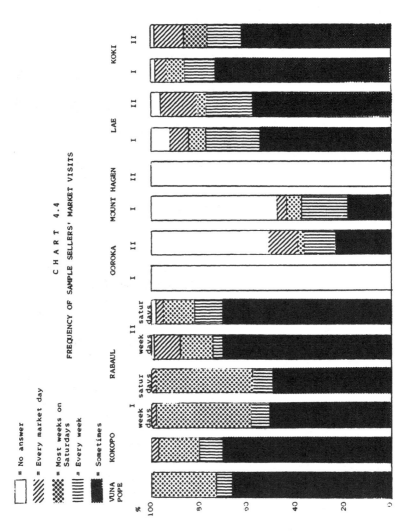

C H A R T 4.4

FREQUENCY OF SAMPLE SELLERS' MARKET VISITS

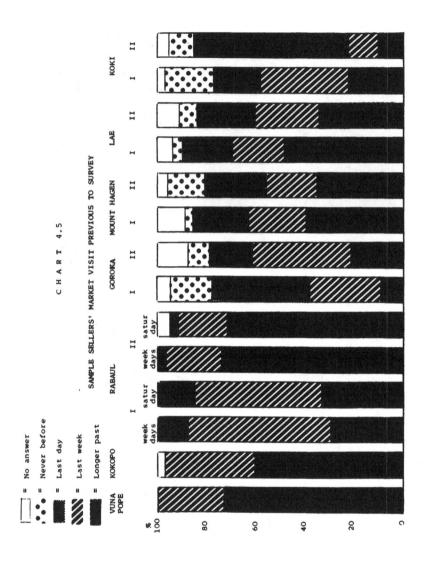

C H A R T 4.5

SAMPLE SELLERS' MARKET VISIT PREVIOUS TO SURVEY

= No answer
= Never before
= Last day
= Last week
= Longer past

156

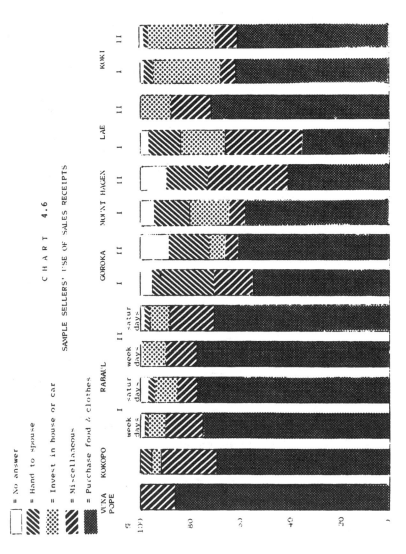

CHART 4.6

SAMPLE SELLERS' USE OF SALES RECEIPTS

= No answer

= Hand to spouse

= Invest in house or car

= Miscellaneous

= Purchase food & clothes

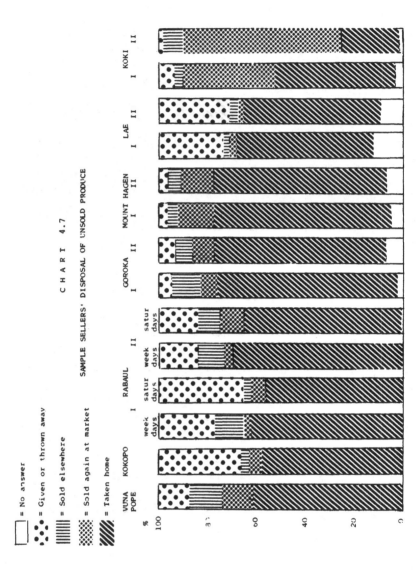

C H A R T   4.7

SAMPLE SELLERS' DISPOSAL OF UNSOLD PRODUCE

☐ = No answer

∴ = Given or thrown away

▥ = Sold elsewhere

▨ = Sold again at market

▧ = Taken home

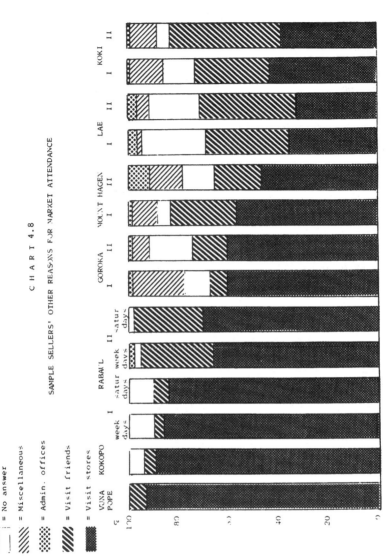

C H A R T 4.8

SAMPLE SELLERS' OTHER REASONS FOR MARKET ATTENDANCE

= No answer

= Miscellaneous

= Admin. offices

= Visit friends

= Visit stores

CHART 4.9: Produce Sold at Papua New Guinea Markets

Common Name	Latin Name
Apple, red prickly	Rambutans (Nephelium Lappaleum)
Avocado	Persea Gratissima
Bamboo Shoot	Bambusa Spp.
Banana, ripe (eating)	Musa Sapientum
Banana, unripe (cooking)	Musa Sapientum
Betel Nut	Areca Catechu
Breadfruit	Artocarpus Incisa
Cabbage	Brassica Oleracea
Capiscum	Capiscum Grossum
Carrot	Daucus Carota
Choco	Sechium Edule
Coconut (dry)	Cocos Nucifera
Coconut (green)	Cocos Nucifera
Corn	Zea Mays
Cucumber	Cucumis Sativus
Custard Apple	Anona Squamosa
Eggplant (Nasivu)	Solanum Melongena
Fivecorner (Ffuit)	Averrhoa Carambola
Ginger	Zingiber Officinale
Granadilla	Passiflora Quadrangularis
Guava	Psidium Guyava
Indigenous Spinach	Abelmoschu Manihot
Lantro Seed	Lucaene Glauca
Lemon	Citrus Limonum
Lettuce	Lacuca Sativa
Mango	Mangifera Indica
Mint	Mentha Viridis
Nula	Gnetum Gnemon
Nut (Galip)	Canarium Sp.
Onion	Allium Cepa
Orange	Citrus Aurantium (C. Sinaysis)
Parsley	Petroselinum Sativum
Pawpaw	Carica Papaya
Peanut	Arachis Hypogaea
Pepper (long)	Piper Sp.
Pepper	Capiscum Spp.
Pineapple	Ananas Sativus
Potato	Dioscorea Spp.
Pumpkin	Cucurbita Maxima
Radish	Raphanus Sativus
Sago	Metroxylon Sago
Sweet Potato	Ipomoea Batatas
Sugarcane (Atup)	Saccharum Officinarum
Sugarcane (Pitpit)	Saccharum Spontaneum
Tagia	Eugenia Malaccensis
Tapioka	Manihot Spp.
Taro	Colocasia Esculenta
Taro (introduced)	Xanthosoma Spp.

Common Name	Latin Name
Tomato	Lycopersicum Esculentum
Watercress	Nasturtium Officinale
Watermelon	Citrullus Vulgaris
Yam (Up)	Dioscorea Spp.

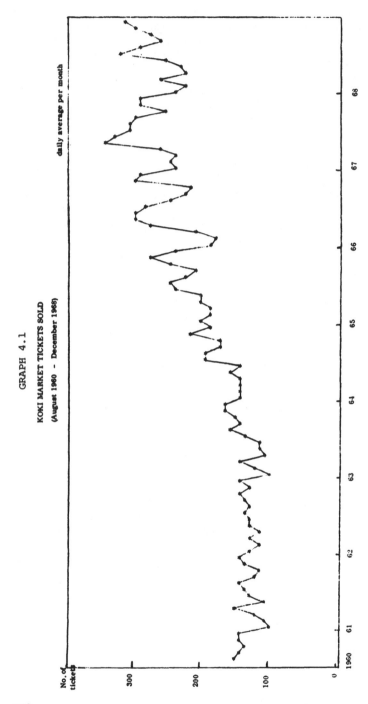

GRAPH 4.1

KOKI MARKET TICKETS SOLD

(August 1960 – December 1968)

daily average per month

162

GRAPH 4.2

NUMBER OF KOKI TICKETS SOLD (7 mths. time lag) AND RAINFALL IN KOKI SUPPLY AREAS

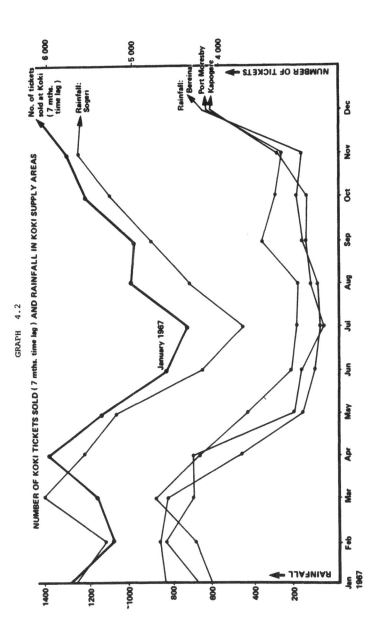

163

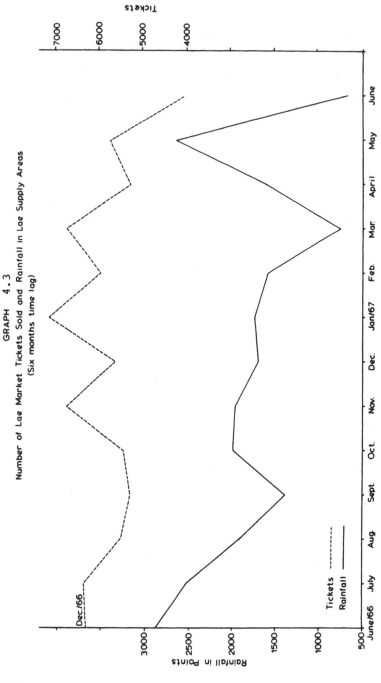

GRAPH 4.3

Number of Lae Market Tickets Sold and Rainfall in Lae Supply Areas

(Six months time lag)

164

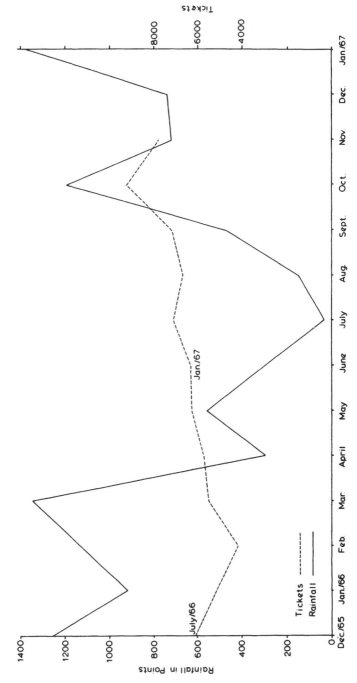

GRAPH 4.4

Number of Goroka Market Tickets Sold and Rainfall in Goroka Supply Areas
(Seven months time lag)

165

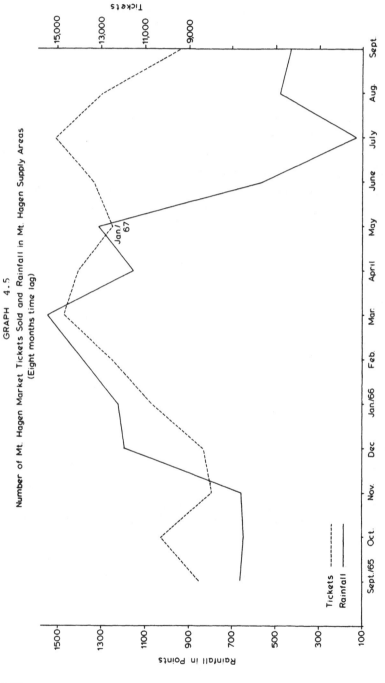

GRAPH 4.5.

Number of Mt. Hagen Market Tickets Sold and Rainfall in Mt. Hagen Supply Areas
(Eight months time lag)

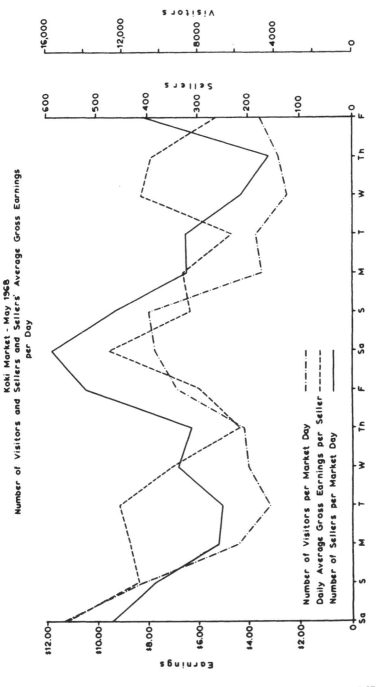

GRAPH 4.6
Koki Market - May 1968
Number of Visitors and Sellers and Sellers' Average Gross Earnings
per Day

Number of Visitors per Market Day —·—·—
Daily Average Gross Earnings per Seller ————
Number of Sellers per Market Day ————————

Visitors

16,000
12,000
8000
4000
0

Sellers

600
500
400
300
200
100
0

F Th W T M S Sa F Th W T M S Sa

Earnings

$12.00
$10.00
$8.00
$6.00
$4.00
$2.00
0

167

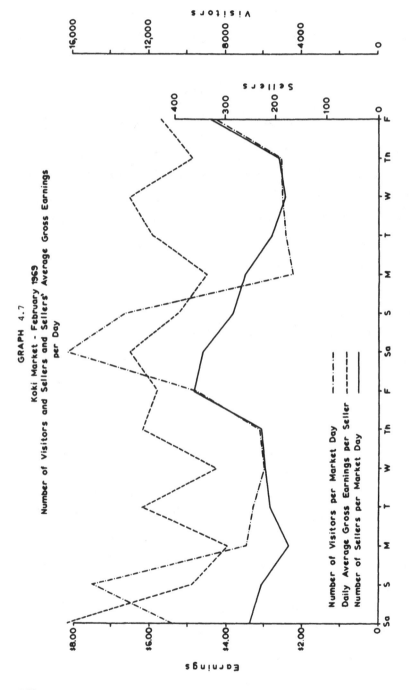

GRAPH 4.7
Koki Market - February 1969
Number of Visitors and Sellers and Sellers' Average Gross Earnings
per Day

Number of Visitors per Market Day —··—··—
Daily Average Gross Earnings per Seller — — — —
Number of Sellers per Market Day ————————

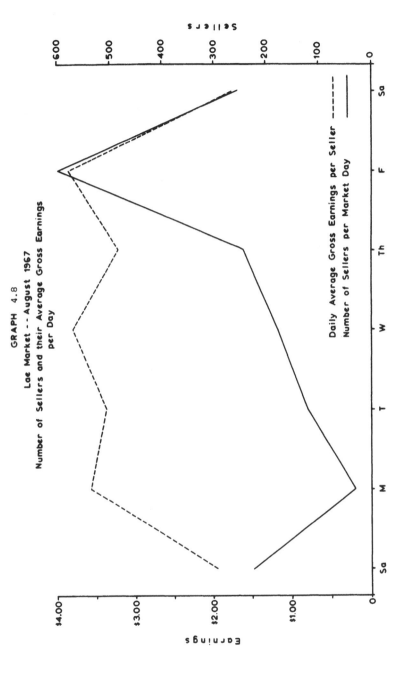

GRAPH 4.8

Lae Market -- August 1967

Number of Sellers and their Average Gross Earnings per Day

Daily Average Gross Earnings per Seller ------
Number of Sellers per Market Day ———

Sellers

Earnings

GRAPH 4.9
Lae Market - December 1967
Number of Sellers and their Average Gross Earnings
per Day

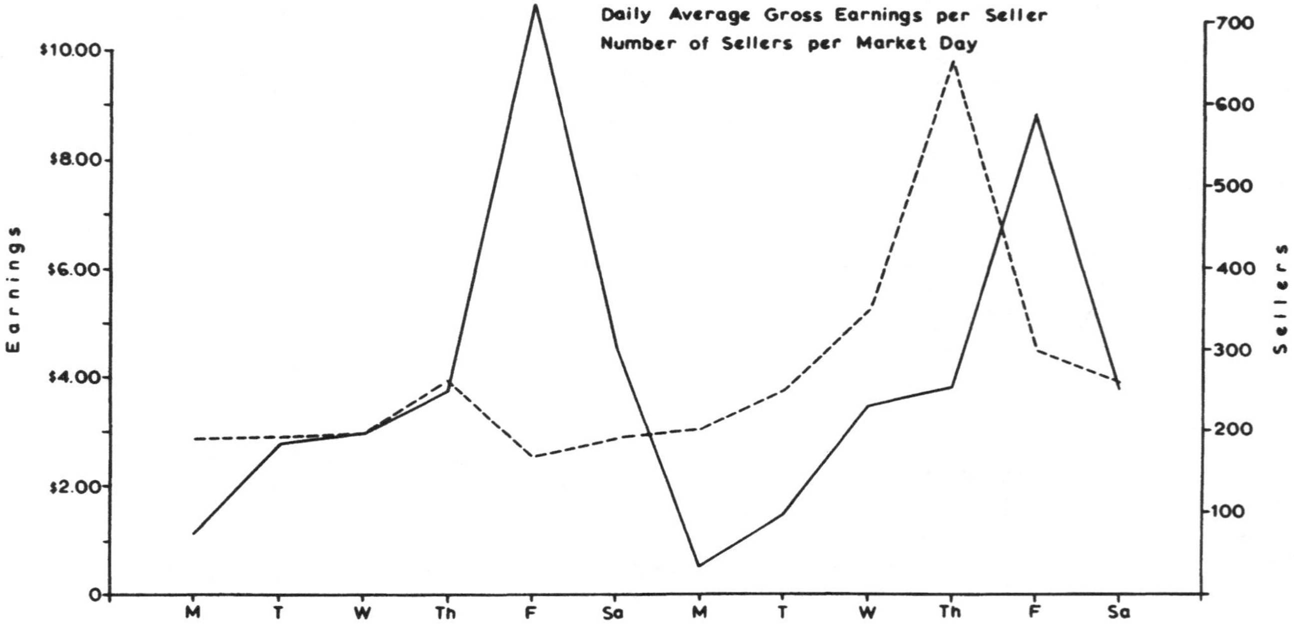

Daily Average Gross Earnings per Seller
Number of Sellers per Market Day

170

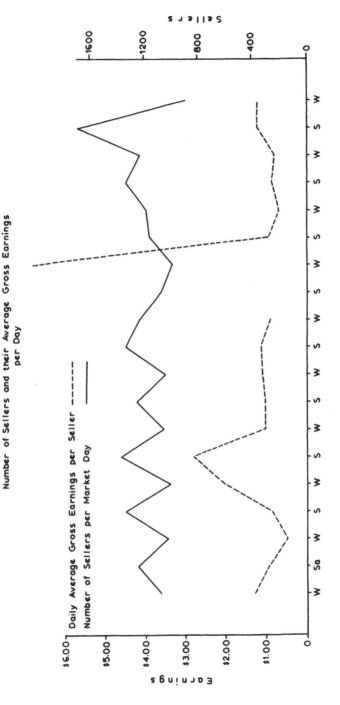

GRAPH 4.10

Mt. Hagen Market - February 1967

Number of Sellers and their Average Gross Earnings
per Day

Daily Average Gross Earnings per Seller — — — —

Number of Sellers per Market Day ————

Sellers

Earnings

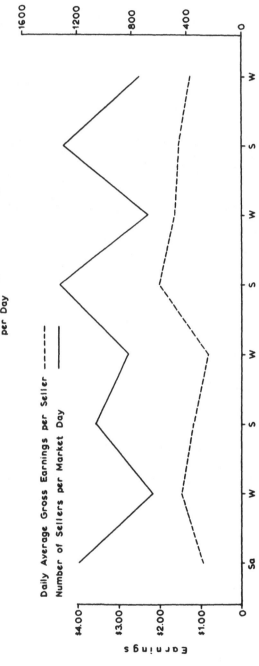

GRAPH 4.11
Mt. Hagen Market - July 1967
Number of Sellers and their Average Gross Earnings
per Day

Daily Average Gross Earnings per Seller -----
Number of Sellers per Market Day ———

Sellers

Earnings

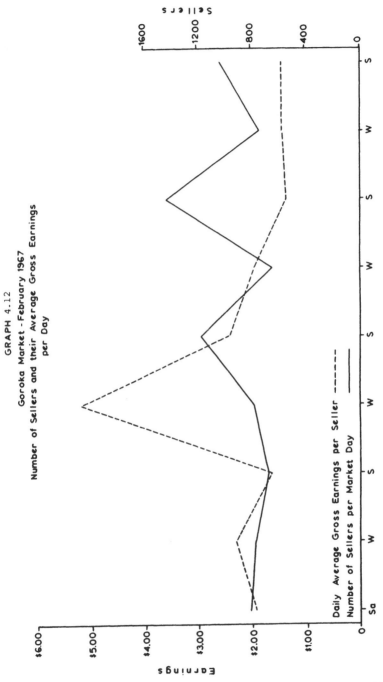

GRAPH 4.12

Goroka Market - February 1967

Number of Sellers and their Average Gross Earnings per Day

Daily Average Gross Earnings per Seller ------
Number of Sellers per Market Day ————

Sellers

Earnings

GRAPH 4.13
Goroka Market -- August 1967
Number of Sellers and their Average Gross Earnings
per Day

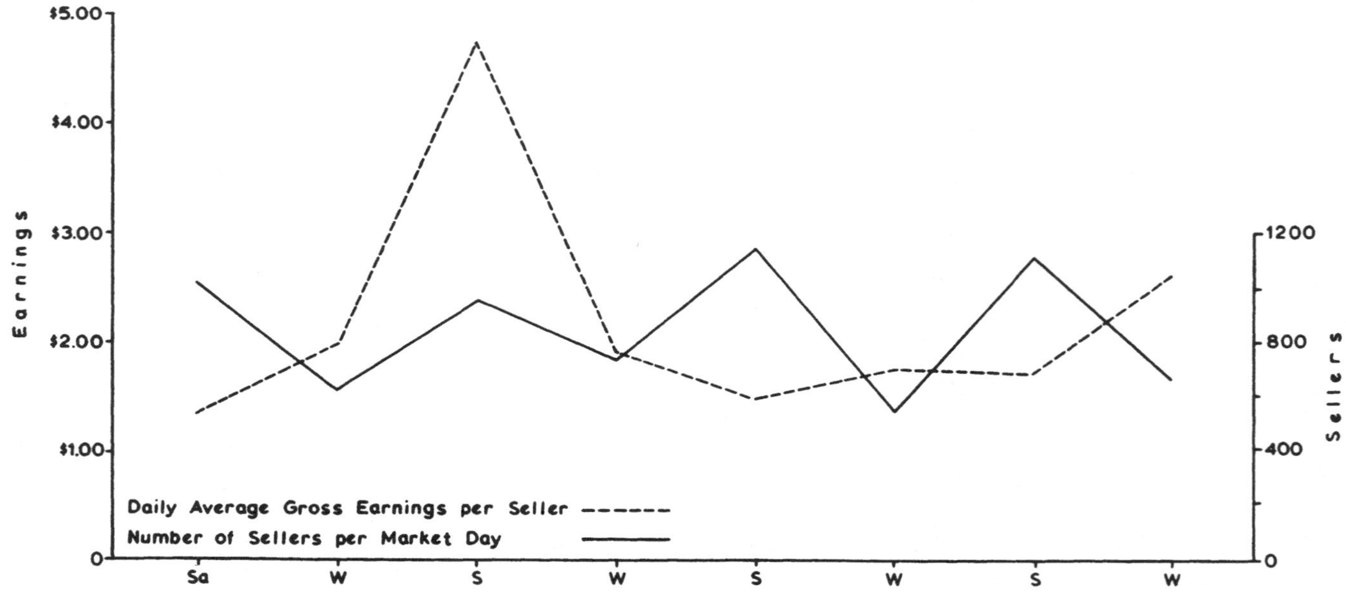

Daily Average Gross Earnings per Seller ------
Number of Sellers per Market Day ———

Sellers

1200
800
400
0

Earnings

$5.00
$4.00
$3.00
$2.00
$1.00
0

Sa W S W S W S W

174

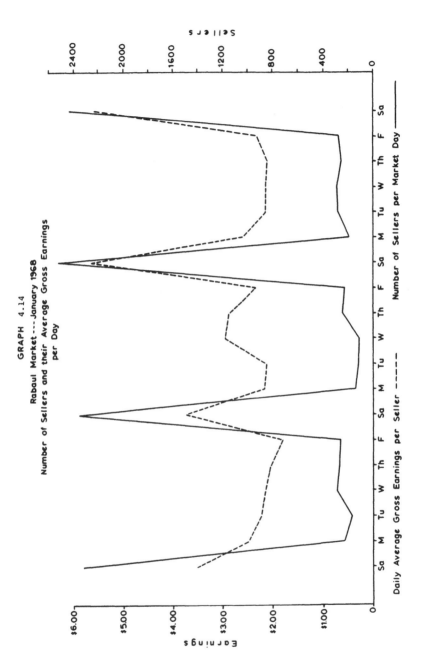

GRAPH 4.14
Rabaul Market---January 1968
Number of Sellers and their Average Gross Earnings
per Day

Number of Sellers per Market Day ———

Daily Average Gross Earnings per Seller - - - -

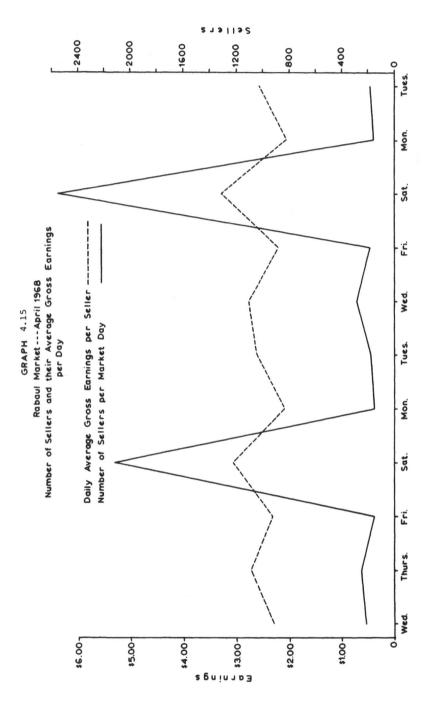

GRAPH 4.15

Rabaul Market---April 1968

Number of Sellers and their Average Gross Earnings per Day

Daily Average Gross Earnings per Seller ----------
Number of Sellers per Market Day ————

Table 4.1: Average Number of Vehicles Arriving
at the Markets per Day

	No.
Vunapope	-
Kokopo	312
Rabaul I:W	1,090
I:S	2,364
II:W	854
II:S	1,898
Goroka (March 1967)	123
Mt. Hagen (March 1967)	41
Lae (August 1967)	64
Koki I	752
II	509

Table 4.2: Value of Unsold Produce Daily by Categories Brought to Papua New Guinea Markets (Percentages)

	Non-indigenous Vegetables %	Indigenous Staples %	Indigenous Greens %	Fruit %	Sundries %	Meat & Eggs %	Fish %	Handi-crafts %	Misc. %	Total %
Vunapope	-	30	18	12	10	-	-	-	-	15
Kokopo	3	5	3	2	31	26	-	47	-	11
Rabaul I:W	24	52	17	23	40	25	25	50	-	39
I:S	14	26	10	25	19	25	25	40	13	21
II:W	16	33	13	17	25	-	4	50	-	25
II:S	8	30	12	21	12	-	10	29	-	21
Goroka	21	-	27	64	18	60	-	-	42	34
	13	3	8	13	12	66	-	38	58	15
Mt. Hagen I	11	-	11	18	1	-	-	-	-	10
II	5	12	7	10	7	11	-	-	4	7
Lae I	33	25	44	38	25	39	9	38	35	35
II	39	28	33	35	25	13	7	29	35	31
Koki I	28	44	15	42	39	27	19	61	40	35
II	28	27	32	30	22	4	14	38	25	24

178

Table 4.3: Value of Produce by Categories Brought Daily to Papua New Guinea Markets (Percentages)

	Non-indigenous Vegetables %	Indigenous Staples %	Indigenous Greens %	Fruit %	Sundries %	Meat & Eggs %	Fish %	Handi- crafts %	Misc. %	Total %
Vunapope	-	29	31	23	15	-	-	2	-	100
Kokopo	4	33	13	11	14	2	-	23	-	100
Rabaul I:W	10	10	6	11	37	1	3	21	1	100
I:S	16	24	17	15	14	5	3	4	2	100
II:W	12	17	8	14	35	-	2	12	-	100
II:S	15	39	13	15	13	-	1	4	-	100
Goroka I	24	6	6	25	10	12	-	1	16	100
II	42	13	10	9	10	4	-	2	10	100
Mt. Hagen I	35	7	19	16	19	3	-	-	1	100
II	46	14	13	15	9	-	-	2	1	100
Lae I	33	16	9	18	10	1	2	3	8	100
II	33	18	9	13	21	2	1	3	-	100
Koki I	2	16	-	34	26	4	15	-	3	100
II	4	18	3	34	17	3	13	1	7	100

Table 4.4: Vendor's Average Earnings and Marketing Expenses per Market Day

		Value brought $	Value unsold $	Value sold $	Transport cost $	Market fees $	Net earnings $
Vunapope		2.21	0.55	1.66	0.35	0.20	1.51
Kokopo		3.35	0.36	2.99	0.35	0.20	2.44
Rabaul	I:W	3.41	1.13	2.28	0.50	0.20	1.58
	I:S	5.98	1.16	4.82	0.74	0.20	3.88
	II:W	3.08	0.66	2.42	0.53	0.20	1.69
	II:S	4.03	0.85	3.18	0.70	0.20	2.28
Goroka	I	2.38	0.39	1.99	0.14	0.05	1.80
	II	3.23	1.00	2.23	0.08	0.05	2.10
Mt. Hagen	I	1.49	0.14	1.35	0.10	0.05	1.20
	II	1.28	0.09	1.19	0.08	0.05	1.06
Lae	I	4.43	1.30	3.13	0.41	0.20	2.52
	II	5.31	1.40	3.91	0.37	0.20	3.34
Koki	I	7.32	1.76	5.56	0.77	0.10	4.69
	II	11.56	4.20	7.36	0.81	0.10	6.45

Table 4.5: Koki: Average Gross and Net Earnings per Vendor According to Tribal Units

	Daily gross earnings per vendor		Cost of transport		No. of days selling at Koki		Cost of transport per day		Market fee	Daily net earnings per vendor		Earnings per market trip	
	May 1968	Feb 1969	May 1968	Feb 1969	May 1968	Feb 1969	May 1968	Feb 1969		May 1968	Feb 1969	May 1968	Feb 1969
	$	$	$	$	No.	No.	$	$	$*	$	$	$	$
Hula	11.78	5.13	-	-	1	1	-	-	0.20	11.58	4.93	11.58	4.93
Mekeo	5.69	6.31	6.81	12.42	8	10	0.85	1.24	0.10	4.74	4.97	37.92	49.70
Rigo	6.59	5.80	3.38	3.58	3	3	1.13	1.19	0.10	5.36	3.51	16.98	10.53
Toaripi	4.02	1.53	1.74	2.65	2	4	0.87	0.66	0.10	3.05	0.77	7.10	3.08
Papuan	7.90	5.24	2.95	3.14	4	4	0.74	0.78	0.10	7.06	4.36	28.24	17.44
Chimbu	13.24	4.03	1.51	2.03	3	3	0.60	0.67	0.10	12.54	3.26	37.62	9.78
New Guinean	6.57	4.41	0.95	2.45	2	3	0.48	0.82	0.10	6.09	3.39	12.18	10.17
Total	7.36	5.56	3.23	3.87	4	5	0.81	0.77	0.10	6.45	4.69	25.80	23.45

*Assuming each vendor pays the market fee which remained unchanged throughout the periods of the survey

Table 4.6: Koki: Average Values of Supplies and Daily Sales per Supply Zone

Distance of home village miles	May 1968			Feb 1969		
	Supplies per seller $	Percentage sold %	Turnover per seller $	Supplies per seller $	Percentage sold %	Turnover per seller $
0 - 35	9.59	74	7.11	7.32	84	6.14
36 - 70	11.78	61	7.15	7.47	74	5.50
71 - 100	11.30	66	7.47	6.62	73	4.86
101 and over	21.53	45	9.60	11.24	61	6.84
Unidentified	10.67	72	7.71	6.56	77	5.06
Total	11.56	64	7.36	7.32	76	5.56

Table 4.7: Male and Female Vendors: Average Earnings and Expenses per Market Day

		Value brought $	Value unsold $	Value sold $	Transport cost $	Market fees $	Net earnings $
Goroka	I:M	4.31	0.18	4.13	0.04	0.05	4.04
	I:F	3.45	1.66	1.79	0.02	0.05	1.72
	II:M	3.02	0.58	2.44	0.16	0.10	2.18
	II:F	1.96	0.32	1.64	0.04	0.05	1.55
Mt. Hagen	I:M	1.04	0.09	0.95	0.07	0.05	0.83
	I:F	1.78	0.17	1.61	0.04	0.05	1.52
	II:M	1.37	0.07	1.30	0.03	0.05	1.22
	II:F	1.49	0.12	1.37	0.03	0.05	1.29
Lae	I:M	5.17	1.70	3.47	0.52	0.20	2.75
	I:F	4.18	1.24	2.94	0.35	0.20	2.39
	II:M	7.74	3.24	4.50	0.58	0.20	3.72
	II:F	4.43	1.30	3.13	0.24	0.20	2.69

Table 4.8: Rabaul: Average Values of Supplies and Daily Sales per Supply Zone

Distance of home village	Jan 1968						April 1968					
	Supplies per seller		Percentage sold		Turnover per seller		Supplies per seller		Percentage sold		Turnover per seller	
miles	W $	S $	W %	S %	W $	S $	W $	S $	W %	S %	W $	S $
0 - 5	3.02	5.12	65	54	1.96	2.78	2.24	4.90	83	66	1.87	3.21
6 - 10	2.96	5.95	76	83	2.25	4.92	2.76	4.17	81	80	2.23	3.33
11 - 15	3.11	5.09	70	78	2.18	3.97	3.16	3.69	79	78	2.51	2.88
16 - 20	4.11	6.67	57	88	2.33	5.85	3.85	4.44	71	81	2.73	3.60
21 - 25	6.37	9.04	54	80	3.46	7.20	4.18	3.86	86	93	3.57	3.59
26 - 30	5.75	2.90	98	83	5.62	2.70	5.12	-	94	-	4.84	-
31 and over	7.23	6.65	52	39	3.76	2.55	-	-	-	-	-	-
Unidentified	3.68	4.79	71	86	2.61	4.18	2.28	2.10	90	64	2.05	1.35

PART THREE:

THEORETICAL AND PRACTICAL IMPLICATIONS

Chapter 5

PRICE FORMATION PROCESS

The producer-seller markets discussed in this volume
all concentrate on supplying fresh food. "There is
little trading in local manufactures or export
crops. Imported produce hardly ever appears in the
market places at all...They exist along side per-
manently established trade stores, shops and department stores operated for the most part by
expatriates and companies; these shops handle some
local produce, but it is only a minor part of their
stock in trade" (Brookfield, 1969:1).

As already mentioned the absence of bargaining
and the largely inflexible prices as well as lack of
competition among vendors are features which distinguish these markets from their urban-based counterparts in Africa (Bauer, 1954), Asia (Dewey, 1962)
and Latin America (Cassidy, 1974). This lack of any
'sales drive' appears to be a widespread phenomenon
in Pacific markets (Brookfield, 1969:2). Yet it is
not restricted to the Pacific but occurs also at
Hinterland-rooted markets in Africa. "In transactions between Tonga, it is left to the one who
desires a commodity to take the initiative. He is
the buyer and therefore the supplicant. The one who
meets the need is the seller and is in a position to
control the terms of exchange" (Colson, 1962:615).
Bauer's discussion of West African markets (1954)
and Colson's account of trade among the Tonga (1962)
suggests that the analytical distinction between
urban-based and Hinterland-rooted markets as well as
between supply and demand stimulated trades may be
meaningful not only in the Pacific region but also
with reference to Africa and possibly other areas
too, where similar conditions prevail.

The detailed account of Papua New Guinea market transactions in the preceding chapters illustrates the nature of locally produced food trade.
It reaffirms what I had found in Rabaul already in

1961. Supplies are still sold almost exclusively by producer-sellers. By contrast in the Philippines "the peasant is more likely to sell to a retailer or carrier than to market his own produce" (Davis, 1973:141). Davis suggests that "producers are likely to become retailers only when conditions result in a strong sellers market" (1973:141). Producer-sellers at Papua New Guinea markets certainly behave as if they operated in a sellers market framework, in spite of the considerable proportion of produce that remains unsold on any one market day (see Table 4.2). Almost all of these vendors give the impression as if they were completely lethargic and could not care less whether.or not they made a sale. Such seemingly irrational behavior is conditioned by a complex system of cultural values interacting with economic variables. Traditional emphasis on reciprocal and fair exchanges (Salisbury, 1970:180), cultural norms denegrating greed (Parkinson, 1907:88), and an integrated social network among suppliers (Epstein, T.S., 1968:163) are some of the important cultural features affecting market patterns. The most significant among relevant economic variables is the marginality of vendors market income. Self-produced food, wage employment, perennial cash crops as well as a variety of tertiary services represent other and more lucrative sources of livelihood which are available to almost all. For most Papua New Guinea vendors the social attraction of market visits outweighs the importance of profit maximization.

In other parts of the world where market trade is more profit-oriented vendors may best be categorized by the different types of produce they sell (see e.g. Cassidy, 1974:66). In Papua New Guinea they are most meaningfully categorized in terms of what motivates them to take their produce to the market. As already mentioned many of them are trippers for whom the market attendance represents a social occasion rather than an economic venture. If any of them failed to sell his produce "one could imagine him shrugging his shoulders, returning home and being none the worse for his day's outing" (Hogbin, 1969:46). Marginalists and buyer-sellers are the other two numerically dominant categories of vendors at Papua New Guinea markets.

Trippers, marginalists and buyer-sellers, the categories of vendors predominating at Papua New Guinea markets are hardly anywhere discussed in the literature. Researchers concerned with markets usually focus on the wholesale/retail trade and regard small producer-sellers of only peripheral importance. Szanton, for instance mentions the existence of barrio-based, small scale irregular producers at a Philippine market, who "cannot however be regarded as engaged in a regular commercial enterprise;...and while they may take advantage of extra items produced by their gardens, there is little attempt to grow things specifically for sale in the market" (1972:20). Yet by virtue of their non-commercial marketing these marginalist vendors may well exert an influence over prices out of proportion with their numbers and volume of sales. The more commercially minded target operators feature most frequently in the literature. For example, Davis discusses Philippine 'target marketeers', who participate in the market only to the extent necessary to attain some specific goal which requires cash" (1973:141), and Cassidy analyses price negotiations of profiteers at Mexican markets (1974:46).

In the rest of this chapter I explore the impact of the different categories of vendors at Papua New Guinea markets on the price formation process. The lack of price flexibility and the absence of competition and bargaining have been noted by all those who studied Pacific markets (Brookfield, 1969). The considerable uniformity of prices charged by the many small vendors for the same product represents another phenomenon which demands explanation. The modal price charged daily per unit weight of some of the most important indigenous crops such as areca nuts, bananas, sweet potatoes, taro, *xanthosoma* and yam, as well as non-indigenous produce such as tomatoes and lettuce applies to more than two thirds of the total quantity of each of these different items brought to Hinterland-rooted markets. How is this remarkable price uniformity achieved without any bargaining and competition? Papua New Guinea vendors appear to operate with two price concepts: the desired price represented by a minimum sized bundle and the minimum acceptable price below which they are not prepared to sell. Cassidy uses similar concepts in analyzing price-making by individual negotiation at markets in Mexico. He refers to Mexican vendor's initial asking price and his minimum price (1974:47) "But this still leaves the question of determining the precise amount of the initial asking price, especially in the vendor's first transaction of the day...Reaching a decision as to a sound initial asking price is much more difficult if a vendor is also the producer of the goods (that is, *a propio*). The reason for this, of course, is that the vendor in this case has no wholesale price to guide him"

189

(Cassidy, 1974:49).

In Papua New Guinea the vendors decide their desired prices before they ever reach the market. Most of them arrange in 10 cent bundles all the produce they intend to sell or prepare the appropriate containers before they leave their village homes, while others make these preparations only during their trip to the market. Most of the vendors as a rule take the sales conditions which operated on their previous visit to the market as guidelines of how much to fetch of what produce and how much to charge. Since their market attendance is highly irregular, there may be considerable discrepancy in the size of the bundles offered for sale by different vendors at the beginning of any one market day. However, most vendors travel in groups to the market. In each of them there is usually one who is the most regular market attendant; she acts as 'price setter' for all their pricing, during their trip, if not before. On arrival at the market these groups each carry their goods to their customary place at the site. The 'pricing leaders' quickly display some of their own produce and then wander round the market trying to gauge prices. If one or other of them discovers that his/her group's bundles compare unfavorably, i.e. they are too small, compared to those offered by competitors they usually decide to wait a little to see if they find buyers prepared to pay the higher price they are charging; if so, well and good, if not then all the members of the group start re-arranging their bundles so as to fall in line with what appears to be the ruling market price. This price can thus be regarded as the desired price agreed by informal consensus among vendors(1).

If in the course of the day the desired price appears too high to attract sufficient buyers vendors may be prepared to increase the size of their 10 cent bundles until they reach their minimum acceptable price. Producer-sellers can hardly ever calculate the cost of the goods they sell. In the affluent setting of Papua New Guinea markets, cost of production forms only a minor part in the complex consideration involved in arriving at the minimum price. Nor do vendors regard the time spent at the market as relevant to their returns. In fact the many trippers are quite happy to pay for the pleasure of their market visits and do not resent returning with their unsold produce, particularly if it is of the kind they can consume in their own households. Therefore, trippers rarely consider lowering their prices. For them the desired price is also the minimum they are prepared to accept. If they fetch non-indigenous produce to the market they simply throw away whatever remains unsold before they depart for home.

Difference in quality of product affects prices charged by vendors only who are prepared to sell below the desired price. However, without any standardization in grading of products, it is practically impossible for an outsider to match difference in quality with difference in prices. Indigenous vendors and buyers though seem to be acutely aware of differentiation in quality of items which form part of their staple diet. They are less conscious of quality variations in produce they themselves are not accustomed to consume.

Prices at Papua New Guinea producer-seller markets on any one day hardly fluctuate in line with changing supply and demand conditions but are basically supply prices which have a lagged relationship with demand.

Short term price fluctuations in response to changing supply and/or demand conditions altogether appears to be only a recent phenomenon at Papua New Guinea markets. The considerable price stability at Gazelle Peninsula markets is due to the tradition of buyer-sellers, while at Highland markets the considerable proportion of trippers and marginalists can readily account for it. Vendors at Hinterland-rooted markets thus tend to act as if they traded on a sellers market, even if they are left with loads of unsold produce. They decide prices at the start of the market and are only rarely prepared to change them later in the day. Trippers and marginalists are not really interested in how much they earn and therefore never re-arrange the size of their bundles. Buyer-sellers are chiefly concerned with equivalence and thus see no advantage in re-pricing their produce, since their counterparts in the sales process would be likely to follow suit.

The climate of a sellers market, though noticeable at *all* the producer-seller markets studied, existed for different reasons at the different markets. At Gazelle Peninsula and Highland markets it exists because of the categories of sellers predominant among suppliers, whereas at Koki and Lae market food requirements create excess demand for fresh foods and thus typical sellers market conditions do exist. Significantly, Koki and Lae are the only markets we studied in Papua New Guinea where a large proportion of sellers come from far afield and stay in town more than one day selling produce at the market for days in succession. Koki even more so than Lae vendors feel certain that they will be able to sell all the produce they fetched and understandably, therefore, are not prepared to lower their prices. Lae is not as much of a sellers market as Koki; supplies of fresh foods are more abundant and demand is less intense at Lae than at Koki. Therefore, the profiteers among Lae vendors, of whom admittedly there are not very many, tend to increase the size of the 10 cent bundles whenever they face slack demand for their produce. But they too operate with a minimum acceptable price in mind below which they do not sell.

SUPPLY AND DEMAND PRICE RANGE

The degree of price flexibility at Papua New Guinea markets varies with the range existing between the vendors desired and their minimum acceptable price: the greater the range the more flexible are prices. The supply price range in turn is determined, by the categories of vendors predominating at the market, the type of produce sold (i.e. indigenous or non-indigenous) and its unit size. The comparatively small proportion of target operators and profiteers at Hinterland-rooted markets, readily accounts for the lack of price flexibility after prices have been fixed in the morning on any one day. These two categories of vendors operate with a wider range between the desired and the minimum acceptable price. Accordingly, their pricing tends to be more demand-responsive than that of others. For products which form part of vendors' regular consumption the supply price range is much narrower than it is for items produced specifically for sale to expatriates. Moreover, the range is also influenced by the different unit size of produce: It is obviously much easier to adjust prices by varying the quantity per 10 cent bundles of tomatoes or areca nuts than it is to adjust prices of 10 cents or multiples thereof for Chinese cabbage or *xanthosoma*. The process of price adjustment is thus much smoother for the former than for the latter type products. Vendors are readier to adjust prices by small percentages, which is possible with products like tomatoes and areca nuts, than to reduce prices by half or one third, which is often what cannot be avoided in changing the 10 cent lots of Chinese cabbage or *xanthosoma*.

Universally sellers have to anticipate demand and decide the price at which they offer their products for sale. All sellers also operate with the concept of the minimum acceptable price, which in some cases may be zero. Whatever the desired and

192

minimum acceptable price, it determines the range of supply prices for any one product.

Buyers on the other hand, also come to the market with an idea of the price they want to pay for the goods they want to buy. This is their desired price. The demand and supply curves usually displayed in economic textbooks (see e.g. Samuelson, 1951:438) assume that buyers invariably think in terms of paying the minimum price, even if this is well below what they expected to have to pay. This is certainly not the case with buyers at Papua New Guinea markets, and may also not represent a realistic picture of demand in many other contexts where supplies are fixed in the short term.

The buyers' desired price is the result of the interaction of several economic and social variables which forms the criterion for the different categories of buyers (see p. 67). Buyers also know how much more they are prepared to pay over and above their desired price, which represents their maximum acceptable price. The distance between buyers' desired price and their maximum acceptable price represents the demand price range.

Market trade takes place only if there is an overlap between the supply and demand price range. If the demand range is altogether below the supply range nothing is bought; on the other hand if it is above the consumer surplus, it is likely that prices are so attractive that all supplies of the product are quickly bought up.

At Papua New Guinea markets the demand price range usually embraces or at least overlaps with that for supply. This also appears to be a more general phenomenon in trade than is often realized.

Non-indigenous Produce: Tomatoes and Chinese cabbage provide typical examples in this context. It is reasonable to assume that the former are more amenable to price variations by altering the size of the 10 cent bundles and have a less elastic demand than Chinese cabbage. If tomato vendors are trippers their desired price is likely to represent at the same time their minimum acceptable price, in which case they may sell only a small proportion of their produce and the rest remains unsold. On the other hand, if we are dealing here with marginalists who are likely to be prepared to sell below their desired price, vendors may sell some of their produce at the desired price and then lower the price slightly to sell more; they throw away their remaining tomatoes. Target operators usually have a lower minimum acceptable price than marginalists and therefore sell a larger proportion of their tomatoes: they are left only with a suitable quantity of unsold tomatoes. Profiteers at markets where supplies at desired price exceed demand, such as for instance IaPilai at Rabaul (see p. 133), try to maximize their returns by accepting the desired demand price for the final portion of their produce which remains unsold towards the end of a market day, to insure selling out. By way of contrast Koki vendors, who operate on a true sellers market can feel confident that they will sell the following day whatever remains unsold on any one day. There the desired supply price coincides with the maximum acceptable demand price. Therefore, Koki vendors can stick to their desired price and yet sell all their produce. Their counterparts at excess supply markets such as Rabaul, who are trippers, do not adjust their prices to demand at the very real risk of being left with considerable quantities of unsold produce.

The elasticity of demand for any specific product obviously determines how much more vendors can sell when they lower prices and in turn is affected by cross elasticities of demand for acceptable substitutes. In Papua New Guinea there is hardly any acceptable substitute for fresh tomatoes which accounts for the comparatively low elasticity of demand for this commodity. Target operators and profiteers act like discriminating monopolists: they begin by selling at higher prices to those who are prepared to pay them and offer lower prices to those who are usually shrewder buyers and come later in the day to the market. Quality obviously also enters here into the consideration: the more attractive tomatoes are usually bought at higher prices before lunchtime by more choosy buyers while some of the lower quality ones are sold at lower prices to buyers who are less concerned with quality and worry more about price. IaPilai had developed her marketing of non-indigenous produce to a fine art: she knew exactly when it was time to increase the size of her 10 cent tomato bundles so as to insure selling out. Unlike IaTuraram, who only fetched a small quantity of tomatoes and mainly sold indigenous produce, IaPilai specialized in selling non-indigenous produce and therefore had learnt the art of marketing this type of commodity.

However, not all profiteers can be sure to sell out all their non-indigenous produce. If demand falls short of supplies at the profiteers' minimum acceptable price then they too are left with unsold produce. The narrower the supply range and the greater the excess of supply over demand at the minimum acceptable supply price the more the produce remains unsold. On the other hand if demand is brisk, unsatisfied demand remains. For instance, at Koki most vendors can sell out at their desired price at which demand often still exceeds supply.

The average weight of tomatoes supplied weekly varies between the different markets. In 1967/68 the estimated weekly average was 75 cwts at Rabaul, 25 cwts at Lae, 10 cwts at Goroka, three cwts at Mt. Hagen and two cwts at Koki. The average proportion of tomatoes remaining unsold also varied from town to town: at Lae 25 percent, Rabaul and Koki 20 percent, Goroka 15 percent and Mt. Hagen 10 percent. The average price per pound of tomatoes was highest at Koki, i.e. about 16 cents, at Rabaul it was 12.60 cents, Goroka 6.50 cents, Mt. Hagen 6 cents and Lae 7 cents.

Tomatoes are thus sold at different prices, which vary considerably between Highland and Lae markets on the one hand and Rabaul and Koki on the other. Yet we did not become aware of any attempt to encourage individual indigenous Highland cultivators to supply tomates to other regions.

The lower elasticity of demand for tomatoes and the greater ease with which 10 cent bundles can be adjusted to vary prices accounts for the much narrower steps in supply price changes as compared with Chinese cabbage. Trippers and marginalists selling Chinese cabbage are likely to keep their desired price disregarding excess supplies. They may thus be left with a considerable proportion of their produce unsold at the end of the market day. Target operators who are prepared to sell somewhat below the desired price may not increase the size of their bundles of Chinese cabbage sufficiently to be able to sell out, simply because this usually involves doubling the quantity. Only profiteers whose pricing is highly demand responsive may manage to sell all or almost all their Chinese cabbage. Vendors usually throw away all their unsold bundles of this produce.

These discriminating price practices are facilitated by the changing clientele visiting the market at different times of the day and by their demand price range. Chinese buyers are the shrewdest of all: some of them come to Rabaul market early in the morning when the different groups of vendors arrive and before standardization of prices has been established. This enables them to pick up bargains from vendors who have arranged larger bundles than the ruling price turns out to be for the day. Other Chinese buyers conduct their purchases late in the afternoon shortly before vendors are due to leave for home and when profiteers are likely to offer bargain sales. The quality oriented expatriate buyers usually turn up in the middle of the morning. They are prepared to pay higher prices for better quality products. Many of the indigenous elite, who consume non-indigenous produce have a lower maximum acceptable price than expatriates. They turn up at the market round about noon or early after lunch, when marginalists and target operators have already increased the size of their 10 cent bundles. These waves of buyers, each with a different demand price range, enables the different categories of vendors to reduce prices according to their own inclinations.

Indigenous crops: Areca nuts and *xanthosoma* provide useful examples for indigenous crops: the former being a conveniently small sized produce to which most people in Papua New Guinea seem addicted and for which demand is less elastic than for the latter, which has bigger sized units and forms part of the diet of large numbers of indigenes. The process whereby the level of the desired price is reached is the same for indigenous as for non-indigenous produce; i.e. by the interaction between the supply and demand price range.

The main difference in pricing between indigenous and non-indigenous crops is the much smaller range between the desired and the minimum acceptable supply price for the former than for the latter. There is thus a much narrower range of acceptable supply prices for indigenous crops, which reduces the likelihood of equilibrium occurring between supply and demand. It is also reasonable to assume a more elastic demand for *xanthosoma* than for areca nuts. *Xanthosoma* is sold in considerable quantities at all the markets we studied; Rabaul and Lae were the most important sales outlets for this produce. About 1,000 cwts were brought weekly to Rabaul of which about half remained unsold; about 250 cwts were fetched weekly to Lae of which about 25 percent remained unsold. *Xanthosoma* is grown in the Highlands also, but only to a limited extent. The most important staple crop there is the sweet potato, whereas coastal people prefer taro and *xanthosoma*. Most of the *xanthosoma* bought at Highland markets is purchased by urbanites originating from the coast. About seven cwts were supplied weekly at Goroka and nine cwts at Mt. Hagen of which 10 percent remained unsold. Vendors fetched a weekly average of about

50 cwts of *xanthosoma* to Koki and sold out all they brought. Average prices per pound of *xanthosoma* ranges from 1.75 cents at Rabaul to 3.50 cents at Lae, 4.60 cents at Mt. Hagen, five cents at Goroka and eight cents at Koki (see Table 5.1).

A more efficient marketing organization could easily dispose of most of the *xanthosoma* surplus at Rabaul. "No attempts have hitherto been made to offer any special protection to local producers of vegetables, fruit and other fresh produce" (Brookfield, 1969:16) nor is there much agricultural extension work done in the field of production and marketing of food crops. Vegetables, fresh, frozen or tinned, are imported on a considerable scale into Papua New Guinea. If *xanthosoma* could be retailed at the various markets for a maximum of 2.5 cents per pound, this would make the crop competitive with rice (see Table 5.2) and would increase the consumption of home produced goods, while reducing the demand for imported foods. The demand price range for *xanthosoma* is greatly influenced by comparable prices of imported substitutes. Even at the lowest price of 6.03 cents per pound of *xanthosoma* charged at Koki market in 1968 it was a luxury compared with rice. 100 calories consumed in the form of *xanthosoma* were about two and a half times more expensive than if eaten in the form of rice. Therefore, only the well-to-do indigenes in Port Moresby could afford to buy *xanthosoma*. Those many laborers, who in 1968 worked in Port Moresby and earned the minimum wage of $6.50 per week could ill afford to consume *xanthosoma* as part of their daily diet. Large numbers of them visited the market at weekends when some of them bought small quantities of areca nuts, bananas and/or *xanthosoma*, which they regarded as a special treat.

The large numbers of Koki buyers who regard their market purchases as special treats accounts for their greater concern with quality of produce rather than price. Mari is typical for this class of buyer (see p. 45).

At the point where prices of indigenous staples become competitive with their imported substitutes, e.g. rice, demand for them becomes highly elastic.

Vendors of *xanthosoma* at Koki even profiteers, rarely sell below their desired price. They face such brisk demand even at the higher prices charged, that they are assured of a sell-out. At the other markets I studied a large proportion of the *xanthosoma* remains unsold (see Table 4.2). Since this produce constitutes an important part in indigenous diet vendors do not really mind having to take large

197

quantities back home. They simply use it for their own consumption. Trippers and buyers at any market hardly ever reduce their prices below the desired level. Marginalists sell more than trippers and buyer-sellers, but some of it at a lower price.

The larger unit size of *xanthosoma* compared with other crops, for instance areca nuts, necessitates bigger steps in price reduction; there are of course different sizes of *xanthosoma,* but even the smallest one weighs considerably more than one individual areca nut. The problem of varying the price by altering the size of 10 cent bundles is obviously more difficult with larger than with smaller sized crops. Target operators are usually prepared to accept even a lower price than marginalists and consequently sell more; they return home with less unsold. The few profiteers who sell *xanthosoma* are the most price conscious of all vendors. If by the beginning of the afternoon they are still left with a lot of unsold stuff they begin to increase the size of their bundles to make them more attractive to buyers. Yet the range between the desired price and the minimum acceptable price is not very large even for profiteers selling *xanthosoma.*

The large proportion of the rural proletarians among buyers at Rabaul and Lae market helps to account for the considerable quantities of unsold *xanthosoma*. Rural proletarians are keen buyers who have a narrower range of demand price than most urban dwellers. For many of them their maximum acceptable price is below the minimum acceptable price asked even by profiteers. Therefore these categories of potential buyers do not purchase any *xanthosma* at the markets.

The pricing process for areca nuts resembles that for *xanthosoma* in terms of being part of indigenous consumption and that for tomatoes because of the small unit size and weight.

Buyer-sellers of areca nuts are unlikely to sell below their desired price which to them represents a standardized equivalence. Trippers behave like buyer-sellers with respect to keeping their prices unchanged throughout the day. Marginalists are prepared to adjust slightly the size of their 10 cent bundles of areca nuts. Target operators are keener than marginalists to earn as much as possible from the sale of their areca nuts and therefore reduce their prices even further: they are therefore left with less unsold nuts.

Profiteers are more price conscious even than target operators, and thus have the lowest minimum acceptable price of all vendors. Unless they

198

operate in a true sellers' market, as at Koki where
vendors usually sell out at their desired price,
profiteers reduce their prices to the lowest acceptable minimum. Yet even the maximum range between the
desired and minimum acceptable price within which
profiteers selling areca nuts operate is small compared to the respective range for non-indigenous
crops. There are only relatively few target operators and profiteers who sell areca nuts; most of the
vendors who do so are buyer-sellers or trippers who
refuse to sell below their desired price and are not
concerned about the quantities of unsold produce
they are left with at the end of their day at the
market. They can always keep the leftover areca
nuts for their own use, or sometimes even sell, at
least part of them for shell money in their own
villages.

As already mentioned some of the Chinese storekeepers in Rabaul regard the market as a source of
wholesale supplies for areca nuts: for instance
they buy 50 or 60 such nuts for 10 cents at the market and resell them in small lots of six or eight
for 10 cents in their trade stores to immigrant
laborers who work throughout the day and are therefore unable to shop at the market. These laborers
frequent Chinese stores in the evenings and regard
the purchase of areca nuts as a treat; they do not
seem to mind paying so much for so few areca nuts.

An incident, which occurred in the course of
our Rabaul market study illustrates the different
approaches to trading displayed by Chinese shopkeepers on the one hand and indigenous vendors on
the other. One of our investigators, a young Tolai
called ToKalaman observed and recorded the sales of
a female vendor called IaMalana, who was selling
mainly areca nuts. Late in the afternoon Mr. Woo,
one of the Chinese storekeepers in Rabaul,
approached IaMalana's goods, carefully examined the
different lots of areca nuts on display, each of
which was offered for 10 cents. He counted the nuts
per 10 cent lot. Then he tried to encourage
IaMalana to join three lots of areca nuts and sell
them for 20 cents altogether. IaMalana refused to
oblige. Although it was already near the end of the
market day and it seemed unlikely that other buyers
would purchase her bundles of areca nuts, she was
unwilling to lower the price. She subsequently
explained to me that she never minded having to take
some of her areca nuts back home again. Her family
and friends were always happy to consume her unsold
produce. Even if they did not pay her, she did not
mind, for she enjoyed being hospitable. Besides,

she expected some reciprocity from those to whom she freely distributed some of her areca nuts. Mr. Woo became exasperated by IaMalana's refusal to lower her sales price and himself tried to increase the size of one of the areca nut bundles.

Though I had strictly instructed our investigators not to interfere in market transactions, and to remain neutral observers, ToKalaman could not resist the temptation to intervene on IaMalana's behalf. He asked Mr. Woo how he would like it if someone buying for instance one pound of sugar in his shop would insist on taking away 1.25 pounds for the price of one pound. Mr. Woo was incensed by this interference and walked away. He returned the following afternoon and tried the same bargaining technique on another seller, who was also observed by ToKalaman and faced a similar response. When he became more insistent ToKalaman threatened to beat him up if he did not leave the vendor alone. The next day the same thing happened only this time ToKalaman lost his temper and hit the Chinese buyer. The police were called. It was only then that I became aware of what had been going on betweem the Chinese buyer, ToKalaman and areca nut vendors. ToKalaman was taken to court and ordered to pay a money fine, which he managed to do easily since all our other investigators contributed a share each.

Subsequently, I had a session with our assistants and reprimanded ToKalaman for having disobeyed my instructions. I appealed to all of them to remain strictly neutral observers rather than interfere in trading transactions. It then emerged how much opposed they all were to bargaining. They reason that vendors fix prices and buyers were free to buy or not to buy; there was no compulsion on buyers to purchase any goods the price of which they thought too high. Like the African Tonga the New Guinea Tolai too thought of sellers as being in a position to control the terms of exchange (Colson, 1962:615). My Tolai investigators pointed out that indigenous buyers visiting expatriate stores always faced fixed prices and were never in a position to bargain. They asked why the same should not hold true for Rabaul market where the roles of expatriates and indigenes were reversed. Thus vendors in particular and indigenes in general regard trading not as "a competition between sellers and buyers each trying to get the better of each other, but as each side providing whatever is available, and exchanging 'fairly' with the other side" (Salisbury, 1970:180). Having themselves produced the goods they offer, producer-sellers take a pride in what they sell. Craftsmen everywhere display similar pride in the goods they produce. Each of our informants from whom we collected background data on the marketing activities stressed that they always selected the best of their crops to take for sale. This helps to explain the generally applicable concept of the desired price and a not much lower minimum acceptable price. With indigenous crops the vendor's pride in the quality of her/his products is particularly important. For instance at Gazelle Peninsula markets, "in sales to other Tolai, where the competition as gardeners, and judges, is relevant, interest by a buyer in, say, a particular bunch of taro may result in the vendor's pointing out borer marks that the buyer did not see, or saying where better taro can be bought" (Salisbury, 1970:183). Such trading practice contrasts with that pertaining in many Asian bazaars, where vendors push their own wares and are pleased when they manage to trick a buyer into purchasing damaged goods at what seem to them high prices. Yet it is likely that even there prices are determined by the interplay between demand and supply price ranges.

Producer-sellers do not only regard their own produce with personal pride but look upon much of their trading activities as delayed exchanges. Though we found no barter transactions conducted at the markets, there certainly is still a barter-mentality surrounding much of the market trade. This helps to account for the lack of price flexibility for individual items, as well as for the high degree of price uniformity prevailing throughout the market. Usually in the afternoons, target operators and profiteers begin reducing their prices in order to attract more customers. What is striking though is the fact that only rarely, if ever, are prices increased in the course of a day. Shortly after trading begins and before vendors have reached a consensus on the desired price level, shrewd buyers may obtain bargains, for sellers are unaware that they are offering produce at a rate below the desired demand price for the day. We found no case where a vendor reduced the size of the 10 cent bundles in the course of the market day however brisk the demand. It seems too risky for individual vendors or groups of sellers to try and raise the price of their produce. They fear that this may jeapordise their market sales altogether.

The more numerous trippers and buyer-sellers are among the total number of vendors, and/or the greater the excess of demand over supplies, the less flexible are prices at producer-seller markets.

Greater proportions of target operators and in particular profiteers tend to increase the supply range as well as price flexibility. At the time of our market studies, target operators and profiteers constituted only a small proportion of Papua New Guinea market vendors, yet there were signs that their importance was increasing.

Our market studies examined the pricing process at producer-seller markets through a magnifying glass so to say. We focussed on short term pricing, when supplies are fixed. Even the briskest demand for a particular produce on any one market day cannot conjure up increased supplies; all that is available for sale is what is fetched at the outset of trading. If vendors could readily increase supplies in response to strong demand, a positive relationship between price and supply might be expected: i.e. the higher price to call forth greater supplies. But in fact this is a purely hypothetical proposition at least as far as Papua New Guinea markets are concerned. Neither does there appear to be a much longer term price-responsiveness displayed by producer-sellers. Only a few profiteers plan their cultivation with expected market prices in mind. The large majority of vendors sell at the market mainly their surplus production exceeding what they consider their consumption needs for indigenous crops. Many of them do also grow non-indigenous produce specifically for sale, but the quantities each fetches to the market are in most cases only marginal additions to their total supplies.

There is thus only little relationship between the market price and the quantity supplied per product, nor does there seem to be evidence for the existence of the reverse relationship. There is no inverse correlation between market supplies and prices at the Papua New Guinea markets. Significantly, Lae market is the only one where we detected a negative correlation between the price and the quantity of some of the produce sold. For instance, there is an apparent inverse correlation between the quantity of sweet potatoes sold and its price per pound throughout the period of our studies; i.e. the coefficient of correlation is -0.42 with a 0.38 significance for August 1967, the respective figures for November 1967 are -0.35 and 0.22. These coefficients do not indicate a high degree of inverse correlation, yet they denote the strongest inverse relationship emerging from all the tests conducted for the markets studied in which I tried to link quantity with price. This relationship at Lae, where it is still somewhat embryonic, is more

pronounced there than at any other market. This can
be attributed to Lae market being in a transition
phase from Hinterland-rooted to urban-based. It has
a higher proportion of profiteers among its vendors
than any of the Hinterland-rooted markets on the one
hand, and is not a true sellers market like Koki on
the other. Profiteers at Lae, of whom there are
more there than at any other market I studied,
except Koki, know that they are operating in a
buyers market. They want to maximize their returns
and are therefore demand-responsive. They tend to
lower their prices, i.e. increase the 10 cent lots,
of sweet potatoes whenever demand falls short of
supplies at the vendors' desired price. At all the
other markets we studied such profiteers' pricing
practice exerted only insignificant influence over
the overall price per product.

PRICE RANGE AND PRICE FORMATION

Commodity prices at producer-seller markets are
established by the interplay between the supply and
demand price range. The supply price range reflects
the difference between the desired and the minimum
acceptable price, whereas the demand price range
indicates the difference between the desired and the
maximum acceptable price. The market price is a
function of the proportions the different categories of vendors constitute: large numbers of trippers and buyer-sellers among all vendors make for
price rigidity, even if supplies exceed demand at the
desired supply price, whereas target operators and
profiteers tend to bring about greater price flexibility if faced with the same market condition.
    Similarly, the extent of the demand price range
is a function of the different categories of buyers
which constitute the market demand. Urban dwellers
contribute the bulk of demand at producer-seller
markets and their importance is growing as the rate
of urbanization increases. Expatriate demand is
likely to decline, at least in its proportionate
importance, as their numbers in Papua New Guinea
decrease. This, however, does not necessarily mean
that the demand for non-indigenous produce will
decline. There are indications that the growing
establishment of an indigenous elite is likely to
result in continuing demand for introduced fresh
foods; indigenes appear to have a considerable income
elasticity of demand for such goods. The extent of
the demand price range is directly correlated with
the income distribution among urban dwellers; the
greater the economic differentiation the greater the

range between the desired and maximum acceptable price. Rural proletarians are often unable to consider paying more than their desired price and if this happens to be below the minimum acceptable supply price they cannot purchase the quantity of goods they would like, which results in a considerable volume of unsold produce. It is only by increasing the purchasing power of rural proletarians or by reducing market prices that their effective demand for staple dietary crops can be increased. Cash cropper buyers on the other hand, are mainly interested in acquiring sundries, such as areca nuts and their accoutrements, peanuts and the like. They are able and prepared to pay a lot more than their desired price, therefore demand for these items is notoriously inelastic at Papua New Guinea markets.

The preceding discussion of price formation at producer-seller markets represents an attempt to explain marketing behavior in terms of vendors' and buyers' own perceptions of trading. Many more studies of this kind are needed to test the various propositions advanced here.

NOTES

1. Similarly, Cassidy reports that in Ghana too, one market 'Queen' "who has been in business for forty years stated: 'We don't meet or have any formal discussion about prices. Somehow a colleague throws in a suggestion and we say let's try and see'. This would suggest that there may be a kind of 'price leadership' in effect in such circumstances" (1974: 80).

Table 5.1: Average Price and Weekly Supplies* for Selected Items at Papua New Guinea Markets

		Areca Nut		Banana (eating)		Corn		Cucumber		Pawpaw	
		Price per lb. cent	Weight cwt	Price per lb. cent	Weight cwt	Price per lb. cent	Weight cwt	Price per lb. cent	Weight cwt	Price per lb. cent	Weight cwt
Vunapope		5.94	1.0	5.17	0.5	12.50	0.6	-	-	4.83	0.6
Kokopo		5.21	12.0	3.75	4.5	-	-	-	-	4.67	9.5
Rabaul	I:W	3.10		4.41		8.93		8.50		3.39	
	II:S	3.24	529.0	3.89	237.0	11.00	6.0	7.46	22.0	4.65	75.0
	II:W	2.98		4.14		8.00		8.95		3.76	
	II:S	3.05	351.0	3.79	123.0	7.59	22.0	10.36	15.0	3.88	67.0
Goroka	I	11.67	81.0	4.74	41.0	3.46	48.0	3.80	35.0	4.15	7.0
	II	10.00	100.0	6.27	36.5	6.66	15.0	5.44	11.0	6.92	11.0
Mt. Hagen	I	10.00	100.0	4.06	48.0	2.35	90.0	6.11	4.0	5.93	4.0
	II	21.25	33.0	5.32	28.0	4.34	48.0	6.95	8.0	5.63	1.0
Lae	I	7.16	112.0	3.86	174.0	6.37	25.0	5.31	43.0	5.02	65.0
	II	8.59	31.0	4.20	133.0	4.75	78.0	5.71	115.0	4.06	45.0
Koki	I	14.86	179.0	8.60	205.0	12.71	33.0	10.62	19.0	6.40	20.0
	II	13.57	35.0	6.83	93.0	9.04	50.0	17.98	36.0	9.13	34.0

		Peanut		Sweet Potato		Xanthosoma		Yam	
		Price per lb. cent	Weight cwt	Price per lb. cent	Weight cwt	Price per lb. cent	Weight cwt	Price per lb. cent	Weight cwt
Vunapope		10.00	0.2	1.03	6.0	1.67	0.5	-	-
Kokopo		9.50	3.5	1.45	65.0	2.92	35.0	4.17	1.0
Rabaul	I:W	7.06	32.0	1.33	758.0	1.64	764.0	5.32	48.0
	II:S	10.50		1.26		1.81		3.54	
	II:W	10.75	10.0	1.31	866.0	2.17	1458.0	4.17	9.0
	II:S	10.50		1.26		1.92		2.25	
Goroka	I	7.13	34.0	2.85	64.0	4.73	5.0	3.83	5.0
	II	12.02	37.0	3.43	134.0	5.55	9.0	1.88	6.0
Mt. Hagen	I	7.18	45.0	5.92	98.0	4.33	10.0	1.49	3.0
	II	6.37	23.0	6.03	17.0	5.12	9.0	-	-
Lae	I	13.33	12.0	3.16	168.0	3.78	280.0	2.50	9.0
	II	8.89	4.0	2.80	260.0	3.27	216.0	5.00	2.0
Koki	I	26.00	14.0	6.78	177.0	10.45	60.0	7.50	40.0
	II	27.15	15.0	7.27	181.0	6.03	36.0	9.67	13.0

*The weights are only approximations as sampling was done on the basis of sellers rather than produce sold.

Table 5.2: Comparative Prices for Certain Starchy Foods

	Rice	Sweet Potatoes	Xanthosoma
Calories per lb.*	1,600	500	400
Price per lb. (cents)			
Rabaul	10	1.05	1.43
Goroka	10	2.85	4.73
Mt. Hagen	10	5.92	4.33
Lae	10	2.80	3.27
Koki	10	6.78	6.03
Price per 100 calories			
Rabaul	0.62	0.21	0.35
Goroka	0.62	0.57	1.20
Mt. Hagen	0.62	1.18	1.10
Lae	0.62	0.56	0.80
Koki	0.62	1.35	1.50

*Calorific values are based on P.P.T., 1965:74

Chapter 6

FOOD MARKETING IN A DEVELOPING ECONOMY

In studying market place trade as an aspect of economic development different social science disciplines have focussed on different aspects of the problem. Economists have been largely concerned with marketing as a "transactional principle" (e.g. Schumpeter,1954). Economic historians investigating trade and markets in their historic contexts questioned the wisdom of trying to apply modern economic prinicples to premarket systems (Polanyi, 1957). This led to the split among economic anthropologists between the "formalists" and the "substantivists". Dalton became one of the major exponents of substantivist theories (1961) which is reflected in the analysis of *Markets in Africa* where the distinction is drawn between "market places" and "market principles" (Bohannan, 1962:3). Geographers, like economists, have until recently limited their attention to export crops; "school geography exemplifies this approach, putting emphasis on the production of major export commodities, but often neglecting local and interregional trade" (Bromley, 1971:124). Social and cultural anthropologists interested in rural markets originally concentrated on studying the socio-economic interactions within the market place. The discussion of the conflicts between peasants and changing coalitions of tradesmen and officials in a Haitian market (Mintz, 1961) represents a typical example of this sort of research.

The analysis of the Chinese marketing pattern as an integral part of a segmentary administrative structure considerably advanced our understanding of indigenous food marketing in Developing Countries (Skinner, 1964). Skinner took his inspiration mainly from Christaller (1966) and analyzed the pre-1949 markets in China in terms of hierarchical systems of centers with hexagonal Hinterland areas. The spatial model of a hierachical market

organization, however, does not readily apply to
many other developing countries, where conditions
are very different. Colonial legacy and ethnic
heterogeneity mitigate against the development of
the Chinease type of centralized administrative
structure. The analysis of the Chinese market system yet provides a useful model particularly because
it is rare inasmuch as it has a country wide per-
spective. Moreover, it emphasises the close linkage
between intra-country trade and the socio-political
setting in which it has developed. In this way
Skinner accounts for the vitality of the traditional
Chinese market system, in spite of the most radical
attempts at re-organization by the revolutionary
authorities. "What hope was there to break these
patterns as long as the units of operation were
precisely the natural, traditionally hallowed communities of village and marketing system?" (Skinner,
1964:24/386).

By contrast with China Papua New Guinea's
traditional socio-political organization reveals
extreme decentralization. The isolation of individual markets from intra-country trade links probably
reflects the traditional dispersion of small
societies and their lack of contact with each other;
the many different languages and dialects spoken by
an indigenous population of less than two million
provides another indicator of socio-economic isolationism. "Study of an internal market system may
provide a lively version of relationships among key
economic and political groups in a society" (Mintz
and Hall, 1960:122). Similarly the absence of an
intra-country system of food distribution, which is
the case in Papua New Guinea, may throw into relief
the serious problem of integrating the many different tribal units into one political entity.

Economic development invariably involves
increasing specialization not only by product but
more so by productive task. Thus it became essential for cultivators to grow a surplus of food and
sell it at reasonable rates to the growing number
of individuals, who no more meet their own food
requirements by household production but instead
produce specialist goods and services. The overall
rate of economic expansion in many Developing
Countries largely depends on the degree to which
the agricultural sector is ready to supply food in
order to sustain an ever increasing number of
specialists. In fact the proportion of the population engaged in tasks outside agriculture provides
a good indicator of a nation's level of development.
"As countries become more commercialized, with an

increasing proportion of their population living in towns, sound internal marketing machinery becomes essential for the satisfaction of food needs at reasonable prices" (Abbott, 1958:2). A number of related problem areas (which are discussed in what follows) affect the establishment of an efficient intra-country system of food distribution.

RURAL FOOD SURPLUS

In Developing Countries food is normally produced by individual farmers who live in small communities where multiplex relations predominate the social scene. It seems well nigh impossible to find a satisfactory biological definition for their basic subsistence requirements. This makes it difficult to measure the surplus food production of an agricultural unit. Harris suggested that "we have been blinded to the fact that food quanta judged superfluous from one viewpoint may be absolutely vital from another viewpoint and that excess quantities for short periods may be accompanied by drastic shortages over a long period" (1959:191). I have similarly argued elsewhere that even stagnant economies produce periodic food surpluses (1967) as a result of environmental conditons over which agriculturists have little or no control. These surpluses provide a minimum risk insurance against the vagaries of climatic changes. "The extra effort annually expended to produce a superabundant crop, some of which will rot in times of abundant rainfall, may just be enough to ward off starvation in years of scanty rainfall" (Harris, 1959:192), provided the crop is storable.

For the purpose of our analysis of food marketing we can define rural food surplus as the *quantity of crops agriculturists make available for sale*. Such surplus may be the result of planned cash cropping or a climatic windfall. It may even be the by-product of land reform, which was the case in Bolivia where "dividing large absentee owned farms into peasant holdings resulted in 'surplus' agricultural production in the countryside plus an unfulfilled demand in the cities" (Clark, 1968:167).

One of the major problems of development is to tap an increasing rural food surplus from an agricultural sector which is declining, if not absolutely, certainly in terms of proportionate size of population.

Most planned socialist economies in existence have struggled with this problem and have so far failed to produce solutions which are generally applicable. It is even more difficult for the many Developing Countries with mixed economies to arrange for incentives which are sufficiently effective to encourage farmers to increase their food surplus.

In countries such as India, where population is already pressing hard on land, intensification rather than extension of cultivation seems the only feasible possibility to increase the surplus of rural food production. By contrast Papua New Guinea, like many other Pacific Island economies, has a tradition of "primitive affluence" (Fisk, 1966:23). Many areas in the country have highly fertile volcanic soils, such as for instance, the Gazelle Peninsula of New Britain where food is in abundance. Under such conditions the rural surplus depends more on the market orientation of farmers than on the technologies of production. Primitive affluence makes individual farmers only marginally dependent on marketing their produce and puts the value of labor at a premium. This is reflected in the narrow supply price range and the high level of minimum acceptable supply prices at Papua New Guinea markets. As already mentioned, only the elite among indigenous urbanites can afford to keep to their staple diet of root crops. The rest have to adjust to eating rice. In terms of calorific value taro, the preferred indigenous staple, is more expensive at all markets than the imported rice. Of all indigenous staples, only sweet potatoes compare favorably in price with rice, but only at Rabaul, Goroka and Lae markets. At Mt. Hagen it is almost twice as expensive to purchase 100 calories in the form of sweet potatoes than rice. This comparatively high price for sweet potatoes at Mt. Hagen is probably related to their high opportunity cost by foregoing feeding them to pigs. At Koki market, where the price differential between rice and sweet potatoes is even greater than at Mt. Hagen, scarcity of fresh indigenous foods accounts for the high price of sweet potatoes (see Table 5.2). "Rice imports into Port Moresby are growing at a much greater rate than that of rice or total goods imported into the Territory as a whole" (Yeats, 1967:IV). The value of total rice imports increased by 27 percent between 1964/4 and 1965/6; overall imports grew by 28 percent while rice imports into Port Moresby grew by as much as 43 percent (Yeats, 1967:2).

Developing economies usually have comparative advantages in the production of agricultural produce. Unless they are rich in oil or other mineral reresources, they can hardly afford the drain on their hard earned foreign currencies by paying for food

imports. Papua New Guinea's recently gained independence is likely to make the country aware of the
waste of resources caused by growing food imports
into what is still fundamentally an agricultural
economy. Only careful stocktaking of the pattern
of existing food production, together with an effective incentive policy relating to agriculturalists,
and an improved intra-country system of food distribution may help to avoid a continuously expanding
value of food imports as urban populations increase.
The necessity and urgency of such measures can be
gauged by the fact that the estimated total annual
turnover for the five major markets in Papua New
Guinea was in 1967/8 $1,770,130 which was less than
the f.o.b. value of white rice alone imported into
the country during 1966/7 (B.o.S., 1967/7).

If market studies like this one of Papua New
Guinea and Skinner's of China (1964)"hold any lesson
for policy makers, it is that national development
requires a...vigorous system of internal exchange"
(Plattner, 1975:79).

INCENTIVES

Economists usually think of productive incentives
solely in terms of prices and cost/benefits. This
approach may be helpful in analyzing productive and
commercial behavior in advanced economies; it may
also apply to countries, such as India, where the
use of improved technologies seems one of the few
available possibilites to increase the food surplus.
Under such conditions cost/benefit considerations
are likely to motivate farmers in the context of
producing more foods. If this is so, then it is
essential for national planners of landshort
economies to channel more investment into the rural
sector, at least temporarily, rather than to continue what has been shown as unjustifiable urban
bias in the application of scarce capital (Lipton,
1977).

Papua New Guinea unlike many of its Asian
neighbors is still well endowed with yet uncultivated fertile lands, though there are certain problem regions within the country where population is
already pressing hard on limited land resources.
Yet on the whole the country seems still comparatively fortunate in terms of availability of cultivable land; large parts of Africa are similarly
fortunate. Whenever there is a growing need for a
rural food surplus and extension of area under
cultivation is readily possible, it may be more
effective to increase the area cultivated per

available unit of labor than to improve the yield per unit of land. Foods for immediate consumption are of course not the only cash crops that can be produced. Indeed the cultivation of perennial export crops such as cocoa, coffee and copra, which are often more remunerative and less labor intensive than the seasonal growing of for instance sweet potatoes and taro, is a serious competitor with food production for the limited availability of indigenous manpower in Papua New Guinea.

Mechanization of agriculture is one possibility worthwhile considering wherever unused land is still available. However, Papua New Guinea agriculture does not lend itself readily to mechanization. The hilly terrain of much of the countryside makes it difficult to use tractors and other such large items of machinery. Moreover, the individual units of cultivation are too small to make mechanization an economic proposition. If the traditional landowning pattern, whereby land is vested in a kingroup, could be perpetuated under modern agricultural practices, this may help to provide large enough units of cultivation which might lend themselves more readily for the use of agricultural machinery. Price incentives do not seem to provide a feasible proposition either for increasing the rural food surplus in Papua New Guinea. As I have shown, only a very small proportion of food vendors are in fact trying to maximize their returns or minimize their losses.

A brief historic review of Rabaul market should help to indicate the rationale for the behavior of present day vendors. As already outlined, the Hinterland ecology encouraged the development of an economically integrated region. Buyer-sellers and producer-buyers were the instigators of market place trade on the Gazelle Peninsula. Trippers and marginalists initially attended only in small numbers. The growth of Rabaul as a town and the availability of imported goods in stores as well as other urban facilities attracted not only larger numbers of trippers and marginalists but also created new categories of vendors, namely, target operators and profiteers. The social aspect of large numbers gathering acts in itself as an important incentive to trippers and marginalists to attend the market. Moreover, urban facilites, such as well stocked stores and cafes, add further attractions. Unfortunately, it was impossible even to estimate the volume of demand for store goods emanating directly from market place trade. Case studies of both buyers and vendors, however, clearly indicate the fact that the existence of the market encourages shop purchases of imported commodities and visits to eating places.

The Gazelle café by the side of Rabaul market is an obvious off-shoot of market place trade. It was started about the beginning of 1965 by a Dutch woman, who personally supervised it. Its kitchen is modern and well equipped with gadgets. The machinery for peeling and slicing potatoes had been imported from Australia and thus could not cope with sweet potatoes and other locally produced crops. This meant that rather than using locally produced items in preparing meals for sale, the café had to import potatoes, onions and rice from Australia. In January 1968 the total value of imported goods purchased by the Gazelle café amounted to about $3,000 per week, whereas its owner bought no more than $100 worth per week of fresh vegetables from local producers. On Saturday, January 13, 1968 the café sold about 3,000 cooked meals, consisting of imported potatoes, rice, tinned fish or meat at 20 cents each as well as sandwiches, drinks, cigarettes and groceries altogether worth about $500. Its owner related that the café's average weekly turnover amounted to about $10,000 of which about one third represented her net profit. She had started the café on the basis of a contract with the Gazelle Local Government Council, which gave her a lease to run the café for 15 years after which she was bound to hand over to the Council without compensation all the buildings and equipment composing the café at that date. When I talked with the owner she had run her business for less than two years, but she had already accumulated such handsome profits that she was eager to sell out. She was then negotiating the sale's arrangements with the Council.

This account of the Gazelle café indicates several important features of Papua New Guinea marketing practices. In itself it represents a success story of private entrepreneurship. It also indicates the conflicts that frequently arise between the interests of private businesses on the one hand and the interest of the nation at large. The Gazelle café benefited from the import of machinery and food items, while the continued substitution of imported for home produced items in the preparation of cooked meals discouraged increasing production and sales of locally grown staple·crops and added to the country's import bill. Moreover, the establishment of a café by the side of the market not only encouraged vendors and buyers to spend some money on refreshments, but it also encouraged more trippers and marginalists to attend the market. Therefore, it also helped to increase the volume of food offered for sale. The positive effects of the Gazelle café were noticeable in the increasing number of vendors that it attracted to the market. Its impact could have been a lot greater had its purchasing policy been more inclined towards locally produced foods rather than imports. Altogether it is worthwhile considering arranging sales outlets through cafés of the bundles of indigenously prepared delicious food, rather than promote the sale of expatriate-type meals at Papua New Guinea markets.

ECOLOGICAL VARIATIONS AND URBANIZATION

The fertile Hinterland in the immediate vicinty of Rabaul insures a regular and abundant supply of fresh foods. The estimated average total weight of produce brought weekly to the market is more than twice as much for Rabaul than for Lae; altogether Rabaul market has the biggest volume of supplies of all the Papua New Guinea market places (see Table 3.1). Indigenous staples constitute about 25 percent of the total value of produce brought to Rabaul of which about one third remains unsold at the end of the day. Vendors cannot help but notice the considerable proportions of food supplies which remain unsold and have to be taken back home again. In the afternoons vehicles queue up by the side of the market waiting to collect for their homeward journeys sellers with their bulging bags of unsold produce. Prices for many of the major items sold are lower at Rabaul than at most other Papua New Guinea markets (see Table 5.1), yet the proportions of the value of produce brought which remains unsold are higher at Rabaul than at all the other markets we studied, where vendors returned home at the end of a day at the market and only rarely tried to sell the produce they have left over after one day's selling (see Table 4.2). This makes food production specifically for the market a risky enterprise and enhances the importance of trippers and marginalists as market suppliers.

Brookfield in his discussion of Pacific market places stresses the importance of risks involved in producing food for sale. He describes Pacific farmers as "multiple insurers who diffuse their inputs through a wide range of enterprises, thus seeming to place more emphasis on the minimization of risk than on the maximization of profit"

(1969:154). Specialization in cultivating food crops for sale is certainly a risky venture for producer-sellers. The marketing structure existing in Papua New Guinea mitigates against such specialization. As long as the intra-country system of food distribution remains unchanged it is unlikely that the rural food surplus will grow in line with increasing urbanization within its vicinity. The number of trippers and marginalists may grow over the years, because of expanding facilities at urban centers, but since each one of them fetches only small quantities of produce and usually refuses to accept anything less than their desired price, locally produced food supplies will increasingly become a luxury which only the wealthiest of the indigenous elite will be able to afford. "If Mt. Hagen's population does continue to grow, even at half the rate it experienced between 1966 and 1971, it will exceed 30,000 by 1980. The increased demand could lead to:

1. Increasing 'imports' of food from coastal areas
2. Increasing use of rice in Mt. Hagen
3. Increasing prices in a limited supply situation
4. A shift towards more specific production of *kaukau* (sweet potatoes) for market and a consequent shift away from pig rearing

or any combination of the above...Whether or not the rural population of the Western Highlands is able to meet an overall rapid increase in urban demand for food, it is very unlikely that it will be able to meet specific increases in demand for taro, bananas, yam and certain types of vegetables coming from urban dwellers of coastal origin, whilst *buai* (areca nuts) and coconuts will have to be entirely shipped into the region" (Jackson, 1974:35). This appraisal of the possibilities of the Mt. Hagen Hinterland being able to meet over the next few years the food requirements of a rapidly growing town seems to indicate that urban markets in Papua New Guinea are likely to develop increasingly more oligopolistic features where demand is strong and supply limited so much so that sellers are assured of selling out at their desired prices. These were the conditions prevailing at Koki markets in 1968/9. By 1990 many more towns are likely to resemble Port Moresby in terms of fresh food supplies at least, unless the market structure is radically changed.

A WEBBED COUNTRY-WIDE PRODUCER-SELLER MARKETING SCHEMA

The absence of wholesale/retail arrangements in
Papua New Guinea may be seen as an advantage inasmuch
as it prevents producers from being exploited by
middlemen and insures a reasonably egalitarian distribution of income from trade. "It is often argued
that conditions of oligopoly place the producers at
the mercy of a few dealers" (Bauer, 1954:212). On
the other hand, the lack of trade intermediaries
increases the risks in producing food such as cash
crops. Except for the informal sales agencies
which seem to operate only among close kin, producers
of a food surplus in Papua New Guinea have little
option but to sell it personally at the market to
the ultimate consumer. By contrast, their Javanese
counterparts for instance can decide where and when
and to whom to sell their surplus garden produce and
fruit. "The farmer's wife may take the goods into
market and retail them herself, but more often she
takes them to the market and there sells them to a
bakul to retail. If the village woman does not want
to go into town herself she may sell the goods to a
woman who specializes in *keban* (garden produce) crops
as a professional or semi-professional first stage
carrier *(bakul)*" (Dewey, 1962:151). The existence of
producer-sellers side by side with small traders at
Javanese markets enables the individual producer to
choose the particular sales outlet which suits her/
himself best. Those producers who are prepared to
take risks and want to attend the market personally
can do so, while others who do not want to travel to
the market and/or are not prepared to run the risk
of being left with some or all produce unsold at the
end of the market day prefer to sell to traders at
less than the market prices. "The small trader can
...substitute his own knowledge, time and labour,
which in view of the high level of unemployment have
a very low opportunity cost (i.e. they have a low
productivity in alternative accessible uses" (Dewey,
1962:86). Many of these small middlemen are only
part-time traders who "have other sources of income.
They can do less trading and can afford to accept a
lower profit margin than the full-time traders, who
must have a certain profit margin and a certain
amount of turnover to support them. Competition
from the part-time traders plus the small volume and
small potential profits, discourages the development
of full-time traders in small-scale local trade or
the penetration of such traders from larger market
centers. So long as local trade can be carried on

218

with little capital and a minimum of skill and experience of wider market conditions, locally based part-time traders will continue to dominate it" (Dewey, 1962:6)

Papua New Guinea markets operate without any' middlemen whatsoever, which is probably connected with the perishable nature of the staple crops, the primitive affluence of the indigenous peoples and their resistence to allow expatriates to participate in marketing their locally produced food. It is also the reason for the lack of any intermarket trade. This market isolationism accounts for the considerable price differentials that exist in the different towns for the same locally produced items (see Table 5.1). This often exceeds by far the transport cost between urban centers; for instance it would pay to air freight areca nuts from Rabaul to Port Moresby.

The absence of trade links between the different food markets in the country penalizes indigenous migrants to the larger towns, particularly Port Moresby. There most items sell at considerably higher prices than anywhere else; it also increases the volume of imported foods. Individual buyers who are familiar with Koki and Rabaul markets, as for instance Madaha (see p. 59) appreciate the advantage of sending goods from lower-priced to higher priced areas. Yet no such commercial links have as yet been established on any larger scale. At the time when I conducted the studies of Rabaul and Koki markets I contacted the respective Local Government Councils and Administrative Departments and discussed with them the possibilities of establishing intermarket trade links. The lack of the necessary training and organizing abilities on behalf of indigenes and the opposition to allowing expatriates to dominate the distribution of food within the country were then seen as the major obstacles to the commercialization of fresh food sales. Moreover, intra-country food trade was considered solely in terms of absolute price differentials, which led to the proposition that Port Moresby only should be supplied with fresh food from other parts of the country. Such arrangement was recognized as an effective means by which not only the cost of living in the country's capital could be reduced but whereby local produce could be substituted for imports. Against this it was held that intermarket trade would put some of the present Koki vendors out of business altogether and as a result promote hostilities between Papuans and New Guineans. However, such drastic economic and political consequences need not necessarily follow an improvement in the country's system of food distribution, if it were to be organized along the principles of *comparative* rather than *absolute advantages of trade.*

The principles of comparative advantages of trade first advocated by Adam Smith suggest that trade can be conducted to the mutual benefit of the two parties even if both produce the same items and one is more productive in all of them, as long as the differentials in productivity vary between the different goods produced. Such conditions prevail within Papua New Guinea (see Table 5.1) and suggest examples of the following area specialization: Koki producer-sellers to supply: corn and bananas; Rabaul: areca nuts and *xanthosoma;* Lae: cucumbers and yams; Goroka: sweet potatoes and pawpaws; and Mt. Hagen: peanuts. Such specialization does not necessitate growers foregoing the advantage of producing their own requirements of items in which their area does not enjoy a greater comparative advantage. All it means is that cultivators should be encouraged to concentrate producing a food surplus of the goods in which they have the greatest comparative advantage. How can this be manipulated without interfering too much with producer-seller practices? It is obviously necessary to build a revised marketing pattern onto the existing socio-economic framework. This requires an integral approach, which takes into account the cultural, economic, educational, geographic, political and other aspects of society. In what follows I outline one such schema for the consideration of planners operating in countries where producer-seller markets prevail.

Subsistence production may continue unimpaired. There is no need to try and interfer with the customary pattern of subsistence production; it can be encouraged to continue along traditional lines.

Training in marketing: There is a great dearth of personnel trained in marketing. "At present the crucial need for marketing education is met in only a few countries, and marketing extension as a consistent public service is still confined largely to North America...The need for specialized agricultural marketing training can be met in two ways: by the inclusion of marketing courses in the normal curricula of agricultural colleges and by offering concentrated marketing training courses on an independent postgraduate basis" (Abbott, 1958:168). Moreoever, basic instruction of marketing practice can be included in primary and/or secondary school teaching as well as adult education. In doing so producer-sellers can be made to realize the advantage of using standard weights and measures rather than continue selling differently sized bundles for the smallest coin in use. This is particularly important because of the widespread practice of selling produce in bundles rather than by weight. Reining reports it for a Zande market in Africa (1962:542). Mintz refers to it in his analysis of sales practices at a Haitian market (1961:34) and Cassidy footnotes it for Mexico (1974:49). Pricing by weight helps to overcome the problem of lumpy products and thereby can improve the efficiency of marketing.

Comparative advantages: The availability of personnel trained in marketing is a necessary precondition of any attempt to restructure a country's system of food distribution. Such an exercise needs a careful study of demand and supply conditions operating in the different parts of the country, Market prices can usually be taken to reflect these conditions. On that basis the comparative advantages, bearing in mind transport costs, can be calculated and a model intra-country trade pattern designed like a jigsaw puzzle along the lines I suggested with reference to Table 5.1 (see p. 220).

Availability of consumer goods: Consumer goods must be readily available at reasonable prices at or near the market site to strengthen the incentive to produce a rural food surplus. "In achieving desired output goals the Rhodesian Grain Board found it expedient to encourage the opening of general retail stores adjacent to buying agencies, and sales on credit to stimulate farmers to bring in more supplies...In West Africa access to corrugated iron and cement for better housing has been an important incentive in production for the market" (Abbott, 1968:103). In Papua New Guinea possible access to specifically desired items encourages target sellers to take produce to the markets.

The establishment of refreshment facilities, like the Gazelle café at Rabaul market, may also play an important part in attracting more trippers and marginalists to service the market. Such refreshment places should be encouraged to use as far as possible locally produced commodities in their food preparations.

Buying Stations: Producer-sellers need to be assured of a sales outlet for the items for which they have the greatest comparative advantage. Such assurance can be provided by the establishment of buying and bulking stations at each of the major markets in the country. If necessary, such stations may first be initiated by an appropriate government agency, but there is no reason why enterprising indigenes should not be encouraged to start such buying operations from scratch or be invited to operate in competition with public buying. The role of these private and/or public buyers is to purchase in bulk from vendors whatever quantity they fetch of the specifically designated items at a price fixed below the one ruling at the market but above the minimum acceptable supply price. Such arrangement would remove the risk involved in producing and selling particular items at the different markets. It is therefore likely to encourage cultivators to concentrate on producing a surplus of the items for which they have the greatest comparative advantage and for which they have an assured sales outlet, which in turn should reinforce their initial advantage, because of possible economies of scale. These buying stations should help to encourage the area specialization of the rural food surplus; they must be prevented from undercutting market prices by retailing locally, instead they should be encouraged to act as countrywide wholesale agents, buying and selling on a commission basis.

Infra-structure: The distribution throughout the country of the different food items accumulated by buyers at the various markets necessitates an infra-structure of rail, road, and/or sea transport. In a country like Papua New Guinea, where there is no rail system in existence and air freight is expensive, communications need to be planned by linking coastal shipping with an inland road system. Public investment in improving the country's infra-structure thus needs to be given high priority in development planning. The advantages derived from building a road and thereby opening up a hitherto untapped supply area are amply evidenced by geographers (see for instance Ward, 1970).

Food retailing: The buying stations at the various markets can also act as wholesale distributors for produce orignating in other parts of the country. Producer-sellers can augment the range of items they sell by buying from these wholesalers and retailing at the market. Moreover, the buying stations may also develop into exporters of indigenous food produce. They will certainly have to explore storage, preservation and processing possibilities to build up buffer stocks so as to compensate for seasonal supply fluctuations. Moreover, if the country's total demand cannot absorb the supplies of a particular commodity offered for sale at producer-seller markets, it will be necessary to explore export avenues for processed commodities, e.g., canned fish or pineapple juice. Root crops may have to be stored in freezing plants to avoid sprouting.

It is therefore possible for producer-seller markets to continue flourishing, being underpinned by the wholesale operations which reduce the risk in producing cash crops in which the specific area has the greatest comparative advantage, and supported by the wholesale of goods originating from other parts of the country. In this way individual small scale producers can be linked with a wholesale/retail pattern without being threatened by commercial exploitation and growing economic inequalities. While accommodating the labor-intensive marketing customary in Papua New Guinea, it also offers a strong incentive by reducing risks to producers to spend more of their time in productive and less in retailing activities. This may give a further impetus to an increasing food surplus.

The schema outlined here streamlines producer-seller markets into a webbed country-wide wholesale retail distribution system. It would seem to offer several attractive advantages. By using considerations of comparative rather than absolute advantages in inter-market trade it designs a linkage between the various parts of the country without ordering them into a hierarchical structure. Such arrangement would be in tune with the country's egalitarian ethos and its strong emphasis on tribal identity. The schema incorporates the social preferences of 'satisficers' as well as the economic priorities of 'risk minimizers'; it should also help to reduce price differentials between different urban centers in the country. By reducing prices of locally produced staple foods it should make them more competitive with imported substitutes.

As long as the buying agencies continue to operate competitively - and this is likely to be ensured by the norm of the minimum acceptable price - the schema should help to avoid the worst evils of economic differentiation which so frequently result from the exploitation of mini-farmers by large scale trade intermediaries. Particularly on markets where the majority of vendors are women it is important to ensure that wholesale/retail trade does not undermine the suppliers economic strength. Otherwise these women who have been enjoying considerable independence are likely to become exploited dependents without their own cash income, which is the unfortunate situation in which the majority of Third World women presently find themselves.

Another advantage of such a schema would be to reduce the risk in trading for vendors thereby encouraging an increasing volume of market supplies, while at the same time enabling the growing numbers of urbanites to purchase the items of staple food at lower prices. In turn this should lower the urban cost of living and facilitate industrial expansion. Most important is the economic integration such a schema would produce. This can be expected to strengthen the political integration of the diverse parts of the country into one political entity, which is after all a major objective of every newly independent nation. Like the Chinese markets fit into the country's hierarchical administrative structure, so it would seem that such a webbed inter-market schema of food distribution in Papua New Guinea should be compatible with its socio-political setting.

The implementation of such a schema undoubtedly will run into many problems. Some can be anticipated. For instance, there is likely to be opposition from those vendors whose trade the schema would make redundant, such as the Mekeo selling areca nuts at Koki. This could be counteracted by imaginative temporary compensation arrangements. Other unexpected difficulties are also likely to arise. Yet unless the schema suggested here is tried out in practice it is difficult to say with any certainty whether it is going to be a success or a failure.

The preceding analysis of price formation and food marketing is based mainly on studies of Papua New Guinea producer-seller markets. The webbed inter-market system of food distribution outlined here also relates particularly to that country. Yet the theoretical and practical propositions emerging from the discussion should be of interest to other Developing Countries also where food production and sales resemble the pattern prevailing in Papua New Guinea.

Chapter 7

SMALL FARMERS, INCREASING FOOD SUPPLIES AND NOVEL
MARKET STRUCTURES

Many Less Developed Countries have been suffering
from chronic food shortages for a long time. Until
recently it was generally thought that the cure for
this ill would lie in increased agricultural production. As a result the world food output has in fact
risen nearly a third in the past decade. This
improvement was not equally distributed, but even
the poorer nations gained at least a quarter. Alas,
their rapid population expansion meant that nearly
the entire increase in food production has gone to
feed more mouths and not to improve nutrition
(Falcon, 1974:4). This experience has dashed the
pious hopes of effecting increased *per capita* consumption in the near future solely by improving agricultural output. Yet this necessarily remains an
important thrust in the sphere of development.
    Population control has now come to be regarded
at least equally, if not more important than agricultural productivity in improving the average standard
of living prevailing in the poorer countries. "There
can be no substitute for agricultural development and
population control in developing countries" (Falcon,
1974:4); although these two variables are not the
only ones affecting development. Increased *per capita*
food output can occur only as part of an overall
socio-economic change, in which numerous variables
are interdependent and interact. It must be stressed
here that societies operate like systems. They have
many separate parts which interact and mutually
affect each other. If one part is changed this
results in ripples running through the total system.
This necessitates an holistic approach to economic
development, particularly in Developing Countries.
Economists, who try to limit their sphere of studies
to the investigation of quantifiable variables and
who insist on single variable analysis by using the
ceteris paribus clause, seem ill equipped to plan

economic development. Unless social and political
as well as economic factors form part of development
models being built for developing economies, they
will neither help to shed light on the process of
development nor on how to implement changes in the
desired direction.

Yotopoulos and Nugent assert that "the legacy
of the neo-classical paradigm of development is probably as much responsible as any other single factor
for the blindness of development economics with
respect to income distribution" (1976:237). They
argue that this paradigm assumes that "as a result
of trade, exchange and factor mobility, economic
development will trickle down and be diffused among
countries, regions, groups and individuals. Except
for differences in initial endowments, there is
little room for wage and income differentials and
for the other signs of dualism. To the extent that
dualism exists it is a temporary aberration attributed to market imperfections and in the process of
development dualism is bound to diminish and ultimately to self-destruct.

Sociologists and anthropologists, on the other
hand, have been much less sanguine on the proposition
that dualism contains the seeds of self-destruction.
They tend instead to view the phenomenon as more
stable and permanent than do economists. The impli-
cation of this view is that development economists
must come to terms with dualism and economic development can take place only within a dualistic society
....Concomitant with rapid development, both dualism
and income inequality tend to persist or even
increase" (1976:253). This critical appraisal of
the neo-classical paradigm of development by agricultural economists indicates the drawback of a strictly
narrow economic approach and points to the need for
interdisciplinary development studies. Ethnic identity, interethnic competition and hostilities have to
be accepted as facts of social life. These are non-
quantifiable, non-economic variables yet they exert
an important, possibly even a determining influence
over the economic behavior of individuals and groups.

Most Developing Countries are culturally and
ecologically heterogeneous. They have though a
common denominator, inasmuch as the large majority
of their peoples live in the rural sector. Most of
them are smaller scale producers whose primary
objective is to meet their own household food
requirements. Such small farms have been found to
be the most efficient production units in agriculture. "In the traditional small family farm, output
and employment of family members relative to out-of-

pocket costs will be maximized. The smaller the farm, the larger will be the output per unit of land. Under conditions of increasing unemployment an optimum size of farm may therefore be that size which is sufficient to provide the family with the means of its own subsistence (which is undoubtedly much smaller than most land redistribution or settlement schemes which have been implemented in LDCs provided) ....A peasant family is hard to beat: the motivation to work diligently and efficiently under the family sharing system is high and shirking can be quickly detected and efficiently penalised" (Yotopoulos, 1974:3). Small farms thus have an obvious advantage over larger production units in terms of productivity per acre. Methods to increase the productivity of small farmers differ between areas with high man/land ratios, such as for instance India on the one hand and regions where uncultivated land is still available in adundance such as Melanesia on the other. Yet the problem of encouraging these small farmers to produce an increasing rural food is present in almost all developing societies.

The small scale of their activities may enable small farmers to maximize output per acre, but it also leads to disadvantages in financial and marketing transactions. "The small farmer suffers from being able to purchase only small quantities of inputs and sell small quantities of output at a time. Market institutions are strained to the breaking point when attempting to collect from and distribute to small farmers" (Yotopoulos, 1974:4). This is certainly true for customary market facilities and makes Yotopoulos argue that "the subsistence small farm must be protected and nutured and this may involve keeping it outside the market; operating at the twilight zone of commercial agriculture. The reason is simple. The traditional small farmer cannot often afford the market and the market cannot often afford him either" (1974:5).

There is ample evidence for the general proposition that yields per acre increase as farm size decreases and labor is applied more intensively. By contrast large farm units benefit from marketing economies of scale which fail to be available to the small farmer. This then poses a dilemma for development planners: they can either promote the maximization of output by means of small farms, which concentrate mainly on meeting their household needs, or they can sponsor the establishment of specialized large scale cash-oriented agriculture. Under existing marketing arrangements these two major objectives appear to be in conflict with each other.

But this need not be necessarily so.

Our market studies clearly indicate that minimization of risk, rather than maximization of profits, is the main motivating force in the activities of small farmers. Risk considerations affect not only Papua New Guinea producer-sellers, but are important determinants of producer practices also in many other developing economies.

For instance, a resettlement scheme in the Middle East ran into trouble because of lack of suitable marketing arrangements. The new settlers had difficulty in finding satisfactory outlets for their produce. They became indifferent to assistance in improving cultivation practices and raising productivity, and reluctant to invest even in small sums or to obtain credit for this purpose (Louwes, 1962).

All this clearly indicates the vital role of marketing in agricultural development. It suggests the need for a radical reorganization of food marketing so as to reduce risks for the small suppliers, without putting them at the mercy of exploitative middlemen. Existing agricultural extension appears to help mainly those farmers who have sufficient land to be able to produce cash crops on a large scale; only little is being done to help the small farmer increase the output of subsistence crops on his small acreage. More important still, hardly any attention is given to improving food marketing arrangements for small scale producers. Export crops are the only items which have featured in planning sales outlets, such as for instance coffee, cocoa or copra Marketing Boards.

The marketing content of most national development plans is at present very low. Although agriculture provides the livelihood for the majority of the population in most Developing Countries, Abbott found that none of the 13 current plans he examined assigned a major role to the marketing of agricultural products in their development strategies. "In only three did the financial allocation of marketing exceed six percent of total expected investment in agriculture" (1968:87). This lack of attention to marketing is a legacy from *laissez-faire* attitudes, which leads to muddled thinking among many planners in Developing Countries. While promoting planning of much of the productive process they glibly assume that marketing arrangements must be left to their own devices and are not to be interfered with. "There is little doubt that the market economy, left to itself in underdeveloped countries, often gives the wrong answers. Prices do not correctly reflect relative costs, opportunities for reducing risks through co-ordinated action are neglected, insufficient allowance is made for the value of knowledge acquired through unprofitable activities" (Abbott, 1968:88). Yet planners still generally leave food marketing out of their considerations.

Lack of market information and weak bargaining power on the part of small farmers inevitably obstruct their response to plan targets. Reports on this subject from the Developing Countries uniformly declare that most farmers are small occasional sellers, ignorant of market values. The practice of standardized equivalences is widespread among these producer-sellers. It is probably as old as trading itself. "Prices in the town market places and fairs of medieval Europe were mostly established by custom by the municipal guilds... Merchants' activities were limited by ordinances of church and town... Those who sold but did not 'produce', it was felt, really contributed nothing to the value of the product. They had no place in a stable society" (Mintz, 1968:173). This moral evaluation of trading practices is still an important social fact in many Developing Countries. It helps to explain the persistence of producer-seller markets and often mitigates against the establishment of an indigenous merchant class. Economic rationality may demand one type of behavior while moral values may lead to another. It is the job of the planner to design a scheme whereby economic changes are compatible with prevailing social values. This is an extremely difficult task, and accounts for the reluctance on behalf of many planners to take a holistic approach to planning. Many well meaning plan measures are never implemented because they failed to be viewed in their total social context. It may well be that agricultural productivity has not risen more simply because of lack of suitable market outlets for food crops. Yet the importance of food marketing as an aspect of agricultural productivity is still generally ignored. Assured markets are more important to small farmers than high prices for their produce. "Following, for example, successful experiments with the production and sale of artichokes in Libya, the Ministry of Agricultural sent an officer to persuade farmers to take up their cultivation. He quoted attractive prices in the market. The farmers' first question was what price could be guaranteed in the village. The officer's silence did not impress the villagers. They later said that if he could guarantee even a quarter of the price he quoted, they would be prepared to undertake the cultivation of artichokes" (Abbott, 1968:100).

Small farmers are chiefly concerned with the cultivation of crops; selling them is of secondary importance to them. They are often unfamiliar with bargaining practices. "The literature on peasant markets is consistent in reporting that foodstuffs are not generally subject to bargaining" (Uchendu, 1967:45). Wherever market trade is embedded in a 'fair exchange mentality', which appears to be the case at most Hinterland-rooted markets, producer-sellers are exposed to the likely exploitation by middlemen. The regulation of local assembly markets in India to ensure fair sales prices and protect producer-sellers against exploitation due to ignorance or weak bargaining power has been shown to have substantial incentive benefits (Chatterji, 1960:7).

The food surplus cultivated by small farmers can be retailed either by themselves or by way of middlemen. "As internal market systems become more sophisticated the importance of direct producer to consumer connections usually decreases and the importance of trading intermediaries increases (Bromley, 1971:127). This may well be the reason for the widespread assumption that the evolution of markets inevitably involves a hierarchical structure. Such structure certainly exists in most developed market systems. Yet there is no inevitability about it, as long as producer-sellers can continue to play an important part in food marketing. This should be possible particularly if Yang is right in claiming that the market "is as much a part of the social and economic routine of the peasants as is their farming" (1944:1). The persistence of producer-seller markets in Papua New Guinea suggests that they represent a distinct marketing pattern which may evolve differently than the usual hierarchical structure.

To integrate the many producer-sellers in one country-wide system of locally produced food distribution poses a complex problem. So much so that there is no one panacea for it. Palliative measures may be all that can be offered in this context. Small farmers need to be reassured of a market for their food surplus at a price which they regard as fair before they can be expected to increase food supplies. At the same time it is essential to ensure that locally produced food sells at prices competitive with imported substitutes. These two seemingly conflicting considerations may be harmonised by organizing a webbed country-wide food marketing system based on the principles of comparative advantages of producer-sellers.

The previous chapter proposes one such new type of market sytem. It may be compatible only with the specific conditions prevailing in Papua New Guinea and other like countries where food staples are root crops which are difficult to store over long periods. By contrast grains are readily stored, which reduces the risk in trading them. This may help to explain the fact that trade intermediaries emerged spontaneuosly in grain producing areas, whereas they seem to be absent from the scene in regions where the staple crops are perishable. Wherever such middlemen already exist, it is important to realise that there is a connection (admittedly neither invariant nor absolute) between their numbers and the cost of the service they provide, since it is by the competition for their business that prices and middlemen profits are kept low (Mintz, 1968:179). "Latin American producers derive considerable benefits from the numerous 'middlewomen' who compete with each other for their trade" (Mintz, 1968:180).

Wherever the local population is reluctant for one reason or another to become sales intermediaries in food marketing either producer-seller markets continue to predominate or outsiders usually from different ethnic origin come to act as middlemen. If indigenous cultivators depend on an outside group for the sale of their produce not only their own but also their country's long term objectives may come into jeopardy. The Fresh Food Marketing Corporation (FFMC) in Papua New Guinea provides a good illustration of this point. In 1976 its directors were four Australian ex-colonial administrators, two Chinese business men and one Papuan official. "The FFMC is setting up a marketing and distribution system completely apart and remote from the customary food marketing arrangements. It tries to buy large scale (for instance at Goroka buying point two thirds of the supplies originate from large scale plantations many of which are owned and operated by expatriates). It tries to sell to large institutions, such as the army and hospitals" (Epstein, T.S., 1978:126).

Large scale buying and selling is the safest immediate strategy to ensure that the FFMC operates at a profit. At the same time it threatens the major overall objective Papua New Guinea has set itself in terms of a reduction of income inequalities. To ensure a benefical effect for the maximum number of Papua New Guineans the FFMC would have to buy from the many small producer-sellers and sell through urban retail outlets where urban immigrants could buy their customary foods at reasonable prices. Only when indigenous private or public enterprise will operate fresh food market ventures is there a chance that the large number of small farmers will be integrated into a country-wide food distribution system.

Market place trade is an integral part of most development processes. It offers several advantages. Regular periodic markets, co-ordinated with visits by service units, make higher order services more widely available in rural areas. The availability of such goods and services in a familiar context, act as a motivating force for increased cash production through more thorough harvesting, greater planting, or use of improved agricultural techniques. The attraction of considerable numbers of people, regularly, to the market center also offers excellent opportunities for the spread of information through extension work and non-formal adult education (Ward, 1974:8). The educational by-product of market place trade is particularly important in countries like Papua New Guinea where the large majority of producer-sellers are women, who usually are less exposed to modernizing influences than are their male counterparts.

The recent focus on involving women more in development programs (Boserup, 1970) together with a new concern with alleviating prevailing poverty (McNamara, 1972) reinforces the need to design new development tactics. To establish an interdependence between markets in different ecological zones may represent one such new tactic. It should help to incorporate the large number of small farmers in a webbed country-wide system of food distribution. In doing so it should promote increased market supplies of food.

The restructuring of food marketing is only one aspect of economic development. Its strategic importance, however, has so far been widely neglected. It represents a serious challenge to planners of Developing Countries, which unless met is likely to threaten the process of development in particular and the world's food supplies in general.

Appendix A

THE CRAFT OF MARKET STUDIES

There still does not appear to be available a text which gives details of the methods used in the conduct of market-place studies. Therefore, I give here a brief summary of the techniques I used in 1961 in what has since come to be regarded as "a pioneer study" (Brookfield, 1969:2) and how I conducted the studies on which this book is based.

It is necessary to emphasize here that in 1961 I was concerned solely with investigating the sellers' side of Rabaul market, while Salisbury studied buyers' behavior. Since most vendors arrived by some means of motor transport, I had one assistant(1) posted at the road corner, which most vehicles entering the market had to pass. He noted the number and type of each vehicle entering the market. Four other assistants were staged at the different sides of the market where vendors were alighting. These investigators recorded the number of sellers arriving per vehicle and the parish from which they came. The rest of my assistants, about twenty in all, were placed randomly all over the market area. Each was equipped with a number of schedules and recorded for three or four sellers the following quantitative as well as qualitative details:

1. Name, home parish, type of transport and fare paid.
2. Time of arrival and number as well as price of each item brought for sale.
3. Particulars of each sale made, indicating time, number and price as well as the ethnic group of each buyer, i.e. whether European, Chinese, Papuan New Guinean or Tolai.
4. The quantity of each item unsold when the vendor left the market.

In order to establish the relationship between the random sample and the total universe from which the sample was drawn, I counted the total number of sellers present at the market at about 9 am on each day of my survey. The count of the women who had come to the market by motor transport yielded a rough idea of the number of vendors. However, not all women who arrived by vehicle were actual sellers, nor did all sellers arrive by motor transport. On the Saturdays surveyed, about five percent of the women vendors walked to the market. The first people arrived at the market about 5 am; the whole market came to life only about 8 am. A count of sellers at 9 am seemed the only reliable way of ascertaining the total number on any one market day, because very few left before that time, nor did many arrive later. However, in order to make certain that my calculations included all market vendors, I made a 10 percent allowance on the total number I counted at the market at 9 am on each survey day. This 10 percent margin sets an upper limit to include all temporary absentees as well as errors in enumeration.

The survey was started on Thursday, June 1, 1961 with the intent to regard the first three days as a pilot study and follow on with a full week's survey. However, on thorough perusal of the first two days' results I was satisfied with the efficacy of the questionnaire as well as with the performance of the investigators. Therefore, I included in my analysis all the data collected on six market days beginning with June 1. On weekdays there was much less activity at Rabaul market than on Saturdays, though weekday trading was steadily increasing. In 1960, the year before my survey, hardly any trade had been conducted during the week, while in June 1961 the average turnover on each weekday was about £110 ($220), by 1968 it had more than trebled. The task of surveying the market during the week, however, was relatively easy. In order to check the reliability of the first Saturday's findings, I conducted another survey on the third Saturday in June. This showed very similar results and thus bears out, at least to some degree, the reliability of the data obtained.

However, before any conclusions can be drawn from the findings of this survey as to the annual market turnover, a few reservations must be made. Firstly, there are seasonal variations in agricultural output, particularly in European and Chinese type produce which are irregular though not very pronounced on the Gazelle Peninsula. Secondly, within the seasonal variations there were random differences from week to week. For instance, during the first week of my survey there was not a single fish offered for sale, whereas on the second Saturday the market was well supplied with fish. Matupi fishermen had been unsuccessful during the first week in June 1961, whereas they managed to make an excellent catch two weeks later. These are important reservations when we come to examine the part the market plays in the overall economy. Moreover, the most important deficiency in my 1961 survey was the lack of data on prices. This would have necessitated the weighing of the bundles of the different produce sold at uniform prices to establish a price per weight of each item. This was a task I then regarded as too difficult for my assistants to tackle. I deeply regretted this decision subsequently for it deprived me of the possibility of comparing price changes over time when I set about restudying Rabaul seven years later.

In 1967 when I began to organise the large Market Study Project discussed in this book I realised that its success depended on establishing rapport with informants. Accordingly, I publicized the planned market studies as widely as possible. For instance, I addressed the Gazelle Native Local Government Council several weeks before the start of our market studies in the area. I explained to the councilors in the vernacular the objectives of our research and appealed to them to pass this information on to their villagers with the request to cooperate with our inquiries. The councilors must have acted upon my request. Indigenous vendors and buyers offered no resistence when my assistants contacted them; most of them seemed to know about our research or at least had heard about it.

We greatly appreciated this cooperation without which it would have been extremely difficult to conduct our market studies. Not all researchers are as fortunate as we were in establishing rapport with informants.

In a market study at Kampala it was found that "the investigator dare not even bring his own scales, for any weighing device is associated with controlled prices and hence with courts" (Mukwaya, 1962: 660).

It is appropriate to mention here that I had joined Tolai women in a mortuary dance in 1960, when I lived in Rapitok, a Tolai village. Traditional dancing is a prestigious activity among Gazelle Peninsula people; particularly those who lead the dance, as I did, are usually renowned in their

society. In 1968 many Tolai market vendors still
remembered my earlier performance. They were
pleased to identify me as the first white woman who
had ever participated in indigenous dancing. This
proved a great advantage inasmuch as it helped to
establish friendly relations with informants and
gain their confidence. It also contributed to making my Gazelle market studies not only a fascinating
exercise, but also a most enjoyable experience.

In market studies of the kind presented here,
it is important not only to establish rapport with
vendors but also with buyers. At the outset of our
Rabaul market study my enumerators encountered some
resistence from some of the Chinese buyers. Because
of this I contacted the Kuomintang Club in Rabaul and
explained to the organizers the objective of our
inquiries. The Club Secretary kindly volunteered to
speak to the Chinese community in their vernacular
over Rabaul radio informing them of the purpose of
the research. His broadcast helped to dispel the
worries of some of the Chinese buyers that our study
may effect price increases at the market; subsequently more Chinese buyers readily answered our
questions.

My personal involvement in the study of Koki
market at Port Moresby was much less than on the
Gazelle Peninsula. I felt at home among my Tolai
friends whereas I was a stranger at Koki. I did
not know any of the Papuan languages nor had I ever
conducted fieldwork in the area. At Koki I depended
on my assistants to help bridge the gap between
myself and our informants. All of the investigators
(2) who helped in the Koki market study were so
interested in it that they managed to secure ready
acceptance from interviewees. During the two weeks
I organised the research at Koki market I got to
know many sellers and buyers. By smiling at individuals, particularly small children, I seemed to
establish empathetic relationships with a large
number of vendors and buyers.

Straatmans had been a Research Officer in Papua
New Guinea for a number of years before he started
on our market studies. He was a fluent pidgin
speaker, and had a wide network of contacts in the
Highlands and at Lae. This enabled him to organize
effectively the collection of the quantitative data
there as well as to compile lots of background
material including taped case studies for those
markets.

We arranged to collect data on the various
aspects of market-place trade at different levels of
inquiry. We reasoned that this would yield a

comprehensive account of Papua New Guinea food marketing. Accordingly, we collected different kinds of data:

<u>Background Data</u>: We searched through all departmental files which might contain material relevant to markets. We copied details of receipts from the sales of tickets to market vendors for as far back as these were available; we familiarized ourselves with the market ecology, collected maps and rainfall details and interviewed appropriate personnel in various Administrative Departments and Native Local Government Councils as well as knowledgeable indigenes and expatriates to learn as much as possible about the background of the markets we were studying.

<u>Market Sketch Maps</u>: We drew sketch maps of the market sites noting the type of produce sold and origin of vendors. We discovered pretty soon that the different tribes or villages supplying the market have usually each carved out an area at the market site to which they stake a claim. This practice helps to put some order into what otherwise might be completely chaotic marketing arrangements.

<u>Transport Inquiry</u>: Since most sellers arrived at the market by one or another means of motorized transport, we checked not only on the vehicles bringing them to town but also on the economics of these transport enterprises.

<u>Total Market Attendance</u>: It was not easy to establish the total number of sellers attending the market on any one day. Most of the markets we studied had the rule which obliged each vendor to buy a ticket. Records of ticket sales gave a rough indication of how many sellers operated on any one day. Yet this was not a wholly reliable indicator: ticket sales per day were often not accurately recorded and a considerable proportion of sellers escaped having to pay their fees. Therefore, we arranged for total counts of number of sellers several times throughout each market day. This yielded a fairly reliable picture of sales attendance.

Counting buyers presented an even more serious problem. This was so particularly on markets which were either not fenced in at all, as is the case on the Gazelle Peninsula, or where there is more than one gate through which people can enter as at Koki, which makes reliable counting of market visitors an extremely difficult task. Moreover, of course it was well nigh impossible to establish the proportion of visitors who had actually bought something at the market, because many people were attracted to the market by its social significance. We coped with this problem as best we could by posting investigators at strategic points at each market and getting them to count with the aid of a tally counter how many people they saw entering the market.

Sampling of Interviewees: It was also easier to sample the sellers than the buyers at the markets we studied. To survey sellers we placed our investigators randomly on the market site; each one recorded daily details of three or four sellers located near him. When the vendor first arrived at the market the investigator had to note his/her personal details, transport cost, motivation in coming to the market, etc. etc.; he also had to establish the total quantity -- in terms of bundles -- of each of the produce the seller had brought along. Moreover, he had to spot-weigh by means of hand spring scales, a number of bundles of each produce and enter all this information on the questionnaire (see Appendix B). Throughout the market day he had to record each sale of the few sellers he was observing and note the ethnicity of buyers. When the seller left the market at the end of the day the investigator had to find out how many bundles, if any, remained unsold of each produce and what was being done with them.

The count of total numbers of sellers attending the market each day of our survey enabled us to calculate the relationship between our sample and the universe it represented. As already mentioned this was not possible with respect to buyers.

We equipped a number of investigators with questionnaires relating to buyers (see Appendix B). The questions were aimed at eliciting personal data similar to what we asked of our sample sellers as well as finding out the type and quantity of produce bought and the price paid. Interviewing buyers was obviously much less time consuming than observing sellers and therefore one assistant could interview as many as 50 or more buyers in a day. We arranged for our indigenous research assistants to tackle those buyers they were best equipped to interview: English speakers interviewed expatriates, pidgin speakers those indigenes whose vernacular they did not know, as well as using the vernacular with their fellow tribesmen. Since we were unable to establish the ethnic composition of the total number of

buyers, nor could we arrange truly random sampling
of buyers because of the problems already mentioned,
we cannot say with any accuracy whether the ethnic
composition of our sample buyers is in fact representative. We estimated the total number of buyers
on the basis of total daily market sales (arrived at
by multiplying daily average takings by the number
of sellers) and divided by the average value of
daily purchases per sample buyer.

Data Processing: In this way we collected a great
many observations on sellers and buyers at each of
the markets we studied which needed processing by
computer. This obviously necessitated coding of all
the answers to our questionnaires. I soon realised
that the only way to handle this big task of coding
all our completed questionnaires and transferring
the data to coding forms was to have it all done on
the spot. Accordingly, at the end of the first week
of my Rabaul market survey in January 1968 I compiled a list of all the coding necessary for the
different produce and villages of origin, allowing
empty numbers for phenomena still to be recorded. I
then arranged for three of the assistants to code
the completed questionnaires and transfer them to
coding forms. They soon got up to date and subsequently the paper work was done the day after the
fieldwork. This enabled us to query with the
investigators any data appearing on our schedules
which needed clarification. I operated in this way
for all the markets I personally studied(3).
      I also tackled the study of Koki market in May
1968. Moreover I arranged for Mr. A. McCullough of
the Department of Trade and Industries, Port Moresby,
to conduct another study of Koki market during
January 1969. He assisted in our May 1968 investigation and was therefore familiar with our
research and processing techniques.

Supervision: I soon discovered that market studies
of the kind we conducted necessitate the close
supervision of research assistants by a senior
investigator. This is important to insure that
interviewees remain on the job and carry out their
inquiries according to the instructions they
received. It also improves the accuracy of the data
collected if spot checks are made of the way the
assistants conduct their questioning and record the
answers. Moreover, it facilitates the sorting out
of queries as they arise. Most important, it gives
the senior investigator personal experience of
market trading, which provides an indispensible

background when it comes to the analysis of the data.

I made it a practice to turn up at the market every day of our studies at about six in the morning shortly before my assistants arrived there. I handed them questionnaire forms, saw to it that each one was posted according to plan and left the market late in the afternoon when all the sellers had left and the interviewers handed me their completed schedules. I took brief breaks during the day away from the market, but my interviewers never knew when I would leave or return and were therefore kept on their toes all the time. Though I must stress here that in the case of most of my assistants such strict supervision seemed hardly necessary. They were themselves fully committed to their inquiries. A brief account of what happened on the first Sunday of our Koki market study should suffice as evidence for this.

Koki market operates seven days a week which necessitated our survey to be conducted without a break throughout two weeks. Those Heads of Departments at Port Moresby, who kindly allocated assistants to me, assured me that my helpers would be credited with their appropriate holiday entitlement. The 26 cooperative college trainees, who were assigned for the Koki market study resided in a hostel at Konedobu about six miles away from the market site. They were fetched daily by an Admininistration truck. I failed to appreciate that Administration drivers do not work on Sundays until I waited in vain at Koki for these 26 assistants on the first Sunday of our survey to arrive as they had done on the preceding weekdays. Just as I was beginning to despair of being able to round up all these young men by means of some transport or other, for I needed their help to cope with the study of the considerably sized Sunday market trade, they all arrived by bus. They related that they too had been unaware that there would be no Administration transport fetching them on Sunday; when they discovered this they held a meeting and decided each to pay his own bus fare to Koki so as not to jeapordize by their absence the success of the survey. Needless to say I refunded their bus fares to them. I was thrilled to realize their commitment to our market inquiry, for they could have legitimately stayed away on that Sunday. This was but one example to illustrate the interest our indigenous helpers displayed in our market study. Partly this was due, I guess, to the enjoyment they derived from being able to spend day after day at the market. But it was certainly also due to their genuine desire to help improve the understanding of indigenous market trade.

240

<u>Profiles of Buyers and Vendors</u>: We thus collected a great deal of quantitative data on both the supply and demand side of producer-seller markets in the Territory. In line with our trying to study markets in greater depth than a mere questionnaire survey could do, we sought to supplement the quantitative data collected at the market site with detailed profiles of individual buyers and sellers. Straatmans and myself either collected these profiles ourselves by getting to know our informants in their home environment or we commissioned others to do this for us. For instance, several students in Departments of Anthropology, Economics and Geography of the University of Papua New Guinea collected such case material relating to Koki market. Standardized guidelines were used for the collection of these profiles (see Appendix C).

NOTES

1.   All my assistants were then Tolai Agricultural Trainees made available by the Department of Agriculture.
2.   At Port Moresby the Department of Agriculture allocated 11 trainees, the Department of Labor sent eight trainees and the Department of Trade and Industry seconded 26 of their trainees to my study at Koki market.
3.   The paperwork for the Highland markets which were studied by Straatmans under Williams' guidance was differently arranged: Straatmans organized the actual market surveys and sent the completed questionnaires to Williams who personally undertook the task of coding the schedules and completing the coding forms. Before he could finish this tedious and time-consuming job he left UPNG and returned to his native New Zealand, taking with him the coding forms and arranging for all the original schedules to be burned. Since he appears not to have had access to a computer in New Zealand he tried to do the calculations manually. This was such a big task that he could only produce a somewhat superficial report on the three markets, the study of which he had supervised. Consequently, I was asked to take over collating the material of all the seven market studies. This was no easy.task, particularly since the coding forms for the Williams -Straatmans surveys were completed in such a way that they did not lend themselves readily to computer processing and also because it was impossible to refer queries to the original questionnaires, as

these had been destroyed. Therefore, it was difficult to standardize the comparison of all the markets since data for Lae and the two Highland markets
were initially processed differently and queries
could not be checked as could be done with the
material where I personally supervised the collection and processing, and where the original
schedules have been preserved.

Appendix B

SELLERS AND BUYERS SCHEDULES

SCHEDULE 1 - SELLERS

Date ....   Interviewer ....

Se. No. ....   Name ....   M( )   F( )

Tribe ....   Village ....

Transport   Time Taken   When last at Market

Plane ( )   More than 1 day ( )   Last market day ( )
Bus   ( )   1 day ( )   Last week   ( )
Truck ( )   ½ day ( )   Longer past   ( )
Car   ( )   Less than ½ day ( )   Never before   ( )
Bike ( )
Boat ( )
Walk ( )

Cost of transport to come ...... to return ....

Do you produce for the market? Yes ( )
                                No ( )

Why do you want to sell?

Buy something ( )
Get money   ( )
Visit town   ( )
Other   ( )

Who gets the money?

Seller   ( )
Husband   ( )
Parent   ( )
Child   ( )
Other   ( )

243

What is the money for?

```
Food          (  )
Clothes       (  )
Car           (  )
House         (  )
Bride price   (  )
Other         (  )
```

How long will you stay in town?

```
½ day         (  )
1 day         (  )
2 days        (  )
longer        (  )
```

What other places will you visit?

```
Admin.        (  )
Stores        (  )
Friends       (  )
Other         (  )
```

What will you do with unsold produce?

```
Eat                      (  )
Sell at market again     (  )
Sell elsewhere           (  )
Other                    (  )
```

PRODUCE FOR SALE

Time	Item	Source			Number of bundles	Number per bundle	Weight per bundle	Price per bundle	Value	Remarks
		Self	rel	bt						
						Unsold Produce				

245

SCHEDULE 2 - SELLERS

Sales Record

Date ....   Interviewer ....   Se. No. ....

Name .... M( ) F( ) Tribe ....   Village ....

246

Time	Item	Number of bundles	Weight per bundle	Price per bundle	Value	Buyer			Remarks
						E	C	Tribe	

SCHEDULE 3 - BUYERS

Date ....   Interviewer ....

Se. No. ....   Name .... M( )   F( )

Tribe ....   Village ....

Transport	Time Taken	When last at market

Plane ( )   More than 1 day ( ) Last market day ( )
Bus   ( )   1 day ( ) Last week   ( )
Truck ( )   ½ day ( ) Longer past   ( )
Car   ( )   Less than ½ day ( ) Never before   ( )
Bike ( )
Walk ( )

Cost of transport to come ...... to return ......

Why do you come?

To buy   ( )
To see   ( )
To meet people   ( )
Other   ( )

Do you look around before buying?   Yes ( )
                                    No ( )

Do you find bundles   Just right ( )
                           Too small ( )

Did you try to get more for   Yes ( )
  your money?   No ( )

Did you succeed?   Yes ( )
                              No ( )

Did you buy

As much as planned ( )
More   ( )
Less   ( )

247

PURCHASES

Time	Item	Number of bundles	Price per bundle	Value	Reason for buying				
					Not grown by self	to resell	Quality	Feast	Other

Appendix C

GUIDELINES FOR SELLERS AND BUYERS PROFILES

SELLERS PROFILES - OUTLINE OF QUESTIONS

Background Data

1. Details of residence (i.e. name of village, distance from market road network etc.)
2. Personal details of seller (sex, age etc.)
3. Religious affiliation and activities (e.g. native catechist)
4. Education (standard achieved, literarcy etc.)
5. Position in Society (e.g. son or wife of elder or 'big' man)
6. Employment history
7. Experience of European contact (through mission, administration or work)

Production for Market

1. Is seller planting crops for the specific purpose of selling at market? If so, why and when was this enterprise started?
2. Does he/she attend market regularly? If not, with what frequency?
3. What factors determine when produce is taken to the market?
4. Does seller take only his/her own produce to the market?
5. Does seller ever buy produce in the rural Hinterland and sell it at the market? If so, is this a regular relationship or a casual arrangement? Who and what decides prices in this context? How much profit does the middle-man expect to make on these transactions? How much does he/she actually make?
6. Does the seller act as sales agent for other villagers? If so, what are the arrangements? Regular or casual relationships? Allocation

of fares and freight? Market fees? Distribution of takings? Who decides the price? Is the sales agent empowered to vary the price according to market conditions? If the seller takes his own produce as well as that of other people does he/she tend to sell his/her own stuff first?

7. What proportion of the village population sell at the market? Regularly? Occasionally?

Transport

1. Availability of roads and motorized transport?
2. Is walking to market a practical alternative to road transport? If so, what factors decide whether seller walks or rides to market? Time taken in walking and riding to market?
3. Is there competition among vehicle operators? e.g. different rates charged?
4. Are fares standardized? i.e. based on distance traveled, or do they vary according to the people concerned?
5. How much are fares? Is return fare equal to going fare?
6. Are children taken to market? If so, what ages? What fares are paid for them?
7. How much are freight rates? What determines freight? (e.g. weight or quantity of produce?)
8. Is return freight equal to going freight?
9. Who pays fares and freight?

Market Facilities

1. If seller has to or wants to stay overnight in market town where does he/she sleep? Does he/she have to pay? If so, how much?
2. Where, what and for how much does seller feed him/herself in town? If fed by relatives in town what are the reciprocal obligations involved?
3. Does seller find market facilities satisfactory? Does he/she have any suggestions for improvement?
4. Who pays the market fee? If seller acts also as a sales agent does he/she allocate part of the charge to the other party involved?

Pricing Mechanism

1. Who decides the sales price?
2. Where is sales price fixed? (Before departure to market, during trip, or on arrival at market?)

3. What factors determine sales price?
4. If market vendor does not alone decide sales price does he/she have the power to alter prices in reply to changed market conditions?
5. Does seller tend to reduce prices (i.e. increase size of bundles) in case of slack demand?
6. Does seller ever attempt increasing prices when faced with brisk demand?
7. Do market prices influence productive activities? e.g. Does a high market price of tomatoes for several weeks encourage the extension of tomato growing? Reversely, does a low market price, or slack demand, discourage further productive activities?
8. Do market prices influence attendance at market? e.g. Do high prices encourage regular sales activities and low prices, or slack demand, discourage this?
9. What is the average turnover for one market day (for particular seller studied)? Collect exact details, where possible of his/her takings for as many market days as he/she can remember; check up on actual takings where possible.
10. What is done with unsold indigenous produce?
11. What is done with unsold introduced produce? (e.g. lettuce)
12. Who keeps the cash taken at market?
13. What is done with the cash?
14. When is market selling regarded as (a) failure, (b) just worthwhile (c) big success?
15. Is market selling a purely economic enterprise for indigenous vendors?
16. Are social considerations also important to induce indigenes to sell at market? If so, what are these?
17. Does vendor also buy things at market?
18. Does he/she pay cash? Or barter?
19. Is the relationship between market vendor and buyer a standing or a casual arrangement? If the former, what is the tie between them?
20. What determines prices in barter transactions?

BUYERS PROFILES - OUTLINE OF QUESTIONS

Background Data

1. Name, age, sex, marital status, size of family household, tribe etc.
2. Place of birth and present residence; if different trace history of migration with reasons
3. Education (standard achieved, literacy etc.)
4. Occupation and fortnightly earnings
5. Employment history
6. Religious affiliation and activities (e.g. native catechist)
7. Experience of European contact (through mission, administration or work)

Buying Pattern

1. When last at Koki market?
2. What was then bought and how much spent altogether?
3. Frequency of market visits; which days of the week and what times of the day?
4. Average weekly market purchases?
5. Are goods usually bought from known sellers (i.e. tribal fellows, friends or relatives); if not, what determines from whom goods are bought (quality, price, convenience, service etc.); do low prices or good quality encourage greater quantities being purchased?
6. Do prices vary between different sellers on the same day?
7. Do prices change throughout the day?
8. Do prices change through the week?
9. Average weekly or fortnightly expenditure on food? How much of this is spent at Koki market?
10. Are goods bought for resale? If so, where, how and to whom are they sold? How much profit is made on the transaction?
11. Is bargaining possible at Koki market and if so, is it successful?

Transport

1. How does buyer get to the market?
2. Cost of transport to and from the market, if any?

Market Facilites

1. Is the buyer satisfied with market arrangements?
2. Would he like an expansion of market selling in

252

the sphere of groceries (e.g. rice and tinned foods) as well as clothes and other commodities?

3. Has buyer any suggestions for market improvements? If so, what are they?

BIBLIOGRAPHY

OFFICIAL PUBLICATIONS AND RECORDS

B.o.S. (Bureau of Statistics) (1966/7). Konedobu, T.P.N.G.
————————————————— (1967). *Imports cleared for home consumption.*

C.o.A. (1924/5). *Administration of the Territory of New Guinea, Annual Report to the League of Nations.*
——— (1927/8). *Administration of the Territory of New Guinea, Annual Report to the League of Nations.*

D.o.F. (Division of Fisheries) (1963). 'Report on Koki Fish Market', Papua New Guinea Administration.

Fenbury, D.N. (1967). 'Memorandum' dated 20.11.1967, Papua New Guinea Administration.

Nachrichten über Kaiser Wilhelmsland und den Bismarck Archipel (1888).

P.P.T. (Project Planning Team) (1965). 'Fresh Food Study', Dept. of the Administrator, T.P.N.G.

Statistical Bulletin, T.P.N.G. (1972). Population Census - July 1971.

OTHER REFERENCES

Abbott, J.C. (1958). 'Marketing Problems and Improvement', *FAO*, Rome.
————————— (1968). 'Marketing issues in agricultural development planning' Reed, Moyer and Hollander, Stanley C. (eds.), *Markets and Marketing in Developing Economies,* Richard D. Unwin Inc., Homewood, Illinois.

Bauer, P.T. (1954). *West African Trade: A Study of Competition, Oligopoly and Monopoly in a Changing Economy,* Cambridge University Press, Cambridge.

Belshaw, C.S. (1957). *The Great Village,* Routledge and Kegan Paul, London.
———————— (1965). *Traditional Exchange and Modern Markets,* Prentice Hall, Englewood Cliffs, New Jersey.

Bohannan, Paul and Dalton, George (eds.) (1962). *Markets in Africa: Eight Subsistence Economies in Transition,* North Western University Press, Evanston, Illinois.

Boserup, Ester (1970). *Women's Role in Economic Development,* Allen & Unwin, London.

Bowman (1946). 'Army Farms and Agricultural Development in the Southern Pacific', *The Geographical Review,* Vol. 36, No. 3.
———————— (1948). 'Prospects for Settlement in North Eastern New Guinea', *State University of Iowa, Studies in Natural History,* Vol. 19, No. 1.

Bromley, R.J. (1971). 'Markets in the Developing Countries: A Review', *Geography,* Vol. 56:124-132.

Brookfield, H.C. (ed.) (1969). *Pacific Market-Places,* Australian National University Press, Canberra.

———————————— and Brown, Paula (1963). *Struggle for Land,* Oxford University Press, Melbourne.

Cassidy, Ralph Jnr. (1974). *Exchange by Private Treaty,* The University of Texas at Austin.

Chatterji, N.P. (1960). 'Agricultural Marketing in India', *Agricultural Marketing,* Vol. 3, No. 1.

Christaller, W. (1966). *Central Places in Southern Germany,* translated by C.W. Baskin, New Jersey, Prentice Hall, Englewood Cliffs.

Clark, R.J. (1968). 'Land Reform and Peasant Market Participation in the North Highlands of Bolivia', *Land Economics,* Vol. 44, No. 2.

Colson, E. (1962). 'Trade and Wealth among the Tonga', Bohannan, Paul and Dalton, George (eds.), *Markets in Africa,* North Western University Press, Evanston, Illinois.

Dalton, George (1961). 'Economic Theory and Primitive Society', *American Anthropologist*, Vol. 63:1-23.

Danks, B. (1887). 'On the Shell Money of New Britain', *Journal of the Royal Anthropological Institute*, Vol. 17.

Davis, G. William (1973). *Social Relations in a Philippine Market: Self-Interest and Subjectivity*, University of California, Berkeley.

Dewey, Alice G. (1962). *Peasant Marketing in Java*, The Free Press of Glencoe, New York.

Epstein, A.L. (1969). *Matupit - Land Politics and Change among the Tolai of New Britain*, Australian National University Press, Canberra.

Epstein, T.S. (1961). 'A Study of Rabaul Market', *Australian Journal of Agricultural Economics*, Vol. 5.
——————— (1962). *Economic Growth and Social Change in South India*, Manchester University Press, Manchester.
——————— (1967). 'Productive Efficiency and Customary Systems of Rewards in Rural South India', in Firth, R. (ed.), *Themes in Economic Anthropology*, Tavistock Publications, London.
——————— (1968). *Capitalism, Primitive and Modern, Some Aspects of Tolai Economic Growth*, Australian National University Press, Canberra.
——————— (1969). 'Buyers and Prices in Indigenous Produce Markets in Papua New Guinea', *The Industrial Review, T.P.N.G.*, Vol. 7, No. 2.
——————— (1973). *South India: Yesterday, Today and Tomorrow*, Macmillan, London.
——————— (1978). 'Some Social and Political Factors Relevant to the Design and Implementation of Agricultural and Rural Development Programmes', *Rural Asia - Challenge - and Opportunity*, Supplementary Papers, Vol. 4, Asian Development Bank, Manila.

Falcon, Walter P. and Timmer, C. Peter (1974). 'Food: War on Hunger or New Cold War', *The Stanford Magazine*, Vol. 2, No. 2.

Fisk, E.K. (1966). 'The Economic Structure', Fisk, E.K. (ed.), *New Guinea on the Threshold*, Australian National University, Canberra.

Galbraith, J.K. and Holton, R.H. (1955). *Marketing Efficiency in Peurto Rico,* Harvard University Press, Cambridge, Massachusetts.

Harris, M. (1959). 'The Economy has no surplus', *American Anthropologist,* Vol. 61:185-199.

Hogbin, G.R. (1969). 'Supplies and Prices on the Market at Kerema, Gulf District, Papua', Brookfield, H.C. (ed.), *Pacific Market-Places,* Australian National University Press, Canberra.

Jackson, R.T. and Kolta, K. (1974). *A Survey of Marketing in the Mt. Hagen Area,* U.P.N.G., Dept. of Geography, Occasional Paper No. 9.

Johnson, E.A.J. (1970). *The Organisation of Space in Developing Countries,* Harvard University Press, Cambridge, Massachusetts.

Leahy, M. and Crain, M. (1937). *The Land that Time Forgot,* Funk and Wagnalla Co., New York.

Lipton, Michael (1977). *Why the Poor Stay Poor: Urban Bias in World Development,* Maurice Temple Smith, London.

Louwes, H.J. (1962). 'Organisation of Markets and Marketing Procedures in Land Reform and Development Programmes', *FAO,* (Paper presented to the Mediterranean Social Science Research Council, Greater Assemby, Cairo).

McNamara, R.S. (1972). *Address to the Board of Governors,* The World Bank, Washington.

Mintz, S.W. (1960). 'Peasant Markets', *Scientific American,* Vol. 203:112-22.
─────────── (1961). 'Standards of Value and Units of Measure in the Fond-des-Negres Market Place, Haiti', *Royal Anthropological Institute,* Vol. 91:23-28.
─────────── (1968). 'Peasant Market Places and Economic Development in Latin America', Reed, Moyer and Hollander, Stanley, C. (eds.), *Markets and Marketing in Developing Economies,* Richard D. Irwin, Inc., Homewood, Illinois.

─────────── and Hall, Douglas (1960). *The Origins of the Jamaican Internal Marketing System,* Yale University Publications in Anthropology, No. 57.

Mukwaya, A.B. (1962). 'The Marketing of Staple Foods in Kampala, Uganda', Bohannan, Paul and Dalton, George (eds.), *Markets in Africa,* North Western University Press, Evanston, Illinois.

Parkinson, R. (1887). Im Bismarck Archipel: *Erlebnisse und Beobachtungen auf der Insel Neu Pommern, (Neu Britanien),* F.A. Brockhaus, Leibzig.
——————————— (1907). *Dreissig Jahre in der Südsee,* Verlag von Strecken und Schröder, Stuttgart.

Plattner, Stuart (1975). 'Rural Market Networks', *Scientific American,* Vol. 232:66-79.

Polanyi, Karl (1957). 'The Economy as Instituted Process', Polanyi, Karl; Armstrong, Conrad M. and Pearson, Harry W. (eds.), *Trade and Markets in the Early Empires,* The Free Press, Glencoe, Illinois.

Reining, Conrad B. (1962). 'Zande Markets and Commerce', Bohannan, Paul and Dalton, George (eds.), *Markets in Africa: Eight Subsistence Economies in Transition,* North Western University Press, Evanston, Illinois.

Salisbury R.F. (1961). 'A Study of Rabaul Market'. (mimeo).
——————————— (1970). *Vunamami - Economic Transformation in a Traditional Society,* University of California Press, Berkeley.

Samuelson, Paul A. (1951). *Economics,* McGraw-Hill Book Company, Inc., New York.

Schneider, O. (1905). *Muschelgeldstudien,* Verein Für Erdkunde, Dresden.

Schumpeter, Joseph (1954). *History of Economic Analysis,* Oxford University Press, New York.

Skinner, G. William (1964). 'Marketing and Social Structure in Rural China', *Journal of Asian Studies,* Vol. 24.

Spinks, G.R. (1963). 'Pilot Survey of Food Consumption and Expenditure Patterns - Two Settlements in Port Moresby', *Papua New Guinea Agricultural Journal,* Vol. 16. No. 1.

Strathern, A. (1971). *The Rope of Moka,* Cambridge University Press, Cambridge.

Szanton, Maria Christina Blanc (1972). *A Right to Survive,* The Pennsylvania State University Press, University Park and London.

Uchendu, Victor C. (1967). 'Some Principles of Haggling in Peasant Markets', *Economic Development and Cultural Change,* Vol. 16, No. 1.

Ward, Gerard R.; Clark, Nancy; Howlett, Diana; Kissling, Christopher C.; Wemand, Herbert C. (1974). *Growth Centres and Area Improvement in the Eastern Highlands District,* Department of Human Geography, RSPS, Australian National University, Canberra.

Ward, Marion W. (1970). 'The Rigo Road', *New Guinea Research Bulletin No. 33.*

Yang, C.K. (1944). A North China Local Market Economy: A Summary of a Study of Periodic Markets Chowping Hsieu, Shangtung, Institute of Pacific Relations, New York, (mimeo).

Yatopoulus, Pan A. (1974). 'A Paramythion of Paracommercial Agriculture' unpublished paper presented at the workshop on "The Role of Intermediary Organisations in the Process of Technology Transfer to the Small Farm Sector in Asia", East-West Centre, Technology and Development Institute, Honolulu, Hawaii.
———————————— and Nugent, Jeffrey B. (1976). *Economics of Development: Emperical Investigations,* Harper and Row, New York.

Yeats, G.P. (1967). 'Fresh Foods Production and Marketing Survey', Project Planning Team, Dept. of the Administration, T.P.N.G. (mimeo).

Printed in the United States
by Baker & Taylor Publisher Services